Civil-Military Relations
and Democracy

A *Journal of Democracy* Book

•

BOOKS IN THE SERIES

Edited by Larry Diamond and Marc F. Plattner

Capitalism, Socialism, and Democracy Revisited (1993)

Nationalism, Ethnic Conflict, and Democracy (1994)

Economic Reform and Democracy (1995)

The Global Resurgence of Democracy, 2d ed. *(1996)*

Civil-Military Relations and Democracy (1996)

Published under the auspices of

the International Forum for Democratic Studies

Civil-Military Relations and Democracy

*Edited by Larry Diamond
and Marc F. Plattner*

The Johns Hopkins University Press
Baltimore and London

Chapters 1, 6, and 9 originally appeared in the October 1995 issue of
the *Journal of Democracy*

The Johns Hopkins University Press
2715 North Charles Street
Baltimore, Maryland 21218-4319
The Johns Hopkins Press Ltd., London

Library of Congress Cataloging-in-Publication Data

Civil-military relations and democracy / edited by Larry Diamond and Marc F. Plattner.
      p.   cm—(A journal of democracy book)
   "Chapters 1, 6, and 9 originally appeared in the October 1995 issue of the Journal of
Democracy"—T.p. verso.
   Includes index.
   ISBN 0-8018-5535-7 (alk. paper).—ISBN 0-8018-5536-5 (pbk. : alk. paper)
   1. Civil-military relations.   2. Democracy.   I. Diamond, Larry Jay.   II. Plattner,
Marc F., 1945–   .   III. Series.
JF195.C59   1996
322´.5—dc20   96-23229

A catalog record for this book is available from the British Library.

CONTENTS

Acknowledgments vii

Introduction, *Larry Diamond and Marc F. Plattner* ix

I. Civil-Military Relations in the New Era

1. Reforming Civil-Military Relations, *Samuel P. Huntington* 3

2. Threat Environments and Military Missions, *Michael C. Desch* 12

3. Military Roles Past and Present, *Louis W. Goodman* 30

II. The Developing World

4. Armies and Civil Society in Latin America, *Juan Rial* 47

5. Controlling Asia's Armed Forces, *Carolina G. Hernandez* 66

6. Security and Transition in South Africa, *Jakkie Cilliers* 81

III. The Postcommunist World

7. Poland's Road to Civilian Control, *Janusz Onyszkiewicz* 99

8. Russia's Fragmented Armed Forces, *Lilia Shevtsova* 110

9. The Postcommunist Wars, *Charles H. Fairbanks, Jr.* 134

Epilogue: The Liberal Tradition, *Joseph S. Nye, Jr.* 151

Index 157

ACKNOWLEDGMENTS

This book had its origins in a conference cosponsored by the National Endowment for Democracy's International Forum for Democratic Studies and the George C. Marshall European Center for Security Studies. Established in 1994, the International Forum has four principal components: a program of research and conferences, the Democracy Resource Center, a small visiting fellows program, and publication of the *Journal of Democracy*. The Marshall Center, located in Garmisch-Partenkirchen, Germany, was established in 1993 as an element of the U.S. European Command and is funded by Congress; it is also supported by the German government and its Ministry of Defense. The Center's primary objective is to assist Europe's aspiring democracies in developing national-security organizations and systems that reflect democratic principles.

On 13–14 March 1995, these two institutions convened an international conference in Washington, D.C., on "Civil-Military Relations and the Consolidation of Democracy." The meeting, attended by some 140 people, featured a keynote address by Samuel P. Huntington that serves as the opening essay of this volume, and concluded with a luncheon address the next day by Joseph S. Nye, Jr., that provides our epilogue. The remainder of the conference was divided into three panel sessions at which initial versions of the eight other chapters included here were presented. Both the authors and the other attendees were fortunate to be able to hear the remarks of a very knowledgeable group of commentators: Andrew Bacevich, Kurt Campbell, J. Kayode Fayemi, Sherman Garnett, Fred Iklé, Rudolf Joo, Erik Kjonnerod, Hernán Patiño Mayer, and Lewis M. Stern. General Ervin J. Rokke, president of the National Defense University, ably chaired the opening panel. A report summarizing the conference proceedings was published in June 1995. The text of this report may also be found on DemocracyNet, the International Forum's home page on the World Wide Web, which is located at http://www.ned.org.

The collaboration between the International Forum and the Marshall

Center was both pleasant and productive. Alvin H. Bernstein, the director of the Marshall Center, played a critical role in bringing the project to fruition, and also chaired a panel at the conference. Debra Liang-Fenton, the Forum's coordinator of conferences and publications, handled the details of the conference and the production of the report with her usual efficiency. Colonel Hans Odenthal, Lieutenant Colonel Hans Bald, and Lieutenant Colonel Peter Missy provided welcome organizational assistance on behalf of the Marshall Center.

The essays by Samuel P. Huntington, Jakkie Cilliers, and Charles H. Fairbanks, Jr., were first published in the October 1995 issue of the *Journal of Democracy*, and thus benefited from the editorial artistry of Phil Costopoulos and the production skills of Miriam Kramer. The remaining essays were edited with great care and thoughtfulness by Richard Shryock, who also provided an excellent initial draft of portions of the Introduction. The copyediting and layout of the book were superbly handled by Annette Theuring. Zerxes Spencer did an admirably thorough job on the index. As usual, Henry Tom and his colleagues at the Johns Hopkins University Press were a reliable source of help and encouragement.

We wish to express our profound thanks to the Carnegie Corporation of New York, which has provided critical financial support to the International Forum, including a portion of the funds that supported this project. (The Carnegie Corporation does not take responsibility for any statements or views expressed in this volume.) We also wish to thank once again the Lynde and Harry Bradley Foundation for its continuing support of the *Journal of Democracy*. Finally, we are grateful to the president and the Board of Directors of the National Endowment for Democracy for their strong support for the work of the International Forum. Special thanks are due to the Endowment's vice-chairman Paula Dobriansky and president Carl Gershman for their active participation in the conference on which this volume is based.

INTRODUCTION

Larry Diamond and Marc F. Plattner

The concluding years of the twentieth century have been marked by three historic developments that have transformed the political world—the spread of democracy, the collapse of Soviet communism, and the end of the Cold War. These closely interrelated phenomena have both overturned the old framework of international relations and profoundly altered the domestic politics of scores of countries. It is therefore not surprising that the perennial question of the relation between political rule and armed force has taken on renewed urgency and often appears in a new guise.

During the Cold War period, two largely separate strands of scholarship focused on the issue of civil-military relations. On the one hand, students of international-security issues were concerned with the influence of the military high command on the making of foreign and defense policy, especially by the two superpowers. On the other hand, students of the developing world (especially of Latin America, with its high proportion of military regimes) were brought to the subject primarily by an interest in the internal politics of the countries they studied, and were often animated by a concern with human rights or democratization. The author of this volume's opening essay, Samuel P. Huntington, is one of very few scholars whose work has bridged this divide.

Today, however, under the impact of the three momentous developments noted above, such distinctions are breaking down. In the first place, the old conceptual division of the globe into the First, Second, and Third Worlds has become obsolete. With the demise of the Soviet Union, not only one of the superpowers but the entire Second World has disappeared. Many (though by no means all) countries that had been considered part of the Third World are now studied under the rubric of "new" or "emerging" democracies, a category that also subsumes the postcommunist countries. In these typically fragile and unconsolidated democracies, the military often represents a potential threat to the effective exercise or even the survival of civilian rule; thus the question of civil-military relations is high on the political agenda of democratic leaders and the scholarly agenda of political scientists.

At the same time, the end of the Cold War has compelled a world-wide rethinking of the roles and missions of armed forces. Militaries that were fashioned mainly with an eye to potential East-West conflict must now be reorganized in a fluid and uncertain international environment in which it is difficult to identify the most significant external threats their countries face. The Soviet collapse also led to a dramatic weakening of most of the left-wing insurgencies that had threatened governments—and preoccupied their militaries—in a number of countries, particularly in Latin America. There has been an understandable worldwide trend toward a reduction in military personnel and expenditures, but this naturally leaves military establishments uneasy. Reducing their resources not only may incline them toward political restiveness, but also makes more difficult the task of adapting to the new era.

Though the key factors that have transformed the issue of civil-military relations are global, the ways in which their impact has been felt differ substantially both from region to region and across countries within the same region. Thus in organizing the conference for which the essays collected in this volume were first prepared, we sought to include both a few general appraisals and a larger number of treatments of particular regions or countries. At the same time, we were also determined to involve participants from a wide range of countries. Thus this volume includes the work of authors from Uruguay, the Philippines, South Africa, Poland, and Russia as well as the United States; the conference also benefited from the perspectives of commentators from Argentina, Nigeria, and Hungary.

This book is divided into three main sections consisting of three essays each. It concludes with an epilogue by political scientist Joseph S. Nye, Jr., that is based on an address he delivered at the conference while serving as U.S. assistant secretary of defense for international security affairs.

The opening section, "Civil-Military Relations in the New Era," looks at the broad global trends that are transforming the relationship between soldiers and civilians. Samuel P. Huntington, the conference's keynote speaker, focuses on the new challenges posed for governments and armed forces by the progress of democratization over the past two decades. There follow two essays, by Michael C. Desch and Louis W. Goodman, that concentrate on the key question of military roles and missions, with Desch emphasizing developments in the United States and Russia and Goodman paying special attention to Latin America (with comparisons to the United States).

The second section focuses on "The Developing World," with essays devoted to Latin America, Asia, and Africa, respectively. All three authors are acutely aware of the great diversity that marks each of these regions. Juan Rial notes the distinct patterns of civil-military relations that prevail in Mexico, Central America and the Caribbean, and the countries of South America. Carolina G. Hernandez, who is careful to take account of the very different national traditions and levels of economic development that characterize the democracies of Asia, gives somewhat more extensive treatment to the very interesting case of her native Philippines. And Jakkie Cilliers not only writes about the general situation in sub-Saharan Africa, but presents a detailed analysis of the special challenges facing the new government and the newly recon-structed armed forces of South Africa.

The third section, on "The Postcommunist World," addresses three very different cases that reflect the extraordinary range of transforma-tions in civil-military relations that have occurred in the former Soviet bloc. Janusz Onyskiewicz, who himself has played a key role in the reform of his country's military both as defense minister and as a member of parliament, focuses on Poland, one of several East European countries that must reorient their armed forces from their former allegiance to Moscow as well as subject them to democratic civilian control. Next, Lilia Shevtsova writes of the quite dissimilar problems of the Russian military, which must adjust to its loss of empire and superpower status while learning how to adapt to life in a precariously democratic environment. Finally, Charles H. Fairbanks, Jr., looks at the most radically altered situation of all—that of the new states and the unrecognized ministates which emerged from the breakdown of the Soviet and Yugoslav federations, and which often lack any semblance of real civilian control over what frequently are very irregular military forces. Taken together, the essays collected in this volume offer a global view of the many and varied challenges surrounding the relationship of democratic governments and their armed forces in the post–Cold War world.

Civil-Military Relations in the New Era

In the opening essay, Samuel P. Huntington asserts that, by and large, third-wave democracies have handled civil-military relations better than they have the other challenges they face. Moreover, civil-military relations in these countries generally are in better shape now than they were under the previous authoritarian regimes (though Russia constitutes an important exception). Civilians have replaced military officers in high political positions, special military governing bodies have been dissolved, and limitations have been imposed on the political involvement of military elites. In addition, organizational changes, such as the creation of civilian-run defense departments, have helped ensure military subordination to elected officials. Great emphasis has been placed on military professionalism, inculcated through the service academies and military schools and formalized in military doctrine, and the armed forces have had to relinquish many of the internal-security and economic functions that they once performed.

Huntington attributes this relative success in reforming civil-military relations to three factors. First, the norms of military professionalism and civilian control are increasingly being accepted around the world—owing, at least in part, to training provided by the United States. Second, political and military elites have come to recognize that the institutionalization of what Huntington calls "objective civilian control" serves the interests of both. Military officials, having learned through their experience in power that many economic, social, and political problems have no easy solution, understand that the demands of political involvement have undermined the military's own coherence, efficiency, and discipline. Politicians, for their part, have seen the high price to be paid for bringing the military into partisan political battles. Finally, civil-military reform has yielded widespread benefits—including reductions in military budgets and manpower requirements, the curtailment of human rights abuses, and the transfer of military-run enterprises into civilian hands—that are popular with society as a whole.

Nonetheless, a number of challenges remain: reducing the likelihood of military coups, curtailing the residual political influence of strong militaries that have withdrawn from direct rule, forging new roles and missions for the armed forces, and reducing the military's isolation from society at large. According to Huntington, economic development, which created the conditions for democratization, also reduces the likelihood of future military coups. He observes that, during the third wave of democratization, coup attempts against new democracies, with a few notable exceptions (Nigeria, Haiti, and Sudan), have generally failed. In fact, the data indicate that there exist coup-attempt and coup-success "ceilings" that can be defined in terms of per-capita GNP. Countries with per-capita GNPs above $1,000 do not experience successful coups, and no country with a per-capita GNP above $3,000 has witnessed even an unsuccessful coup attempt. Successful coups have occurred only in those countries with per-capita GNPs under $1,000.

Militaries still wield considerable influence behind the scenes in those countries where they yielded power more or less voluntarily, as occurred in Brazil, Chile, Nicaragua, Turkey, and South Korea. Civilian governments have nonetheless made considerable progress in asserting their control over military budgets, personnel, and force structures and in curtailing many of the military's long-held privileges. The main sticking point remains the handling of past human rights abuses by the armed forces, as governments are under considerable popular pressure to rewrite the amnesty agreements that served as the foundation for the military's withdrawal from politics.

The end of the Cold War and the concomitant spread of democratization means that many countries around the world face declining external-security threats. Both old and new democracies must therefore redefine the roles and missions of their military establishments. This poses a particular problem for the smaller new democracies, especially those in which the military has long played a role in internal as well as external security. Huntington suggests that international peacekeeping may be one viable alternative, as it is both close to the military's traditional war-fighting role and conducive to developing collaborative international relationships. Combating drug trafficking and other criminal activity and quelling domestic unrest are other possible alternatives, although they run the risk of undermining the military's professionalism.

Finally, Huntington notes that the development and diffusion of new military technology along with the decreasing likelihood of all-out war have reduced the need for large standing armies recruited through conscription. The negative side of this development is that it undermines the "close identification between citizen and soldier, people and army" that dates back to the French Revolution. The movement away from the concept of a citizen army requires a rethinking of the link between the military and society.

Huntington concludes that future developments in civil-military relations will depend in large part on the actions of the civilian leadership in the new democracies. The greatest problems will be seen in countries where democratic institutions and leaders prove incapable of promoting economic development and maintaining law and order. In those countries, civilian politicians may be tempted to use the military in their quest to further their own political ambitions.

The next two essays, by Michael C. Desch and Louis W. Goodman, both focus on the core question of military missions and how these affect civil-military relations. According to Desch, military missions can be distinguished according to whether the key tasks undertaken by the armed forces are external or internal—that is, whether they are primarily oriented to fighting interstate wars or extend to such domestic tasks as nation-building, internal security, economic development, humanitarian relief, and social-welfare provision. Military missions in turn are determined in large part by the threat environment that a nation faces; however, in the absence of either a significant internal or external threat, or in the presence of both, the prevailing ideas about national security embodied in a country's military doctrine may also play a significant role in determining missions.

Desch argues that sound civil-military relations are most likely to be found in countries confronting a clear external threat. In such cases, civilian authorities tend to be less factious and more likely to adopt objective control mechanisms with respect to the military; for its part, the military is focused on the external danger and dependent on the civilian leadership for support in mobilizing human and material resources. Civilian leaders grant the military substantial autonomy in making combat-related decisions in return for the military's political loyalty. The United States and the Soviet Union during the Cold War exemplified this model of civil-military relations.

In contrast, the worst civil-military relations are generally to be found in countries that face significant internal threats. Here civilian authorities are most likely to be split along factional lines and are often tempted to bring in the military to settle domestic political disputes. The end result is often a military coup and an extended period of military rule, as happened in Argentina, Brazil, and Chile during the 1960s and 1970s.

Finally, when a country faces both external and internal threats, the prevailing ideas about national security can directly influence the country's military doctrine and hence the nature of its civil-military relations. In the case of France during the 1950s and early 1960s, military strategists, following France's defeat in Vietnam, came to view the Cold War not mainly as a battle between the military forces of East and West but rather as an ideological, political, and economic struggle for the hearts and minds of civilian populations. The doctrine of "revolutionary war" changed the military's mission from one of external and conventional war-fighting to one of nonconventional, counterrevolutionary warfare. Only through the strong leadership of General Charles de Gaulle was France able to extricate itself from the morass of the Algerian conflict and refocus its military once again on external defense.

The changing security environment of the post–Cold War era has jeopardized the healthy civil-military relations that the United States and the former Soviet Union long enjoyed. In both, the external threat that once gave the military an outward focus has been removed at the same time that governmental institutions have come under increased strain owing to popular pressures and financial constraints. Civilian authorities in both the United States and the former Soviet Union are beginning to intervene in spheres normally reserved for the military, and the military seems increasingly willing to challenge political decisions. Civil-military tensions are particularly pronounced in Russia, where the military is being drawn inexorably into partisan political infighting.

Desch recommends that civilian authorities in the United States and Russia act decisively to refocus the military's attention on external, combat-related activities. This means promoting a climate of military professionalism and eschewing such nonmilitary missions as internal policing, counterterrorism, and social-welfare provision. Moreover, it entails reminding the civilian population that the end of the Cold War has not eliminated international conflict or the need for a military whose primary mission remains fighting wars.

Goodman agrees with Desch that the military's core mission must remain that of providing protection from external threats and that nothing should be allowed to interfere with the military's maintaining its combat readiness. Nonetheless, he contends that historically many of the world's militaries have undertaken noncombat roles, including disaster relief, internal security and policing, economic development, and social-welfare provision. In some countries, such as the United States, these noncombat missions have not led to military intervention in politics or diminished the military's ability to defend the country against external aggression. Moreover, given the reduced security imperatives occasioned by the end of the Cold War and by the spread of democracy, many nations have little choice but to find alternative missions for their military establishments.

Latin American militaries in particular have demonstrated a propensity to expand their missions beyond external war-fighting. Armed forces throughout the region have been involved in public works (laying roads, building dams, and constructing buildings), civic action (delivering education, health, and other services to disadvantaged groups), internal policing (including antidrug and antiterrorist activities), and even economic activity (running both military-related and consumer-oriented enterprises). Democratization has pushed the issue of the military's proper role to the fore and led some governments to scale back at least the military's involvement in the arms industry.

Goodman argues that, while it may be neither possible nor wholly desirable to restrict the military to its traditional combat role, there is a need for criteria by which to evaluate the appropriateness of noncombat missions. He suggests that the military not undertake a given activity if *any* of the following conditions hold: 1) the military's involvement would prevent other groups from undertaking the activity in question, thus hindering civilian organizations' ability to develop critical skills and expand their role in society; 2) the military would gain additional privileges that it would be subsequently reluctant to give up; and 3) the armed forces might become so involved in noncombat activities that it would neglect its core defense mission.

Yet there are times when the military must take on noncombat missions owing to special circumstances, as during natural disasters or in response to terrorist campaigns. What is essential in such cases is that the new noncombat mission be understood by all concerned as purely transitional, that a firm timetable be put in place for its return to civilian control, and that checks be put in place requiring civilian authorization of any extensions. Each nation's fundamental laws should include provisions that restrict the military's mission under normal circumstances and specify under what conditions exceptions can be made. The constitutional provisions in many countries that allow the military to exercise "extraordinary powers" in situations of "national emergency" usually do not meet this standard and create dangerous situations in which civilian rule is "carried out under the constant threat of military intervention."

Finally, Goodman identifies the lack of civilian defense-policy expertise as a key problem in many consolidating democracies. The importance and complexity of the military's core mission in the modern world demand close collaboration between military officers and civilians who understand the military's needs. Only under such circumstances can civilian authorities exercise proper oversight of the military's activities.

The Developing World

In Latin America, as Juan Rial documents in his essay, both the end of the Cold War and the progress of democratization in the region have led to a gradual withdrawal of the military from politics and a normalization of civil-military relations. From the 1960s through the 1980s, Latin American militaries faced few external military threats but encountered serious challenges from internal guerrilla movements, often inspired or supplied by the Soviet Union or Cuba. Moreover, the domestic political scene was frequently marked by high levels of political conflict between parties on the left and the right. The military, especially in South America, saw itself as a "moderating force" that intervened to defend the constitutional order against any damage that might be caused as a result of either political infighting between civilian factions or confrontation with insurgent movements. Although military officials justified seizures of power as temporary measures designed to foster a "cooling-off period" before the restoration of civilian rule, most countries in the region witnessed frequent military coups and prolonged periods of either *caudillist* (personalist) or institutional military rule. In Central America the armed forces or national guards (quasi-military police forces) played much the same role, even though they developed from different traditions than their South American counterparts. Only in Mexico and Cuba was the military firmly subordinated to the ruling party and committed to maintaining the party's hold on power.

Several trends in the region helped facilitate a return to civilian rule and a withdrawal of the military from an active political role. First, Latin America in this century has escaped large-scale interstate armed conflicts; the border clashes that have occurred have been limited in extent and duration. Second, as external support for revolutionary movements has diminished with the collapse of the Soviet Union and the economic crisis besetting Cuba, guerrilla and insurgent forces have declined in significance throughout the region, except in Peru, Colombia, and Mexico. Third, Latin American militaries by and large did not attempt to establish "foundational" regimes that constituted real alternatives to civilian rule; rather, the justification and legitimacy of military regimes rested on their pledge to restore civilian rule as soon as the threat to the constitutional order subsided. Thus as the crises that compelled military intervention abated, the military withdrew to the barracks. Finally, beginning with the Carter administration, the United

States began to criticize South American military regimes for human rights abuses, thus isolating these regimes internationally and helping to persuade their leaders to hand over power to elected civilian officials.

According to Rial, two things must happen in order for civil-military relations in Latin America to be normalized to resemble those in the advanced industrial democracies: the armed forces must be given a new mission appropriate to the post–Cold War world, and mechanisms must be established to ensure civilian control. Although some Latin American countries have abolished their armed forces altogether (Haiti, Panama, and Costa Rica), most continue to maintain a military force. These militaries carry out a wide variety of missions. First, they guard against border violations by neighboring countries, especially in disputed regions. Second, several Latin American armed forces still face challenges from active guerrilla movements, particularly in Peru, Colombia, and, most recently, Mexico. Third, several armed forces (notably those of Mexico, the Andean countries, and some Central American countries) assist the police in combating illegal drug trafficking; some also help maintain public order in times of social unrest. Fourth, Latin American militaries often help the government carry out "civic-action" programs, usually in an effort to counter the popular appeal of guerrilla movements in poor areas or to improve the military's public image. Fifth, a few Latin American militaries (notably Argentina's and Uruguay's) participate in international peacekeeping operations. Finally, many Latin American militaries engage in a variety of economic activities as a means of self-financing, although the trend here is to move away from arms-related industries and toward more commercial activities.

Traditionally, civilian authorities in the region have exercised only weak control over their national militaries. Civilian defense ministries have served as "little more than a clearinghouse for personnel management, logistical support, and basic services (such as health care) for military personnel." The military establishment has usually controlled the education and promotion of the officer corps, although some appointments require formal approval by the executive or legislative branch. Legislatures have not used their control over appropriations to exercise oversight of the military, but rather have limited their involvement to debates over the military's human rights abuses and its involvement in peacekeeping operations.

Rial argues that, for the foreseeable future, most Latin American countries will need to maintain a military force. While the military's primary mission should be to provide external defense, some of the region's armed forces inevitably will be called upon to assist the police in countering threats from insurgent movements and in combating the illegal drug trade. The troops given these assignments should be well equipped, well trained, adequately funded, and limited in number so that the military does not become increasingly "policified." The military may also benefit from participation in international peacekeeping operations, which will help them gain a deeper appreciation of the world's cultural diversity and will bring them into closer contact with Western militaries that are firmly under civilian control.

Finally, civilian authorities must exercise greater oversight over their military establishments. Many Latin American governments have recently moved to exert this control by sharply reducing the military's budget; this has the effect, however, of undermining the military's readiness and pushing the armed forces into illegal economic activities. In addition to articulating a new mission for the military through a clearly defined defense policy, civilian authorities should set clear legal guidelines for military involvement in domestic-security matters and establish institutional mechanisms, such as effective defense ministries, to provide oversight and control. In order to accomplish this, Latin American governments need to be able to call upon civilian experts who are knowledgeable about military issues. Finally, as many Latin American militaries remain largely isolated from civil society, governments should attempt to bridge this gap through confidence-building measures and other forms of civil-military interaction, such as educational exchange.

Carolina G. Hernandez raises similar issues in her essay on civil-military relations in East, Southeast, and South Asia. Military regimes have been common to these regions of Asia, owing in large part to the inability of civilian governments in the 1950s and 1960s to manage the diverse challenges posed by nation-building and economic development. As in Latin America, the failure of military-backed authoritarian regimes to foster economic growth, eliminate corruption, or ensure political stability, together with the emergence of a significant middle class, has recently given rise to a trend toward democratization in such countries as Pakistan, Bangladesh, Thailand, and the Philippines. In South Korea and Taiwan, by contrast, the very economic success achieved under authoritarian regimes created social and economic forces that led the push for democratization. Unlike in Latin America, however, military regimes have continued to hold on to power in many Asian countries, and the armed forces still exert a powerful behind-the-scenes role in many of the newly emerging democracies.

Changes in the global and regional security environment have also had a major impact on the military's role. The end of superpower competition and the decline in external support for indigenous communist movements have generally diminished both external and internal threats in many countries, although a few countries still face significant external threats (notably Taiwan and South Korea). Two other factors have had opposite impacts on civil-military relations in the region. On the one hand, the expansive view of security long prevalent in the region—according to which the military is responsible not only for external security but also for internal security, nation-building, and economic development—makes it difficult for civilian governments to curtail the military's domestic role. On the other hand, several external powers—notably the United States, Great Britain, and Japan—have tried to further the democratization process by tying development aid to a diminution of the political role of the military and a reduction in the defense budget.

Unlike many of their Latin American counterparts, Asian militaries have been fairly successful at defending their economic interests. Military budgets continue to rise, even in the newly emerging democracies. Moreover, the military has penetrated the domestic economy in a variety of ways. Military elites have gained access to lucrative positions in the public and private sectors (notably in Bangladesh, Pakistan, Thailand, Indonesia, and the Philippines), engage in a variety of rent-seeking activities like natural-resource extraction and cross-border trade (in Thailand, Indonesia, and the Philippines), and are heavily involved in corruption. Efforts to reduce the armed forces' influence by cutting military budgets thus either encounter stiff resistance or impel the military to seek other ways of financing its activities.

Nevertheless, new democratic leaders upon coming to power often enact policies designed to reduce the military's domestic influence. In addition to cuts in the military budget, such actions include curtailment of the military's autonomous economic activities, removal of military elites from civilian positions, forced retirement of high-ranking officers, and prosecution of military officials for human rights abuses and criminal activities. Some governments may even intrude into what the military regards as its own professional sphere (by placing restrictions on the military's ability to carry out such functions as counterinsurgency) or may appoint civilians whom the military finds unacceptable to top government positions. As the experience of President Corazon Aquino in the Philippines demonstrates, this confrontational approach may backfire, antagonizing the military command and prompting military intervention in politics. The contrasting approach taken by Aquino's successor, Fidel Ramos, shows that civilian leaders need to be sensitive to the military's concerns and might be better off pursuing a policy of reconciliation between the military and democratic forces.

Hernandez agrees with Rial that civil-military relations can be improved if civilian leaders help promote the military's professional autonomy by articulating a well-defined military mission, guaranteeing the armed forces an adequate defense budget, and refraining from undue interference in the military's sphere of competence. She concurs with Goodman that the military can be assigned missions other than providing external security, such as disaster relief and the building of infrastructure, if their involvement in such nondefense matters is strictly delimited and of short duration, does not involve extensive interaction with the civilian population, and is under the strict control of civilian authorities.

She, too, sees participation in international peacekeeping as an appropriate mission for national armed forces in the post–Cold War world. Finally, Hernandez seconds Rial's contention that institutional mechanisms need to be established through which civilian authorities can exercise effective control over the armed forces.

Jakkie Cilliers offers a more pessimistic assessment of the prospects for democratization and normalized civil-military relations in sub-Saharan Africa, a region that has been wracked by violence, including several major civil wars and various ethnic conflicts. Economic problems, brought on by crushing foreign debt and the loss of traditional export markets, have exacerbated the suffering brought by war and lawlessness. With the passing of the Cold War, the major powers have lost interest in the region, which means that they are no longer there to provide significant foreign aid or to ensure the inviolability of borders. Movements of thousands of refugees fleeing war or poverty and the existence of large exile communities constitute additional sources of strain. Some rays of hope can be found, however: the waning of external support for proxy wars and authoritarian regimes and the increase in the number of countries "groping toward democracy."

As Cilliers emphasizes, most African societies lack the foundations for healthy civil-military relations. In the West, "citizen armies" were intimately linked to the nation-building process, and military service became part and parcel of republican citizenship: "The citizen army backed by civilian reservists served not only as a shield against foreign enemies and an instrument of national will, but also as a means for keeping the professional military class under political control." In contrast, African militaries, formed in most instances from colonial-era units at the time of independence, stand apart from society at large and have become "instruments for gathering, guarding, and dispersing largess—they exist, in short, to help maintain political or ethnic power."

Moreover, Africa lacks the political foundation upon which to build the type of "effective, voluntary security cooperation" found elsewhere in the world: no clear distinction between free and unfree countries or between market and centrally planned economies exists upon which to base an alliance system, nor is there a grassroots base of informed citizens supporting a culture of nonviolence. Rather, African countries are riven by a multitude of ethnic divisions and a glaring disparity between a very rich elite and the poverty-stricken masses. The rule of law has little meaning, family and traditional authority are in sharp decline, and social norms have eroded—all of which helps breed violence and allows gangs and warlords to thrive.

Cilliers argues that sound civil-military relations are the product of "longstanding national tradition and a complex set of formal and informal measures that affect the government, civil society, and the military itself." In addition to formal laws regulating the military, these include the role of the media and independent academic establishments and the military's own doctrine and internal culture. If civil-military relations are to be given a sound framework, it is vital that the state clearly demarcate the limits of the military's role and that both the broad public and the military feel that such a role is legitimate. This requires that civilian leaders take the lead in defining the military's overall strategy and defense planning, in laying out the armed forces' roles and missions, and in regulating the military's budget, recruiting and training practices, force structure, and level of armaments. As Africa too suffers from a "knowledge gap" in the areas of strategic studies, national security, and conflict management, indigenous research institutions and nongovernmental organizations need to take up these issues and engage in vigorous debates. The developed world can help by forging closer ties between its own military forces and those of Africa, by undertaking comprehensive civic-education programs for military personnel, and by providing assistance with demobilization programs.

The prospects for democratization and the establishment of sound civil-military relations are better in southern Africa, where several countries are making progress toward democracy. With this region's major conflicts seemingly resolved, the outlook appears much brighter now for a prolonged period of peace and stability. Much rests on South Africa's ability to bolster economic and social development in the region. South Africa's fate, in turn, depends in large part on the future political stability of its neighbors.

Cilliers argues that a "crisis of effectiveness is threatening the police and the military in South Africa." Despite the progress that has been made since the ending of apartheid, South Africa still faces serious and potentially destabilizing social problems. For the foreseeable future, the South African Police Service will need the help of the South African National Defence Force (SANDF) in domestic law enforcement. This blurring of police and military roles is unhealthy in the long term, however, as it can produce interservice rivalry, politicization of the armed forces, and a lowering of professional standards. In addition, the armed forces are already overburdened by the support that they are required to provide to socioeconomic development programs. Instead of relying on the military for police duties, the state should shift resources from the military to the civilian police forces. In particular, greater resources need to be allocated to public-order policing and border security, as violent crowd incidents, mass protests, illegal immigration, and cross-border smuggling of arms, narcotics, and other contraband are on the rise. Moreover, greater emphasis must be placed on increasing the professional competence of the police and armed forces, which, Cilliers argues, must take precedence over such issues as achieving racial and gender balance within the services.

With respect to the armed forces, progress has been made in

integrating the apartheid-era South African Defence Force (SADF) with the former guerrilla armies of the African National Congress (ANC) and the Pan-Africanist Congress (PAC) as well as the armies of the various "homelands." Nonetheless, much work remains to be done. Approximately 50,000 troops will have to be demobilized and provided vocational training before they are released into an economy suffering nearly 50 percent unemployment. Moreover, many former guerrillas have not reported to designated assembly points, nor have they turned in their weapons. The existence of significant numbers of disaffected former guerrillas represents a potential law-and-order problem, even if it does not constitute a revolutionary threat.

Despite the fact that it is still dominated by a white officer corps, the SANDF has demonstrated its loyalty to the ANC-led government on a number of occasions. In early 1994 the SADF defused a revolt by right-wing rural Afrikaners in the Bophuthatswana homeland and helped restore order in the East Rand and KwaZula-Natal, which had been torn by factional and ethnic violence. In addition, the SADF helped distribute ballots to rural areas during the run-up to the April 1994 elections. Notwithstanding the progress to date, strong leadership is needed to bolster morale within the armed forces, help formulate a sound defense policy, and subordinate the military to civilian democratic institutions.

Cilliers believes that regional security must be built from the ground up. Individual African nations need to focus first of all on resolving their own security problems and establishing political stability. Bilateral and limited multilateral cooperation, first between countries in each region and then between regions, can then take place on common security issues that hinder development. Only when these efforts have been successful can the groundwork be laid for general security cooperation for Africa as a whole. The developed world can best help this process not by focusing on halting the proliferation of nuclear, biological, and chemical weapons in Africa but by fostering military cooperation between African and Western militaries in order to raise the professional standards of African armed forces.

The Postcommunist World

Prior to the collapse of communism, the former Soviet Union and the countries of Eastern Europe had in place a stable system of civil-military relations in which the armed forces remained strictly subordinate to communist party authorities. Under the communist system, the party exercised its control over the military first of all by means of political commissars, who served as party watchdogs reporting not to the military high command but directly to the party central committee. In addition, the party attempted to recruit into its ranks as many soldiers, particularly officers, as possible. Party dominance was backed up by extensive surveillance of the military by the security forces. Moreover, the armed forces of most East European countries were subordinated to the Warsaw Pact command in Moscow.

Janusz Onyszkiewicz shows how Poland's efforts to elaborate a new system of civilian controls over the military were an essential aspect of the ongoing democratization process. The Polish military had a long tradition and enjoyed a high level of popular esteem, but in the past had demonstrated a penchant for interfering in domestic politics. In fact, during the various national uprisings in the nineteenth century and the political crises that marked the interwar period, military leaders like Marshal Józef Piłsudski often assumed near-dictatorial powers. Even during the communist era, the military often had to be called in to put down worker revolts (notably in 1956, 1970, 1976, and 1981).

Thus one of the first priorities of the Solidarity-led government that came to power in 1989 was to reform the military and establish a new system of civilian controls. In the short term, this entailed six principal goals: 1) securing the military's loyalty to the new government; 2) dismantling Communist Party controls within the military; 3) bringing the armed forces under solely national control; 4) instituting personnel changes in the high command; 5) recasting the military's mission; and 6) reforming the various special services. Much of this agenda was implemented successfully and relatively quickly, as the military found it expedient to take a resolutely apolitical stand during the period of political and economic transition and because President Wojciech Jaruzelski chose not to interfere in the process.

From 1991 on, reform proceeded on two tracks: 1) elaboration of measures to ensure the political neutrality of the armed forces, and 2) implementation of organizational changes within the defense ministry to facilitate civilian oversight of the military establishment. These reform efforts, promoted by the government and the parliament, ran into difficulties as a result of opposition from the president and of the military's desire to maintain some autonomy from civilian control. Although legislation passed in 1991 prohibited political organizing and propaganda among armed-services personnel and directed that no military personnel still in active service could run for political office, President Lech Wałęsa in 1993 actively solicited military support for his political movement, the Nonparty Bloc in Support of Reform. Similarly, the attempt to establish a truly operational defense ministry functioning according to civilian guidelines and subordinating the military hierarchy to civilian governmental officials met with resistance, as President Wałęsa insisted that the General Staff report directly to him in his capacity as supreme commander in chief.

Onyszkiewicz remains cautiously optimistic that, although reform of civil-military relations in Poland has proceeded by fits and starts, the mechanisms are now in place that can ensure civilian control of the military. If Poland is to make further progress down this road, the budgetary process must be reformed, guidelines must be established for the role of the military during domestic emergencies, and, most important, civilian officials must become better informed on military issues.

According to Lilia Shevtsova, Russia faces even greater challenges than its former Soviet bloc allies when it comes to establishing a new system of civil-military relations. The country has had to confront a number of problems simultaneously—state-building, democratization, free-market reform, and the forging of a new national identity—and the methods for dealing with these different problems have often been incompatible with one another. Moreover, the struggle for power between political factions and between the executive and legislative branches has been more intense than elsewhere in the former Soviet bloc.

Early in the transition process, the Russian military found itself confronting a situation in which the political elites were locked in combat, social forces were disorganized, crime was on the rise, and national morale was at a nadir. The military itself was beset with problems, including woefully inadequate pay and social benefits, spreading corruption and other criminal activity, aging of equipment, poor training and discipline, and growing divisions between regular and elite troops, officers and enlisted men, volunteers and draftees, and new recruits and veterans. The armed forces, particularly the officer corps, were also divided ideologically, with chauvinistic, conservative, and statist tendencies prevailing. The fall of communism and the collapse of the Soviet Union have left the Russian military without a sense of mission and have engendered feelings of frustration and defeat.

Shevtsova argues that two events—the September 1993 armed conflict between the president and his parliamentary opponents, and the war in Chechnya—have drawn the military inexorably into politics. Prior to the September 1993 events, the armed forces had avoided taking sides in the political infighting that characterized Russian domestic politics. They remained on the sidelines, despite the virtual absence of effective mechanisms of civilian control, the persistence of institutional conflict, widespread military opposition to many of the regime's foreign and domestic policy initiatives, and the concerted efforts of the various political factions to draw them into the fray. Shevtsova attributes the military's neutrality primarily to its disenchantment with all the contending political parties and institutions and to its own internal divisions. Indeed, divisions within the ranks made it difficult to ascertain the military's corporate interests and threatened to generate internal conflict in the event that the military intervened. In Shevtsova's view, the military's reluctant intervention on the side of Yeltsin in the September 1993 crisis resulted not from loyalty to the president but rather from opposition to the parliamentary leadership and its efforts to undercut the authority of the military high command. In the wake of these events, however, the military became much more assertive in pressing its own policy agenda on the Yeltsin administration, particularly with regard to the so-called near abroad.

The war in Chechnya, launched by the president's inner circle of advisors and not by the military high command, further alienated the armed forces from the Yeltsin administration. Key military officials spoke out strongly against the conduct of the war and the decision-making process within the Kremlin and the Ministry of Defense. The war revealed major problems within the military establishment: 1) a growing gap between the ruling political elites and most of the officer corps; 2) divisions among top military elites; 3) the hostility of much of the officer corps toward the defense minister; 4) the army's inability to carry out its mission successfully; and 5) the incompatibility of the country's strategic objectives and the military's organizational structure and mode of operations. The failure of the initial Chechen campaign generated resentment within the armed forces, while prompting Yeltsin to initiate organizational reforms designed to bring the military command more firmly under his personal control.

Given these developments, Shevtsova is led to ask what the prospects might be for a military coup. She puts forward three preconditions that would have to be present before the military would either launch a coup itself or back a civilian-led coup: 1) the availability of a charismatic leader (preferably drawn from the armed forces); 2) the existence of a political organization capable of planning such a coup and providing it with ideological cover and an agenda; and 3) a willingness on the part of civilian co-conspirators to grant the military a significant degree of autonomy under the new regime. Shevtsova believes that, although potential leaders of a coup could be found and the public might support it, the political organization necessary to organize a coup does not exist. The internal divisions within the military and the complexity of the problems confronting the country also act as barriers to military involvement.

In fact, Shevtsova sees the primary danger to Russian democracy as emanating not from the military but rather from the security forces. Yeltsin has moved relentlessly to build up a variety of security forces as a counterweight to the military (as well as to one another) and to subordinate them to his personal authority. The president has simultaneously reduced the influence of the former KGB and the Ministry of Internal Affairs while creating his own security forces, notably the Main Protection Administration and the Presidential Security Service, both under the command of his close political associates. This development has coincided with a shift of decision making from open to shadow political organs, the growing isolation of the president from his political base, and his increasing use of authoritarian methods of rule. In Shevtsova's view, the Yeltsin regime is coming increasingly to resemble the personalist regimes of Alfredo Stroessner in Paraguay and Anastasio Somoza in Nicaragua, albeit in weaker form. It could also be headed in another direction, however; if the security forces lose confidence in Yeltsin's ability to survive, they may plan a palace coup to ensure their own survival in a post-Yeltsin era—a scenario that would put them in a struggle for power with the military.

Charles H. Fairbanks, Jr., emphasizes the importance of looking beyond the traditional military establishments in the postcommunist world and of examining the nature and role of new military formations in the new states and breakaway ministates that have emerged out of the former Soviet Union and Yugoslavia. Only Russia, Ukraine, Belarus, and the Serb-Montenegran remnant of the former Yugoslavia inherited formal armies when the Soviet and Yugoslav federations collapsed. In the Baltic states, Armenia, Croatia, and Slovenia informal militias formed prior to independence and became the subsequent building blocks of national armies. Elsewhere, especially in the unrecognized ministates, the situation has been much more chaotic, with the formation of a wide variety of armed units, including party or movement militias, ethnic or regional militias, armed criminal groups, bandit formations, and warlord bands. Under such conditions, few of our conventional assumptions about the nature of relations between the government and the armed forces still hold.

Scholars usually take it for granted that the military consists of "a group or groups of armed men, raised, trained, and commanded by the state, with a fixed organization and terms of service," and assume that the legal government controls all the means of coercion (including police, security, border-patrol, and paramilitary forces). This is not the situation that prevails in much of the former Soviet Union and Yugoslavia today, however. What is to be found in many of the breakaway states and all the unrecognized ministates "is not the modern military formation structured by impersonal commitment to the state and the chain of command, but rather a loosely bound group—often with a charismatic personality at the center—that one joins or leaves spontaneously." Even those formations that are nominally units of regular armies are either "ignorant of or have abandoned the technical skills and routines that modern armies ordinarily employ." National armies are replaced by "nongovernmental irregular formations, nongovernmental formations with official patrons, and armed formations that move in and out of the government's ambit." Whatever loyalty these militia-like formations manifest is not to a formal state but rather to an ethnic group, a region, a political party or movement, or an individual warlord. This lack of formal organization, training, and mission explains in great part why the conflicts in which these soldiers are involved are marked by plundering, vandalism, sexual predation, ethnic cleansing, and general disregard for human rights.

According to Fairbanks, in both the former Soviet Union and Yugoslavia it is difficult to draw a clear line between regular and irregular military formations. Several explanations can be given to account for this phenomenon. First, the fraying of the bureaucratic chain of command during the last years of communist rule meant that the military and security agencies began to turn into independent organizations commanded by their own bosses. Second, political factions competing for state power began to use the military and security agencies for their own partisan ends. Third, the various state bureaucracies had sufficient resources to create their own private military forces. Fourth, the armed services often began to rely on their own form of informal financing. Finally, the trend toward "antipolitics" has meant that individuals are increasingly reluctant to serve under regular military command but are willing to fight with irregular units for their ethnic group or for a charismatic leader.

Fairbanks criticizes democrats in the West and in the newly independent states for failing to recognize the importance to the democratization process of formal, publicly controlled military forces. Governments throughout the former Soviet Union and Yugoslavia today are often the hostages of these irregular military formations. Militia-driven secessions, coup attempts, and rebellions have occurred throughout the region, even if full-fledged military rule has not yet taken hold anywhere. Fairbanks questions whether the conventional Western model of civil-military relations is applicable under such circumstances. Civilian supremacy may not even be desirable if the existing government is neither liberal nor democratic. Perhaps what is needed is armed forces that can stand apart from both the civilian government and criminal elements, intervening when necessary to combat nonpolitical crime and to safeguard the community against imminent threats to its survival.

The book concludes with an epilogue by Joseph S. Nye, Jr., based on a speech that he gave in his former capacity as U.S. assistant secretary of defense for international security affairs. Nye outlines a series of U.S. foreign-policy initiatives designed to promote better civil-military relations in nations around the world. He concurs with Michael Desch that military overreach is the primary threat to stable civil-military relations in the post–Cold War world and that the military's mission should not be internally focused. He is encouraged, however, by the efforts being undertaken in Latin America, Eastern Europe, and the former Soviet Union to create new mechanisms for civilian oversight of the military, and argues that the United States has a vital role to play in encouraging what he calls the "liberal military tradition." Nye's presentation offers a revealing look at the perspective of a senior government official on the issue of civil-military relations—and a welcome sign that political leaders are coming to recognize the importance of this issue for the consolidation of democracy.

Toward Civilian Supremacy

The essays in this volume provide real grounds for hope that one of the most difficult obstacles to stable democracy—the intervention of the military in politics—can be overcome. As several of our authors observe, a number of countries have made visible progress in recent years toward establishing civilian supremacy over the military, or what Huntington terms "objective civilian control." If this progress is to spread throughout the new democracies of the third wave, clear lessons must be drawn about the conditions for achieving a lasting, democratic pattern of civil-military relations.

The first lesson is to be clear about goals. Civilian supremacy entails more than simply minimizing military intervention in politics. It requires establishing the primacy of elected, civilian authorities (executive and legislative) in *all* areas of policy, including the formulation and implementation of national defense policy.[1] Thus the head of government, working through a civilian-led and authoritative ministry of defense, must have the capacity to determine budgets, force levels, defense strategies and priorities, weapons acquisitions, and military curricula and doctrines; and the national legislature must at least have the capacity to review these decisions and monitor their implementation.

Capacity is a crucial concept. It involves not just statutory authority but the knowledge, understanding, and experience to make these decisions effectively, in a way that will earn credibility, respect, and acceptance (if not always enthusiastic agreement) from the armed forces themselves. This is why several of our authors place such great emphasis on training civilian defense officials and strategists, and on building up a larger fund of national-security knowledge in civilian universities, think tanks, the mass media, and other organizations of civil society.

As several of our authors note, democracies must subordinate military to civilian authority while still granting significant scope for the military to exercise its professional judgment and competence within the broad policy parameters that civilians set. This will involve considerable autonomy for the military in officer promotions (except at the highest level), training of soldiers, war-fighting tactics, and so on. Moreover, if civilian politicians are to be effective in winning and maintaining military acceptance of their supremacy, it will also involve substantial participation by the military in the budgeting, procurement, strategy, and policy decisions that civilians ultimately make.

This underscores a second and perhaps paramount lesson for democracy. Above all, military role expansion and military coups are *politically* driven processes; by the same token, the achievement of civilian supremacy over the military must be *politically* led.[2] Military establishments do not seize power from successful and legitimate civilian regimes. They intervene in politics (whether by coup or by a more gradual expansion of power and prerogatives) when civilian politicians and parties are weak and divided, and when their divisions and manifest failures of governance have generated a vacuum of authority. The January 1996 military coup in Niger was a classic instance of an opportunistic military's seizing upon a deadlock in civilian politics to reclaim power. Similarly, the failure of civilian politicians and parties in Nigeria to unite against the annulment of the 12 June 1993 presidential election allowed the military to terminate the democratic transition that it had itself managed just before the moment at which it was supposed to step down. And as Shevtsova notes, the efforts by Russia's civilian political factions and leaders, including President Yeltsin, to use the military in their power struggles have eroded military professionalism and detachment from politics. Thus the greatest imperative for avoiding a military coup is effective democratic governance, and what Juan Linz has termed "loyalty" to the democratic system on the part of all major democratic actors. Such loyalty includes "a rejection of any 'knocking at the barracks door' for armed forces support" in situations of political crisis and conflict.[3]

Just as the weakness and inefficacy of civilian politics invite military intervention, so can strong political institutions and unity of democratic purpose among civilian political elites—backed by broad and manifest citizen support—help to roll back the political prerogatives of the military. The structure of the political-party system can be an especially crucial variable in facilitating (or obstructing) coherent government. But these conditions can merely help. Where the military itself has controlled the pace and character of the transition from authoritarian rule, establishing civilian supremacy is a much more formidable task. Particularly where the military has a long tradition of intervention and rule and has acquired substantial domains of power in the state and the economy—as in Latin America, Africa, and much of Asia—narrowing military prerogatives can be a risky business, requiring for success all of the classic instruments of effective politics: broad coalitions, persuasive communication, a clear vision of ultimate goals and a sequential strategy for achieving them, deft balancing of costs and rewards, and a shrewd sense of timing. Establishing civilian supremacy, then, depends in part on the quality of civilian political leadership and strategy. The more entrenched is the military's role in politics, the more crucial these political variables become.

The political dilemma is heightened by the contradictory nature of the imperatives confronting civilian political leaders in democracies with politically powerful militaries. On the one hand, civilian supremacy requires reducing military prerogatives and restricting the military to a much narrower, defense-centered professional mission. On the other hand, political stability requires keeping civil-military conflict to a minimum. Reducing military prerogatives and power almost invariably generates conflict between civilian and military authorities; thus it is difficult to maximize both these goals simultaneously.[4] This is particularly true in the current era, when, as Desch and other contributors to this book note, the ebbing of external threats leaves military establishments in much of the world hard-pressed to identify a conventional (national-defense) mission that would justify large force levels, officer corps, and expenditures. In these circumstances, retaining a veto in domestic politics and an active role in national development and the national economy (especially arms production) may appear to the military vital to defending its viability as an institution. Barring some event that dramatically reduces the military's power and standing in society, democratization of civil-military relations therefore needs to rely on processes of bargaining, dialogue, cooperation, and consensus-building that gradually diminish military prerogatives and redefine and professionalize the military's mission through a series of incremental steps.

These incremental steps are aimed at two broad transformations: disengaging the military insofar as possible from the political realm, including such nonmilitary issues and projects as rural development, domestic intelligence, policing, and participation directly in the cabinet; and subjecting even the military's national-defense functions to civilian oversight and control. The timetables for these transformations will overlap, but there is an obvious logic to an early emphasis on the constriction of the military's role, with a more gradual construction of a new framework for civilian control over military and defense matters.

On the political side, civilian leaders should move quickly after the inauguration of democracy to purge potentially disloyal officers and replace them with officers respected by their peers but less associated with the previous military regime. More generally, elected governments should act boldly to attain difficult but circumscribed goals when their popular support is high (as at the start of a democratic regime and early in the term of a new administration). As soon as possible, the military must also be removed from surveillance, policing, mediation, and intimidation of domestic political life. This may well require a far-reaching reorganization of the intelligence apparatus, with institutional separation between foreign intelligence and domestic criminal and antiterrorist intelligence, and ultimately civilian control and leadership of the foreign-intelligence component as well. It also often requires substantial professional enhancement and training of the civilian police (and possibly creation of an intermediate riot-control and antiterrorist force). Combating crime and controlling violent or illegal domestic protests should not be the business of the military. The more it is called upon to perform these sensitive internal-security functions, the greater the risks of its becoming embroiled in domestic political conflicts, and of its wielding democratically unaccountable power in civic life.

The same logic holds for extended military involvement in economic and social development, including "civic action" to reduce poverty and develop marginalized areas. If such involvement is generalized and ongoing (as opposed to limited and intermittent, to address humanitarian emergencies or very specific logistical and engineering needs), it erodes the boundaries of the military's distinct professional role as a combat force, and immerses the armed forces in a myriad of domestic political issues and conflicts. This threatens the corporate unity of the military as a professional defense force. Worse still is the symbolic implication. "Non-combatant domestic roles convey to the armed forces that their involvement in broad economic, political and social problems is legitimate."[5] Thus these domestic roles must be sharply restricted or terminated. This goes as well for military ownership and control of industries and major mass-media outlets.

The second broad set of initiatives involves extending civilian control to more strictly military functions of preparation for and engagement in combat, including multilateral peacekeeping and peacemaking. An early imperative here is to consolidate authority over military affairs in a civilian-led and (increasingly) civilian-staffed ministry of defense, with ultimate authority resting with the civilian head of government, who should be clearly designated as commander in chief of the armed forces. Over time, civilian officials must acquire control over top military promotions and assignments as well as military budgets and acquisitions, while reorienting the military mission—and thus officer-training curricula and force deployments—around the goals of defending external borders and sea lanes and participating in regional and international peace operations. In many young democracies facing declining external threats, this will necessitate a reduction in force levels. Yet if the more limited goals of national defense and international security are to be realized, if civilian commitment to these goals is to be perceived as credible, and if the military is to be effectively reoriented around these limited professional missions, new expenditures will typically be needed to modernize weaponry and equipment, to train forces to use them, and to permit the types of transnational, cooperative training exercises that will enhance regional security.

This transition to a much leaner, more agile, technologically sophisticated, and professionally constrained military will be protracted. Practically speaking, it takes time to prune a bloated officer corps, to devise new missions and doctrines, to revise longstanding programs of training and education, and to reorganize force structures around new types of weaponry and equipment. As we have stressed, however, gradualism is also desirable for political reasons. Time is needed for civilian and military elites to adapt to new structures of authority and to develop confidence and trust in one another. Military officers in particular need to become convinced that expanding civilian control will not compromise the nation's security or the institutional prestige and integrity of the military. Time is also needed for what Alfred Stepan terms "civilian empowerment," whereby civilians develop the substantive competence to manage and monitor military budgets, acquisitions, training, promotions, and operations intelligently and responsibly. Building up sufficient civilian expertise to staff the defense ministry, the foreign-intelligence bureau, and legislative oversight committees and to provide the more informal guidance and scrutiny that must come from the academy, the policy community, and the mass media is a long-term process. So is the generational change that sees old-line commanding officers, who may bear responsibility for human rights violations under authoritarian rule, succeeded by younger officers better able to adapt to a more constrained military role. The overarching logic of incrementalism has been well articulated by Felipe Agüero: "Untimely civilian effort to initiate military reform may prove counterproductive. The need to reassure the military during the first years [following a democratic transition] may . . . demand postponement of reform measures, particularly in those areas deemed most sensitive. Civilian expertise is most effective if put into practice when at least some degree of confidence between the new authorities and the military has developed."[6]

Beyond gradualism, some obvious principles of political strategy will further smooth the way for democratization of civil-military relations. At each point along the path of reform, civilian political leaders must endeavor to reduce the costs and neutralize or diminish the threats that the military perceives from the proposed changes. In part, this is what a shrewd and careful process of bargaining is all about—probing for the limits of tolerable change at any point in time. In addition, however, civil-military conflict can be controlled and confidence enhanced if civilian leaders always accord the military a position of high status, honor, and income. Military officers and soldiers who are being asked to accept difficult changes in their functions, in their institutional size and resources, and in their fundamental conception of their national role and mission should be reassured that their roles under the new arrangement will be greatly valued by the country, and that their service is honored and appreciated. Soldiers should be paid decently, and they should never have to worry about *whether* they will be paid (no matter how dire the fiscal crisis of the state). Officers' incomes and pensions should be competitive with private-sector management positions, not only to induce loyalty to the reform process, but to deter corruption. Increases in military pay and pensions should be able to be offset over time by overall reduction in the number of soldiers, and especially officers. Yet even though military spending in many countries must be reduced in the medium to long run, new democratic governments may deem it wise to defer that goal as a temporary concession to win military confidence.

As Huntington and many other scholars emphasize, civilian officials must also act with restraint in their relations with the military. Not only must they resist the temptation to turn to the military for support in situations of political conflict, or as an instrument of first resort to quell unruly domestic protests, but they must also repay respect with respect, granting the military the autonomy to conduct its training and operations and assign and promote its officers in accordance with professional standards and criteria, without political interference at the micro level.

If democracy works in other respects, it is likely over time to bring progress in civil-military relations as well. As democratic institutions sink firm roots and popular commitment to the constitutional system deepens, the scope for the military to intervene in politics, or even to rattle its sabers menacingly, diminishes. As economic development proceeds, the society becomes more educated and complex, and the possibility of its being successfully managed by a military government recedes. The political culture also changes, promoting tolerance and the peaceful resolution of conflict, as well as greater resistance to authoritarian styles of governance. These factors no doubt help to explain the national income ceilings on coups and coup attempts that Huntington identifies in this volume. Moreover, if democracy can facilitate distribution of the benefits of development across the country and resolution of the society's key conflicts through peaceful accommodation, it will preempt the forms of violent protest—left-wing guerrilla insurgencies, ethnic secessionist movements, religious fundamentalist mobilization—that have brought military coups or political interference in many civilian regimes throughout the world. Finally, as new democracies become established and more economically developed, they become more viable partners for participation in democratic collective-security arrangements that generate powerful additional pressure —political, normative, and structural—for civilian supremacy over the military. The North Atlantic Treaty Organization (NATO) has been the classic instrument of such influence, and it is likely that the incorporation of emerging East European democracies like the Czech Republic, Poland, and Hungary as full members will advance consolidation in those countries as it did in Spain, Portugal, and Greece.[7] Even the more limited association with NATO brought by participation in the Partnership for Peace program appears to have had some effect in diffusing the model and norms of civilian supremacy. Also helpful have been international education and training programs like those operated by the George C. Marshall Center in Garmisch-Partenkirchen, Germany.

These positive concomitants of democratic change, and the general progress in civil-military relations that Huntington notes in Chapter 1, do not, however, lessen the importance of a coherent reform strategy and the difficulty of implementing it in many new and troubled democracies. Unfortunately, a number of new democracies have not made substantial progress toward consolidating democratic institutions. In those cases, public respect for parties and politicians is low, and political violence, terrorism, and insurgency invite military intervention. Such countries cannot afford to wait for military influence in politics to ebb by some "natural" historical process. Indeed, the continued involvement of the military in politics and social life may be intimately bound up with other obstacles to democratic consolidation. By acting positively, through a coherent incremental strategy, to reform civil-military relations, such democracies may realize more general improvements in their political institutions and legitimacy. Even where, as in Chile, democracy is generally performing well in most respects, the autonomous power of the military may persist as an isolated but significant affliction, diminishing the quality and stability of democracy.

In short, as so many of the essays in this volume emphasize, the most dangerous thing that democrats can do is to take the military for granted, or to assume that the problem of civil-military relations will eventually take care of itself. For many years to come, most of the new democracies that have emerged in the past decade or two, and some older ones (like Sri Lanka, Venezuela, and Colombia) that have become embattled and destabilized, will be struggling to achieve the deep legitimacy and stability that come with democratic consolidation. Even with the diminished likelihood of military coups, democratic reform of the military remains a major component of the challenge they face. And civilian supremacy remains a vital goal.

NOTES

1. On this and other dimensions of the concept of "civilian supremacy," which is closely related—but not identical—to Huntington's "objective civilian control," see Felipe Agüero, "Democratic Consolidation and the Military in Southern Europe and Latin America," in Richard Gunther, P. Nikiforos Diamandouros, and Hans-Jürgen Puhle, eds., *The Politics of Democratic Consolidation: Southern Europe in Comparative Perspective* (Baltimore: Johns Hopkins University Press, 1995), 126–27; and *Soldiers, Civilians, and Democracy: Post-Franco Spain in Comparative Perspective* (Baltimore: Johns Hopkins University Press, 1995), 19–23.

2. On the latter point, see Alfred Stepan, *Rethinking Military Politics: Brazil and the Southern Cone* (Princeton: Princeton University Press, 1988), 138–39.

3. Juan J. Linz, *The Breakdown of Democratic Regimes: Crisis, Breakdown, and Reequilibrium* (Baltimore: Johns Hopkins University Press, 1978), 30.

4. Stepan, *Rethinking Military Politics*; Wendy Hunter, "Contradictions of Civilian Control: Argentina, Brazil, and Chile in the 1990s," *Third World Quarterly* 15 (1994): 633–53.

5. Hunter, "Contradictions of Civilian Control," 646.

6. Agüero, *Soldiers, Civilians, and Democracy*, 33.

7. On the positive effects of NATO membership for the development of civilian supremacy and the consolidation of democracy in Spain, Portugal, and Greece, see ibid.

I.
Civil-Military Relations
in the New Era

1.
REFORMING
CIVIL-MILITARY RELATIONS

Samuel P. Huntington

Samuel P. Huntington is Albert J. Weatherhead III University Professor and director of the John M. Olin Institute for Strategic Studies at Harvard University. He has also been affiliated with Columbia University and has served in the White House as coordinator of security planning for the National Security Council. His many books include The Soldier and the State: The Theory and Politics of Civil-Military Relations *(1957) and* The Third Wave: Democratization in the Late Twentieth Century *(1991).*

As we all know, the last two decades have seen a remarkable political revolution in which transitions from authoritarianism to democracy have occurred in roughly 40 countries. The previous authoritarian regimes varied considerably. They included military governments in Latin America and elsewhere; one-party regimes in the communist states but also in Taiwan; personal dictatorships in Spain, the Philippines, Romania, and elsewhere; and a racial oligarchy in South Africa. The transitions to democracy also differed greatly. In some cases, including many military regimes, reformers came to power within the authoritarian regime and took the initiative in bringing about the transition. In other cases, the transition came as a result of negotiations between the government and opposition groups. In still others, the authoritarian regime was overthrown or collapsed. In a few instances, intervention by the United States brought the fall of the dictatorship and its replacement by a regime based on elections.

Virtually all of these authoritarian regimes, whatever their type, had one thing in common. Their civil-military relations left much to be desired. Almost all notably lacked the kind of civil-military relations characteristic of the world's industrial democracies, which I once termed "objective civilian control."[1] This involves: 1) a high level of military professionalism and recognition by military officers of the limits of their professional competence; 2) the effective subordination of the military to the civilian political leaders who make the basic decisions on foreign and military policy; 3) the recognition and acceptance by that leadership of an area of professional competence and autonomy for the military; and 4) as a result, the minimization of military intervention in politics and of political intervention in the military.

Civil-military relations in the authoritarian regimes differed from this model to varying degrees. In the military regimes, no civilian control existed at all and military leaders and military organizations often performed a wide variety of functions only distantly related to normal military missions. In the personal dictatorships, the ruler did everything he could to ensure that the military was permeated by and controlled by his cronies and agents, that it was divided against itself, and that it served his purpose of keeping a tight grip on power. In the one-party states, civil-military relations were not in quite the same disarray, but the military was viewed as the instrument of the party, military officers had to be party members, political commissars and party cells paralleled the normal military chain of command, and ultimate loyalty was to the party rather than the state.

The new democracies have thus faced a daunting challenge in the need drastically to reform their civil-military relations. This challenge, of course, is only one of many. They also have had to establish their general authority with the public, draft new constitutions, establish competitive party systems and other democratic institutions, liberalize, privatize, and marketize command economies or economies heavily dominated by the state, promote economic growth while curbing inflation and unemployment, reduce fiscal deficits, limit crime and corruption, and curb tensions and violence among ethnic and religious groups.

How well have the new democracies dealt with these problems? Overall, their record has been spotty at best, lending credence to the arguments of those, like Singapore's former premier Lee Kuan Yew, who criticize democracy for breeding inefficiency and indiscipline. In many cases, economic performance has declined. Economic reform has been stymied, has become unpopular with publics, and has been manipulated to benefit members of the old authoritarian elite. Crime and corruption have increased. Human rights guarantees in new constitutions have been routinely violated. The press has been controlled or subverted. Political party systems have been fragmented and personalistic, incapable of producing either effective governments or responsible oppositions. The removal of authoritarian controls has permitted and even helped to stimulate heightened communal consciousness and violence. With some exceptions in some areas in some countries, new democratic governments have not been all that good at producing good government.

This democratic deficiency has generated authoritarian nostalgia, as people in country after country look back with longing at dictators who provided for basic needs and made things work. This desire to return to authoritarianism was dramatically illustrated by a 1993 poll in which 39 percent of the residents of Moscow and St. Petersburg said that life was better under communist rule, while only 27 percent said that it was better under democracy.[2] If that describes opinion in Russia's two best-off cities, then one can only assume it is even less prodemocratic elsewhere.

Against this general pattern of failure or mediocre performance, the record of new democracies in dealing with civil-military relations stands out in pleasant contrast. Obviously, major differences exist from country to country, and significant problems still confront new democratic regimes. Yet overall, much progress has been made. With one soon-to-be-mentioned exception, it is hard to think of any new democracy where civil-military relations and civilian control of the military are in worse shape now than they were under authoritarian rule. Civil-military relations are a dramatic exception to the lackluster performance of democracies in so many other areas. The story here is one of a decline in military power in politics and in political intervention in the military along with slow, halting, but nonetheless real progress toward the creation of systems of civil-military relations resembling those that exist in the established industrial democracies. My argument is, in short, twofold: first, the new democracies have overall done better with civil-military relations than they have with most of their other major problems; second, with probably one exception, civil-military relations are in better shape in the new democracies than they were in the authoritarian regimes that these democracies replaced.

The truth of these propositions is clearly evident in Eastern Europe. Over the years, Anton Bebler of Slovenia has probably been the most perspicacious observer of East European civil-military relations. The changes in those relations since 1989, he observed in 1994, have been a "development of historic proportions." He listed 11 main components of this change:

(1) increased transparency of defense policies and often a greater supervisory role by parliaments and public opinion; (2) civilianization of defense ministries; (3) radical personnel changes in the upper echelons of the armed forces; (4) national emancipation from Moscow and resultant new security doctrines; (5) partial redeployment of and an altered profile for the armed forces; (6) a greater stress on participatory managerial styles within military establishments; (7) relative political neutralization of the armed forces; (8) discontinuation of the military's internal-security role; (9) ideological pluralization; (10) abolition of obtrusive discrimination against religious believers; and (11) decriminalization of conscientious objection.[3]

Comparable changes have taken place in the new democracies in Southern Europe, Latin America, East Asia, and elsewhere. Incoming democratic governments have purged top military leaders almost across the board. Limitations on political involvement and other constraints have been imposed on the military. Organizational relationships have been restructured with the creation of defense ministries and central staffs to exercise control over the military. The defense portfolio is not held everywhere by a civilian—Russia and some other important places remain exceptions—but the trend is in that direction. Special military bodies exercising political power such as the Council of the Revolution in Portugal have been eliminated. Civilians have replaced military officers in high political office, such as the presidencies of Turkey and Portugal. Overall, there are fewer serving officers in positions that one would normally think of as political. In the postcommunist countries, communist-party control of the military has ended and major efforts have been made to depoliticize the military.

Together with these developments, in most of the newly democratic countries there have been efforts to restructure and redirect the military toward military missions and to get them out of a wide range of less-than-strictly-military activities. These include the activities that two decades ago Alfred Stepan referred to as the new military professionalism in Latin America, and which involved the military's promoting national development and focusing on internal security.[4] In Latin America and elsewhere, the military performed tremendously important economic functions and ran substantial industries, including many not concerned with national defense. These extramilitary activities have not been totally eliminated, but in a large number of countries they have been very substantially cut back by governments privatizing military-run businesses and industries. The Argentine government has been very active in this area.

In almost all cases, military forces in new democratic regimes have been reduced in size. Whether or not this was wise in all circumstances, it was certainly an indication of some form of civilian control. In general, the emphasis in the new democratic regimes has been to rewrite the doctrines and revise curricula in service academies and military schools so as to emphasize military professionalism. The new regimes have, insofar as possible, acquired more modern equipment for their armed forces and attempted to bring them up to international standards of competence. Such moves mark a broad trend toward enhancing military professionalism and reducing the roles that military forces have played in society.

Reasons for Success

Why have new democracies generally been so successful in restructuring their civil-military relations? Several factors have probably played a role. First, there has been a broad diffusion and acceptance of the norms of military professionalism and civilian control by militaries around the world. In past cases where Latin American military personnel have attempted coups or have been unmasked as torturers, liberal U.S. congressmen and journalists have immediately cited these acts as consequences of their education in U.S. military schools. That U.S. military officers could teach their Latin American counterparts how to organize a coup or torture prisoners, however, seems highly improbable. In fact, exposure to the U.S. military and training in its schools have been major factors in the diffusion and acceptance by military officers elsewhere of the liberal democratic norms of military professionalism and civilian control. The George C. Marshall Center in Bavaria represents an important extension of this effort into the post-Soviet world.

Second, movement toward objective civilian control has been in the interest of both military and civilian leaders. Military officers have learned that there are no easy solutions to the intractable economic, social, and political problems confronting their respective countries, and that sustained involvement in politics has disastrous effects on the coherence, efficiency, and discipline of the army. It sacrifices, in Stepan's terms, the military as institution to the military as government, which is one reason why so many military regimes in Latin America voluntarily surrendered power.[5] Elected political leaders, on the other hand, recognize that playing politics with the military is playing with a two-edged sword and that a politically neutral professional establishment is most congruent with their interests. As a result, opposition to progress in civil-military relations has generally been limited to small groups of disaffected midlevel officers and to extreme-nationalist civilian politicians on the margins of the political arena.

Third, unlike economic reform, civil-military reform imposes few costs on society and produces widespread benefits: reductions in military service, cuts in military spending, curtailment of military abuses of human rights, and the transfer to private hands of military-run enterprises. These measures are obviously popular and arouse little or no opposition from groups outside the military.

The comparative success of new democracies in reforming civil-military relations does not mean that there are not major civil-military problems in some countries, and less urgent but still significant problems in many others. Two countries, in particular, face rather unique challenges. South Africa is struggling to integrate the guerrillas of the African National Congress's force, the Umkhonto we Sizwe (MK), with the South African Defense Force, a force with an overwhelmingly Afrikaner officer corps and a tradition of commitment to apartheid. The government of President Nelson Mandela has undertaken efforts at integration that have produced a significant, presumably temporary, increase in the military budget. It appears that the integration of MK officers is proceeding reasonably well, but the integration of the rank-

and-file guerrillas has produced demonstrations, a protest march on President Mandela's headquarters, small-scale mutinies, large-scale absenteeism, and warnings from Mandela that he will not tolerate "an army of criminals" and will discharge from the military those former guerrillas unwilling to accept the discipline required in a regular force.

In South Africa, the central problem is the military's integration; in Russia, the central problem is its disintegration.

In South Africa, the central problem is the military's integration; in Russia, the central problem is its disintegration. As Benjamin Lambeth has pointed out, unlike any other contemporary military establishment, the Russian military has lost not only manpower, money, and mission, but also a war, an alliance, and a country.[6] The result is a thoroughly disorganized and demoralized military, which is not only incapable of conducting a war but also so divided against itself that it is, in all probability, incapable of conducting a coup. The Russian armed forces seem to be thoroughly politicized and divided into factions and personalistic cliques. To compensate for a lack of funds, soldiers increasingly turn to commercial activities and the sale of military supplies. They are overwhelmingly contemptuous of both President Boris Yeltsin and Defense Minister Pavel Grachev and await the appearance of a new leader who will provide leadership and discipline. That leader could be a civilian but—as General Aleksandr Lebed suggested, stopping just short of naming himself for the role—could also conceivably be a general like Chile's Augusto Pinochet. At the same time, however, politicization of the military has been accompanied by the broadening of civilian influence in the form of much greater transparency, supervision by the Duma, public and legislative debates over issues of policy regarding the military, and diffusion of military expertise beyond the limited confines of the general staff. Nonetheless, it would be hard to argue that civilian control mechanisms in Russia today are in better shape than they were in the Soviet Union.

Let me briefly refer to four general problems affecting civil-military relations in various new democracies: military intervention in politics, pre-existing military privileges, the definition of roles and missions, and the development and diffusion of new military technology.

First, there have been, by my count, somewhere between 30 and 40 coup attempts against newly democratic governments. In some states like Argentina, the Philippines, Spain, and Greece, there have been multiple coup attempts. With a few exceptions—Nigeria, Sudan, and Haiti being the most notable—the coup attempts have failed. The interesting question is why. If well-established military forces are challenging new regimes, which have a somewhat fragile existence and are potentially unstable, why have they gone down in defeat? The answer to that question lies primarily with each country's level of economic development and modernization.

The process of economic development from the 1950s through the early 1970s laid the basis for the movement toward democracy beginning in the mid-1970s. Economic development has also ensured the failure of almost all of the subsequent coup attempts. Without embracing absolute economic determinism, one can cite a useful economic guideline. There is a coup-attempt ceiling and there is a coup-success ceiling, both of which can be defined more or less in terms of per-capita GNP. Countries with per-capita GNPs of $1,000 or more do not have successful coups; countries with per-capita GNPs of $3,000 or more do not have coup attempts. The area between $1,000 and $3,000 per-capita GNP is where unsuccessful coups occur, while successful coups in Nigeria, Sudan, and Haiti were in countries with per-capita GNPs under $500.

Coup attempts against democratic governments, including the two in 1992 in Venezuela, are a legacy of underdevelopment. They are acts of desperation. Almost all of these coups have been led by lieutenant colonels, which is significant. In the Philippines, Argentina, and Venezuela, the same lieutenant colonel tried again and again. In Venezuela the lieutenant colonel was jailed after the first coup attempt in February 1992, but somehow he smuggled out a manifesto to certain units that provoked them to revolt again on his behalf in November. He then reportedly began planning another coup, which failed to materialize. Coups led by lieutenant colonels, however, are not likely to be successful. What commanding general or chief of staff wants to have to take orders from a lieutenant colonel who has seized the presidential sash? The danger to new democratic governments from coups has been overestimated.

Second, where military governments have given up power more or less voluntarily, those militaries will continue to have substantial influence in their society after their withdrawal from power. Notable examples are Turkey, South Korea, Nicaragua, Brazil, and Chile. Yet Humberto Ortega is out in Nicaragua, General Pinochet's power has been steadily reduced, and the political influence of the Brazilian military is not what it used to be. Gradually, Latin American and other governments are asserting their authority over personnel, budgets, and force structures; centuries-old military privileges are being whittled away; military personnel are being subjected to the normal legal order; and challenges are even being made to the amnesties that the military demanded as the price for returning to the barracks, in effect rewriting the terms under which the military exited from power. As the confrontation in Chile involving Generals Manuel Contreras and Pedro Espinosa has shown, however, the better course than valor for new democratic governments on the issue of prosecute-and-punish versus forgive-and-forget remains: "Do not prosecute, do not punish, do not forgive, and, above all, do not forget."[7]

The Question of New Missions

The threat of military intervention comes from militaries that are politically weak; the legacy of military privilege comes from militaries that are politically strong. A third problem, that of roles and missions, confronts almost all militaries in the post–Cold War world. It is perhaps least difficult among major powers, like the United States, Russia, and China, which are reshaping their forces to deal with regional contingencies. For smaller new democracies, particularly those which have been susceptible to military coups, the problem is more serious. Insofar as the thesis that democracies do not fight democracies is valid, the proliferation of democracies in the world enhances the problem. While under military rule, Argentina did fight a war with Britain and came close to fighting one with Chile. Now that all three countries are democratic, amicable relations exist among them. What functions then exist for the Argentine armed forces? Peacekeeping is clearly part of the answer; Argentine troops have been deployed on such missions to the Persian Gulf, Croatia, Cambodia, Angola, Morocco, and the Sinai. Other new democracies have also moved in this direction. While a peacekeeping mission is obviously different from a warfighting mission, it does, nonetheless, involve the deployment of armed forces abroad in situations where they could be called upon to fire or be fired upon. The involvement of the military in new alliances and collaborative relationships can also provide military establishments with constructive and demanding missions. Further removed from traditional military missions is the use of military forces to combat drug mafias, crime, or domestic unrest. Precisely because they are becoming increasingly professional, military forces typically resist such assignments (as has happened in both Russia and Iran).

Fourth, the development and diffusion of new military technology and the decreasing likelihood of an all-out war requiring national mobilization are altering the relations between military establishments and their societies in new democracies, old democracies, and continuing dictatorships. Conscription is slowly on the way out. In Spain, Germany, and Russia, half or more of the potential conscripts find ways of avoiding service. Virtually all the Central and East European countries have significantly reduced the length of required service. Belgium has abolished conscription, and Venezuela, Argentina, and South Africa are in the process of doing so. Even Russian military leaders briefly considered the possibility of having a volunteer force. The era of the conscript army, which began with the French Revolution, would appear to be fading into history. With it, presumably, will go the close identification between citizen and soldier, people and army. At least some theorists of democracy have argued that such close identification is highly desirable—"every citizen a soldier, every soldier a citizen," in Jefferson's words—and the movement away from that ideal requires rethinking the nature of civil-military relations in a democratic society.

Future problems in civil-military relations in new democracies are likely to come not from the military but from the civilian side of the equation. They will come from the failures of democratic governments to promote economic development and maintain law and order. They also will stem from weak political institutions and ambitious political leaders who may enlist the military as their accomplices in undermining or destroying democracy, as Alberto Fujimori did in Peru and as Boris Yeltsin, Lech Wałęsa, and others might be tempted to do in their own countries. The new democracies have been more successful in dealing with civil-military relations than with most of the other major challenges they face. Sustaining that success now depends on their ability to make progress in dealing with the ills that lie outside their militaries and within their societies at large.

NOTES

1. Samuel P. Huntington, *The Soldier and the State: The Theory and Politics of Civil-Military Relations* (Cambridge: Harvard University Press, 1957), 83–85 and passim.

2. Robert Arnett, "Russia After the Crisis: Can Civilians Control the Military?" *Orbis* 38 (Winter 1994): 50.

3. Anton Bebler, "On the Evolution of Civil-Military Relations in Eastern and Central Europe," *Inter-University Seminar Newsletter* 23 (Fall 1994): 9.

4. Alfred Stepan, "The New Military Professionalism of Internal Warfare and Military Role Expansion," in Stepan, ed., *Authoritarian Brazil: Origins, Policies and Future* (New Haven: Yale University Press, 1973), 47–65.

5. Alfred Stepan, *The Military in Politics: Changing Patterns in Brazil* (Princeton: Princeton University Press, 1971), 253–66; and Stepan, *Rethinking Military Politics: Brazil and the Southern Cone* (Princeton: Princeton University Press, 1988), 30ff.

6. Benjamin S. Lambeth, "Russia's Wounded Military," *Foreign Affairs* 74 (March–April 1995): 86ff.

7. Samuel P. Huntington, *The Third Wave: Democratization in the Late Twentieth Century* (Norman: University of Oklahoma Press, 1991), 231.

2.
THREAT ENVIRONMENTS AND MILITARY MISSIONS

Michael C. Desch

Michael C. Desch is assistant director and senior research associate at the John M. Olin Institute for Strategic Studies at Harvard University. He is the author of When the Third World Matters: Latin America and U.S. Grand Strategy *(1993), as well as many articles on military issues, and serves on the editorial board of* Security Studies.

The end of the Cold War paradoxically has coincided with a deterioration of civil-military relations in both the United States and Russia. Since the abortive August 1991 coup and the subsequent collapse of the Soviet Union, recurrent concerns have been raised about the erosion of civilian control of the Russian military. Questions are also being aired in the United States about whether American civil-military relations are currently in a state of "crisis." While neither military can yet be said to be outside of civilian control, civil-military relations in both countries, once considered models of stability, have certainly taken a turn for the worse.[1]

This may seem surprising given that most of the literature on civil-military relations shares Harold Lasswell's contention that the military's influence should be highest in a challenging international threat environment and lowest in a relatively benign one.[2] The end of the Cold War thus should have made it easier, not harder, for civilians to exert control over the military establishments. In this essay, I examine why the opposite has turned out to be true. As far as the Russian and American cases are concerned, the root of the problem is that neither nation's military has fully adjusted to the new, less challenging international security environment. Nor has either nation yet articulated a new mission for its armed forces that would be as conducive to good civil-military relations as were the former Cold War missions.

As will be shown, different combinations of external and internal threat environments shape the military's "mission" and hence the pattern of civil-military relations. Missions can be distinguished according to whether a given military's key tasks are internal or external and whether they are limited to war-fighting or include such nonmilitary functions as nation-building, internal security, humanitarian relief, and social-welfare provision. External military missions are the most conducive to healthy patterns of civil-military relations, whereas nonmilitary, internal missions often engender various pathologies. States confronting both external and internal threats, or neither of these, face less determinate threat environments. In such cases, other factors, particularly the ideas underlying a state's military doctrine, can play an independent role.

I draw on four case studies to support this argument. The respective experiences of the Soviet Union and the United States during the Cold War show that external military missions produce healthy (if different) patterns of civil-military relations. In contrast, the former military dictatorships of Latin America's Southern Cone illustrate how internal, nonmilitary missions can lead to poor civil-military relations, and France's experience during the Algerian crisis of the late 1950s and early 1960s shows how a challenging external and internal threat environment can complicate civil-military relations and how the ideas informing a state's military doctrine can play an important role. Then I discuss the experience of the United States and Russia since the end of the Cold War to show what new challenges may arise. Finally, I conclude with some remarks concerning the future of civil-military relations and offer some basic policy guidelines to democratic politicians on how best to redefine the military's mission in the post–Cold War world.

Objective versus Subjective Control

Political analysts who study civil-military relations often cannot agree as to what criteria should be used to characterize them as either "good" or "poor." Some scholars suggest that good civil-military relations exist when the military stays strictly within its professional realm and that poor civil-military relations occur when the military strays outside that realm. In the extreme case, countries in which coups—direct seizures of power by the military—have occurred would be said to have the poorest civil-military relations. Other scholars suggest looking at whether a given system produces sound policy choices in the military realm. In my view, however, the best way to gauge civil-military relations is to examine how civilian and military leaders handle policy differences between them: the best civil-military relations are to be found in those countries where civilian authorities are able to prevail in policy disputes with the military.

The *mission* that a nation's military is assigned has a major impact on civil-military relations. A military's mission denotes its primary task in terms of both the nature of the threat (military or nonmilitary) with which it must deal and the location of that threat (internal or external).

The best way to identify a military's mission is to examine its doctrine, which can be understood as the software that runs the military hardware.[3] A particular military's mission is determined largely by the international and domestic security environments that the nation faces.

As stated above, the threat environment that a nation confronts determines in large part the military's mission and hence military subordination to civil authority. A state facing a traditional, external military challenge is likely to have stable civil-military relations. Such a threat environment forces the institutions of civilian authority to become more cohesive and thus makes them better able to deal with the military in a unified fashion. The civilian leadership under such circumstances usually adopts *objective control* mechanisms, which involve granting the military substantial autonomy in the narrow military realm in return for complete political loyalty. Samuel Huntington argues that such objective civilian control is most likely to produce healthy civil-military relations.[4] Moreover, the external threat orients the military outward, making it less inclined to meddle in domestic politics, since it depends on the state's unwavering support, especially in this age of total warfare.[5] Civilian leadership enjoys greater legitimacy under such circumstances and has a greater capacity to provide the resources necessary to conduct a successful war. In short, an external focus ought to produce the optimal pattern of civil-military relations—one in which the civilian leadership can rely on the military's obedience.

In contrast, if a country faces significant internal threats, the institutions of civilian authority will most likely be weak and deeply divided, making it difficult for civilians to control the military.[6] Civilian politicians often cannot resist the temptation to bring the military into the domestic political arena, both to support their particular faction in its struggle with rival groups and to ensure their group's control of the armed forces. Huntington argues that this extreme form of *subjective control* inevitably leads to unhealthy civil-military relations.[7] Subjective control refers to the effort to control the military by politicizing it and making it more closely resemble the civilian sector. A significant domestic threat also induces the military to adopt an internal orientation, making military intervention in politics almost inevitable. Since the military organization in this situation has little need to call upon the nation's civilian leadership for support, it is less likely to obey those leaders. In short, a nonmilitary and internal mission will produce the worst pattern of civil-military relations.

A state facing both external and internal threats will generally experience difficult civil-military relations, although they will not be as bad as in a state facing only internal threats. When faced with both internal and external threats, the military ought to be relatively focused and cohesive, although its particular orientation may be uncertain. In these circumstances, if the military turns its attention inward, then civil-military relations will usually turn out to be quite poor; however, if the military concentrates on the external threat, relations with civilian authorities may be satisfactory. Governmental institutions are often quite divided in such a threat environment, and therefore civilian authorities may turn to subjective control mechanisms. In such situations, other factors can often play a role in determining just how problematic civil-military relations will be.

A wide range of civil-military relations can be found among states facing neither internal nor external challenges. Sometimes, without a significant external threat to force them to come together, civilian authorities may not be very united and may not have a strong incentive to adopt objective forms of control. Similarly, without a clear external military mission, the military has less incentive to subordinate itself to civilian authority. Yet in other cases civilian institutions remain fairly cohesive, civilian leaders adopt objective controls over the military, and the military retains its external orientation. Thus in this indeterminate threat environment, other factors may explain the pattern of civil-military relations that emerges in a particular nation-state.

The objective threat environment, while often playing an important role, does not alone determine a military's mission, especially when both internal and external threats are present or neither is. To explain the particular pattern of civil-military relations in such cases, we need to consider the role played by the prevailing ideas about the military's proper mission and its role in society. Such ideas are usually embodied in a state's military doctrine.

External Missions: The Cold War Rivals

Two cases—the United States and the Soviet Union during the Cold War—strongly support the proposition that traditional, external missions produce excellent civil-military relations. While these two protagonists differed significantly in terms of their political systems, cultures, and histories, they had two important things in common: the militaries of both nations had traditional, external military operations as their primary mission, and both nations proved to be models of military subordination to civilian control.

The American case.[8] During the Cold War, the United States confronted a significant external threat from the Soviet Union. While some decision makers in the United States saw the Soviet challenge as primarily psychological and nonmilitary in nature, most civilian and military leaders viewed it in strictly military terms.[9] The American military, unlike its French counterpart, as we shall see, embraced the more conventional, external mission, which in the end proved conducive to healthy civil-military relations.

On a whole host of issues, from military strategy to social policy,

American civilian leaders regularly imposed their will on the military. For example, President Harry S. Truman was committed to racial integration of the armed forces and to that end issued Executive Order 9981 in July 1948. Although the military initially resisted carrying out this order, the personnel shortages of the Korean War eventually led military leaders to realize that integration, far from undermining military efficiency, actually enhanced it.

The Korean War also witnessed one of the greatest Cold War challenges to civilian control of the military. General Douglas Mac-Arthur, the commander of both U.S. and UN forces in Korea, against strict orders publicly criticized the limited nature of the war effort and sabotaged the administration's efforts to initiate negotiations. Enraged by the challenge to his authority, President Truman in April 1951 ordered that MacArthur be relieved of his command. Despite strong Republican and public support for MacArthur, the Joint Chiefs of Staff backed President Truman, and the challenge to civilian authority posed by this "old soldier" quickly "faded away."

President Dwight D. Eisenhower had to overcome military resistance both to his military strategy of massive retaliation (with its high reliance on nuclear weapons rather than conventional forces) and to his austere military budgets. During his term in office, President Eisenhower forced the Joint Chiefs to accept military budgets that were much lower than they thought prudent. Indeed, throughout most of the Cold War, American civilian leaders managed to keep the military on a much shorter budgetary leash than the military would have liked.

Although serious tensions in U.S. civil-military relations did emerge during the Vietnam War, the fact that they were resolved underscores just how strong civilian control was throughout the Cold War. The American military showed some initial reluctance to become involved militarily in Southeast Asia, but obeyed orders once civilian decision makers concluded that supporting a noncommunist South Vietnam was in the national interest. During the war itself, many military leaders had deep reservations about civilian-imposed limitations on the conduct of the ground and air wars. At one point, military discontent became so intense that the Joint Chiefs even discussed resigning en masse. In the end, however, they decided that they could not quit when the country was in the midst of war.

In a few minor instances the military did successfully resist civilian authority, but these proved to be the exceptions to the rule. Indeed, civilian officials nearly always prevailed over the military leadership on those issues about which there was serious disagreement. This stemmed in large part from the fact that the American military embraced a traditional, external military mission during this period.

The Soviet case.[10] While there is some debate on the matter, most analysts agree that the Soviet Union enjoyed relatively good civil-military relations during the Cold War.[11] Several factors were at work. To begin with, the central institution of civilian rule—the Communist Party—proved to be quite strong and cohesive, particularly after the death of Stalin. In addition, the party leadership generally relied upon objective mechanisms to control the military. Finally, although the armed forces did on occasion play a role in domestic politics, becoming marginally involved both in internal policing and in several power struggles between communist elites, they nonetheless maintained their primarily external war-fighting mission.

The real puzzle is why the Soviet military not only went along with perestroika *but sometimes even embraced it enthusiastically.*

The strength of Soviet civil-military relations was evident in the fact that, despite the turmoil of the Gorbachev period, the Soviet military remained subordinate to civilian authority, at least up to the August 1991 putsch. This occurred despite several developments that could have been expected to strain civil-military relations. For instance, Mikhail Gorbachev's policies of *perestroika* and *glasnost'* gave the military's critics relatively free rein to air their complaints about the armed forces. The spread of nationalist and secessionist movements seemed to threaten the very unity of the state, undoubtedly generating considerable concern within military circles. For his part, Gorbachev, while slashing the defense budget, departed from longstanding objective control arrangements and began to meddle in many areas of military competence. In addition, his new foreign policy made significant arms-control concessions to the West, acquiesced in the breakup of the Warsaw Pact, and allowed the reunification of Germany.

The real puzzle is why the Soviet military not only went along with *perestroika* but sometimes even embraced it enthusiastically. The answer lies in the fact that the Soviet military viewed many of Gorbachev's reforms as militarily essential. By the late 1970s, many Soviet military theorists had come to believe that a high-technology military revolution was in the offing. Only a revamped civilian sector could provide the cutting-edge technologies that they believed would become increasingly critical in modern warfare. Military elites believed that the external military threat to the Soviet Union had already increased owing to the widening technological gap with the West. Thus, for many of these officers, particularly onetime chief of staff Marshall Nikolai Ogarkov, radical reform seemed to offer the only solution.

The Soviet case thus further shows how a traditional, external military mission can produce good civil-military relations. That the Soviet military weathered the tumult of the Gorbachev period and the eventual breakup of the Soviet Union without intervening significantly in Soviet domestic politics (the events of August 1991 notwithstanding) is a tribute to the strength of civilian controls.

Internal Missions: Argentina, Brazil, and Chile

The military dictatorships that in the 1960s and 1970s characterized the Southern Cone of Latin America illustrate how the predominance of internal over external missions contributes to poor civil-military relations.[12] Indeed, Argentina (1976–83), Brazil (1964–85), and Chile (1973–89) all experienced many of the pathologies that we would expect to find in states where an internal threat environment prevails.

In each of these states, the institutions of civilian rule proved to be quite weak. Argentina witnessed the tumultuous return of Juan Perón in June 1973, the rise to power of his third wife (Isabel) upon his death in July 1974 and her subsequent removal in March 1976, and the emergence of guerrilla movements such as the Montoneros. In Brazil, the leftist regime of João Goulart (1961–64) turned out to be quite weak and ineffective. Finally, in Chile the democratically elected socialist government headed by Salvador Allende (1970–73) came increasingly under fire from both the Left and the Right before falling to a military coup in 1973.

The civilian regimes in these countries often sought to control their militaries by politicizing them. For example, throughout the 1960s and 1970s, various Argentine civilian politicians turned to the army for support against other civilian factions. In Brazil, civilian opponents of the Goulart regime actively encouraged the military to play a more direct role in domestic politics. In Chile before the coup, Allende himself contributed to politicizing the military by bringing military officers into his Popular Unity government. In short, subjective control was the norm immediately before military seizures of power in Argentina, Brazil, and Chile.

Finally, the militaries of these countries embraced missions that were primarily internal and frequently nonmilitary. Beginning in the 1950s, Brazilian military thinkers at the Escola Superior de Guerra (Supreme War College) began to view Brazil's strategic problems in ways that departed significantly from the classical theories once imported from Europe. Previously influenced by German geopolitical thinkers promoting social-darwinist theories of interstate competition, Latin American military strategists by the 1960s began to turn to French theorists who advocated the new idea of "revolutionary war."[13] First the Brazilians, and later the Argentines and the Chileans, developed their own versions of the French theory and incorporated it into their national-security doctrines.[14] These doctrines continued to view international communism as the key threat, but, reflecting French rather than American thinking, saw the streets and plazas of their own countries and not the North German plain as the principal field of battle. According to this perspective, the threat posed by international communism emanated from domestic left-wing movements that would try to exploit social, economic, and political problems in their effort to undermine the state, the Catholic Church, and the military itself. The triumph of the Cuban Revolution in 1959 and the subsequent explosion of rural and urban terrorist movements across Latin America during the 1960s and 1970s lent credibility to these fears. To combat this threat, military officers could not rely solely on traditional weapons and tactics but would instead have to learn about political and psychological warfare, economic development strategies, social-welfare provision, and even national administration.

The link between the prevailing national-security doctrines and the most overt expression of a breakdown in civil-military relations—clearly manifested in military seizures of power and prolonged military rule—has already been well established.[15] The key point to be made here is that these cases provide further evidence of the link between internal, nontraditional military missions and poor civil-military relations. The emergence of military dictatorships in the Southern Cone of Latin America shows that internal military missions produce pathologies in civil-military relations.

Dual Missions: France from 1954 to 1962

The Algerian crisis that gripped France between 1954 and 1962 illustrates how a challenging external *and* internal threat environment can complicate civil-military relations.[16] The new doctrine embraced by the French military in the 1950s led the armed forces to adopt internal, nonmilitary missions. This in turn helped produce a breakdown in civil-military relations, which was rectified only when President Charles de Gaulle introduced a new military doctrine that reemphasized the military's traditional, external mission. The French case illustrates how, in a structurally indeterminate threat environment, ideas can play a crucial role.

For most of the nineteenth and twentieth centuries, the French military had been a model of military subordination to civilian institutions. Indeed, it played such an insignificant domestic political role that it became known as *la grande muette* (the great mute). What happened to transform this model of stable civilian control into a new reality that threatened the very fabric of French democracy?

First, beginning with the fall of the Popular Front government in the 1930s, continuing with the establishment of the collaborationist Vichy government in Paris and the rival Free French exile government in London following France's defeat in May 1940, and concluding with the foundation of the ill-fated Fourth Republic in the immediate postwar years, French governmental institutions progressively weakened and lost much of their popular legitimacy. A second related development was that French civilian leaders adopted subjective mechanisms of civilian control of the military. During the Second World War, General Charles de Gaulle and Marshal Philippe Pétain vied for the allegiance and support of French military units, which only served to divide the military and draw it increasingly into domestic affairs. This pattern continued during the short-lived governments of the postwar Fourth Republic.

> *The doctrine of* **guerre revolutionaire** *changed the French military's mission from external war-fighting to internal counterrevolutionary warfare.*

When Germany's defeat in the Second World War greatly diminished the threat from France's traditional rival in Europe, the French, unlike most other Europeans, did not shift their security focus to the new conventional military threat emanating from the USSR. Whereas the Americans and most of the rest of Europe focused their efforts on confronting the danger posed by the 175 Warsaw Pact divisions poised to strike at the heart of Western Europe, the French turned their attention to the internal and nonmilitary aspects of the communist threat. This stemmed in part from the domestic challenge posed by the French Communist Party, one of the largest and most pro-Soviet communist parties in Western Europe. Yet the French also came to see the wars of national liberation that began to break out throughout the vast French colonial empire as provoked by internal agents of international communism. In other words, French civilian and military leaders came to regard the Cold War as an internal and largely unconventional conflict.

That France experienced a crisis in civil-military relations during the Algerian conflict should not be surprising. The Algerian war came in the wake of France's defeat in Indochina at the hands of the communist Vietminh. The French military believed that the war in Indochina had been lost because the French had tried to fight it using traditional military doctrine and tactics. Thus, following the defeat at Dien Bien Phu in 1954, the French officer corps came up with a new doctrine, which they called *guerre revolutionaire*. The crux of this new doctrine of "revolutionary war" was that the Cold War was not a conventional military conflict like the Second World War fought against an external adversary using infantry, armor, and artillery. Rather, the Cold War was a political, economic, and ideological conflict that would be waged partially by force of arms but primarily through propaganda, economic reform, and political persuasion. In short, the doctrine of *guerre revolutionaire* changed the French military's mission from external war-fighting to internal counterrevolutionary warfare, which entailed significant nonmilitary activities.

Algeria seemed to be the perfect laboratory for testing this new doctrine. Most French people regarded Algeria as an integral part of metropolitan France (it even made up two of France's *départements*). Opponents of a French Algeria, though supported by the forces of international communism and radical Arab nationalism, were largely indigenous—Algerian Arabs made up the bulk of the National Liberation Front (FLN). In addition, many in France believed that the country's hold on Algeria was being undermined by domestic enemies in metropolitan France, primarily on the left. In short, the French saw the Algerian war as essentially an internal affair that would be waged by largely nonmilitary means.

France experienced a series of serious civil-military conflicts between 1954 and 1962, at a time when the army operated according to the mission articulated in the doctrine of revolutionary war. In June 1958, the military played a central role in bringing down the moribund Fourth Republic and returning General de Gaulle to power. In January 1960, having lost faith in de Gaulle's commitment to the cause of French Algeria, significant portions of the military supported the "revolt of the barricades" in Algiers. In April 1961, four generals led a military rebellion that, while unsuccessful, nonetheless helped give birth to the Secret Armed Organization (OAS). The OAS, a terrorist organization based in Algeria (with cells in metropolitan France) and made up of hard-line military officers and right-wing civilians opposed to Algerian independence, constituted a serious challenge to civilian, democratic rule in France. Given the growing gap between the military and the government in this period, only de Gaulle's skilled maneuvering managed to avert a complete breakdown in civil-military relations.

De Gaulle's plan for reestablishing stable civil-military relations had two key components. First, he successfully persuaded most of the French people that Algeria should not be considered an integral part of France, which had the effect of undermining popular support for the French settlers in Algeria (the *pieds-noirs*). The terms of debate thus shifted from saving the *pieds-noirs* by keeping Algeria as part of France to finding a way to get them out of Algeria and acquiescing to Algerian independence.

Second, de Gaulle fundamentally reoriented French military strategy by changing its primary mission from internal counterinsurgency back to external warfare. The French nuclear program, as the centerpiece of this effort, was designed simultaneously to reestablish France as a major European power and to give the French military a more traditional external focus. De Gaulle's new defense strategy (*tous azimuts*) hypothesized that France could face an external threat from any direction—not only from the East but also from the West. In the wake of this policy shift, military interference in French domestic politics receded.

The French case thus provides further evidence that internal, nonmilitary missions can prove disastrous for civil-military relations, whereas traditional, external military missions provide the basis for a sound relationship between the military and civilian authorities.

After the Cold War

In contrast to the Cold War period, in which both the United States and the Soviet Union served as models of stable military subordination to civilian authority, the post–Cold War era has witnessed a marked deterioration in civil-military relations in both cases. It is not accidental that this should coincide with the end of the Cold War, as the changed international security environment has undermined longstanding Cold War military missions. To date, neither Russia nor the United States has confronted a really challenging internal threat environment, although Russia faces many more potential dangers than does the United States.

The "crisis" of American civil-military relations. Recently scholars in the United States have begun to question whether the country is witnessing a significant deterioration in civil-military relations. Members of the "crisis school" point to such factors as the unprecedented political role taken on by General Colin Powell, former chairman of the Joint Chiefs of Staff, the frosty reception given President Bill Clinton by various military units, and the general climate of distrust and mutual recrimination surrounding relations between the Clinton administration and the military leadership.[17] In contrast, other scholars and former policy makers argue that nothing has really changed.[18] Who is right?

While talk of a "crisis" in U.S. civil-military relations is premature, some evidence suggests that civilian control of the American military is not as firm as it once was. On the positive side, civilian leaders have persuaded the military to accept major reductions in defense spending. Moreover, both President George Bush prior to the Gulf War and President Clinton during the period leading up to the Haitian operation successfully overcame initial military reservations about intervention. On the negative side, the military appears to have prevailed in more policy disputes with the administration than it did during the Cold War. For example, military reluctance about direct intervention in Bosnia kept the United States on the sidelines of that conflict for over three years. The military also initially resisted Senator Sam Nunn's efforts to initiate a major reassessment of military roles and missions. The military's objection to the "win plus hold" strategy (i.e., maintaining sufficient forces to contain a second aggressor while winning a major regional war) forced the administration to embrace the more ambitious and costly strategy of fighting and winning two major regional wars simultaneously. In addition, the military has balked at civilian efforts to open more combat specialties to women, and, with the aid of its congressional supporters, it thwarted the Clinton administration's efforts to end the exclusion of homosexuals from military service. Several potentially serious issues still loom on the horizon, including deeper cuts in defense spending and implementation of the conclusions of the roles and missions study. Although these issues have yet to be resolved, the trend in civil-military relations appears to be moving in the wrong direction.

Several changes brought about by the end of the Cold War have affected civil-military relations. For example, American civilian institutions, while still robust, have nonetheless come under considerable strain in recent years. Moreover, politicians seem to have abandoned the previous policy of objective control and are now trying to influence several policy areas previously within the exclusive purview of the military. Finally, and most important, the external war-fighting mission, which during the Cold War served to keep the military outwardly focused and subordinate to civilian authority, is becoming less central. The various external missions that remain increasingly entail such nontraditional tasks as peacekeeping and humanitarian intervention. In addition, civilian leaders are asking the military to take on a greater domestic role in such areas as counterterrorism, antinarcotics operations, disaster relief, riot control, and even social-welfare provision. These nontraditional and internal military missions are less conducive to maintaining the prior pattern of healthy civil-military relations.

Obviously, little danger exists that the American military will stage a coup and attempt to seize power. Nor do I expect the armed forces to become openly insubordinate and disobey direct orders. Despite the weakening of America's governmental institutions, these remain much stronger than their counterparts in the coup-plagued nations of the Third World. Nor has the U.S. military really embraced the sort of nontraditional, internal mission adopted by the French army during the Algerian crisis or by the "new professional" military dictatorships of Latin America.

A key factor in the deterioration of American civil-military relations is uncertainty about the military's post–Cold War mission. The diminished international threat environment has weakened the domestic institutions of civilian authority, caused the civilian leadership to move toward subjective control, and left the U.S. military in a quandary about its international and domestic missions. Given these changes, the U.S. military will most likely be less obedient to civilian leaders than it was in the Cold War period.

The breakdown of Russian civil-military relations. A similar debate has ensued about the state of Russian civil-military relations in the post-Soviet era.[19] Some scholars, basing their judgment on the Soviet Union's long record of relatively good civil-military relations, predict that Russian civil-military relations will remain fairly stable.[20] Others argue that Russian civil-military relations have deteriorated significantly since the end of the Cold War.[21]

My own perspective is more in line with that of the latter camp. Russia has witnessed several troubling developments in recent years. For example, the military has blocked several foreign-policy initiatives undertaken by the Yeltsin government. The Russian military undermined the Yeltsin administration's efforts to negotiate a return of the Kuril Islands to Japan and delayed its deal with Ukraine to divide up the Black Sea fleet. Similarly, despite civilian support for the Conventional Forces in Europe treaty, the Russian Ministry of Defense has threatened to unilaterally abrogate those parts of the treaty that it believes run counter to Russian security interests in the Caucasus. Moreover, the military's strong objections to any Western plans to admit East European countries into the North Atlantic Treaty Organization have forced the government into a similarly firm stand. Finally, Defense Minister Pavel Grachev and his military allies seem bent on settling the Chechen conflict by force and sabotaging any civilian efforts to negotiate a peace accord.

The military has flexed its muscles in other ways as well. It won important changes in the conscription laws in order to halt evasion of the draft by potential military recruits. The military has also resisted repeated civilian efforts to promote significant military reform. Moreover, Grachev's demand that all military forces be placed under the control of the Ministry of Defense may soon be met. The Ministry of Defense has even taken an active electoral role, putting up 123 officers as candidates in the parliamentary elections of December 1995.

Individual military leaders have demonstrated their staying power. Grachev so far remains in place as defense minister despite recurrent calls for his removal following the military's operational problems in Chechnya and his personal implication in several corruption scandals. Retired general Aleksandr Lebed—known for defying civilian politicians, questioning whether Russia is ready for democracy, and openly expressing admiration for Chile's former military dictator Augusto Pinochet—is one of the most popular political figures in Russia today. All these signs suggest that all is not well in Russian civil-military relations.

Several factors are at work here. Russian civilian institutions in the post-Soviet era remain weak. The Communist Party, although currently undergoing an upswing in popular support, no longer functions as the central institution of civilian rule, and nothing has emerged to replace it in this role. Moreover, Yeltsin and other politicians have begun to adopt subjective control mechanisms. The events of September–October 1993, when both the Yeltsin regime and its parliamentary opposition tried to win the armed forces over to their side in what became a violent confrontation, illustrate the increasing willingness to politicize the military.

More important, the military has lost the traditional external mission that played such a central role in maintaining the healthy pattern of civil-military relations during the Cold War. The remaining missions for the Russian military are neither clearly external nor distinctly military. The new military doctrine adopted in late 1993 reflects the ambiguity of the military's post–Cold War mission. While the doctrine does outline several traditional, external war-fighting missions, more than two-thirds of the document deals with such nontraditional and internal missions as law enforcement, counterterrorism, and combating ethnic separatism, narcotics trafficking, and tax evasion.[22] In addition, much of the military's attention focuses on the newly independent states of the former USSR, which make up what the Russians call the "near abroad"; in particular, military officers have expressed concern over the status of ethnic Russians living in these areas. Technically, this mission is external because it deals with what are now sovereign states, yet many Russians, including a substantial number of military officers, believe that these territories should be part of a greater Russia, so in that sense it could be regarded as internal. Indeed, an apt comparison can be made between the Russian military's mission of protecting ethnic cohorts in the near abroad and the French military's defense of the *pieds-noirs* in Algeria. This type of mission, which, as we have seen, had deleterious consequences for French civil-military relations, could have a similar impact in Russia.

The end of the Cold War and the consequent loss of traditional, external military missions helped bring about a deterioration of civil-military relations in both the United States and Russia. Admittedly, Russia's problems are far more serious, although even there a military coup still seems unlikely. Nonetheless, we need to ask what Russian and American civilian leaders should do to try to improve the state of civil-military relations.

Policy Recommendations

I have argued that a state whose military has a clear, traditional, external mission is likely to have good civil-military relations (defined in terms of the civilian leadership's being able to impose its will upon the military). A state facing a challenging external threat environment is likely to have strong and cohesive institutions of civilian rule, a civilian leadership that relies on objective control mechanisms, and a military organization that is externally focused. In contrast, a state whose military has an internal and nontraditional focus is likely to have problematic civil-military relations. A state facing primarily internal threats is likely to have weak and divided institutions of civilian authority, a civilian leadership that resorts to subjective control mecha-nisms, and a military that is internally focused.

The United States and Russia in the post–Cold War era appear to fall between these two ideal types. For both countries, the end of the Cold War has witnessed a weakening of governmental institutions, albeit to different degrees. Both American and Russian civilian leaders have also moved away from objective control toward some type of subjective control. Finally, both nations' militaries face almost an existential crisis regarding their mission, as the end of the Cold War has seriously called into question their *raison d'être*. As both militaries struggle to find a new post–Cold War role, they are unfortunately moving or being led toward nontraditional and internal missions. As the French case clearly shows, such missions are unlikely to be conducive to maintaining healthy patterns of civil-military relations.

The challenge for civilian and military leaders in both Russia and the United States is to find new military missions that are both appropriate to the changing international security environment of the post–Cold War world and conducive to a desirable pattern of civil-military relations. As the post–Cold War international security environment is indeterminate, civil-military relations could go either way. Under such circumstances, the ideas that inform policy choices can play an important role. Civilian leaders in both countries should keep in mind the following guidelines.

First, they should be careful about assigning the military a larger internal role. While historically the armed forces of several nations have been able to exercise some internal-security functions yet remain subordinate to civilian authority, those countries whose militaries retained the traditional, external war-fighting focus have on balance enjoyed better civil-military relations. Therefore, civilian leaders in both the United States and Russia ought to be circumspect about the type of internal missions that they assign to their militaries. Obviously, the use of the military during natural or man-made disasters is appropriate; however, the regular assignment of military units to tasks involving internal security, counterterrorism, law enforcement, or social welfare (e.g., provision of health care in inner cities) is undesirable in terms of maintaining both military readiness and good civil-military relations.[23] In both countries, civilian leaders have moved in the wrong direction in recent years. The Yeltsin administration's use of the military in October 1993 to seize the parliament building has made the military a major player in Russian domestic politics.[24] Recent suggestions by members of the Clinton administration that the American military be used for the provision of domestic social welfare and infrastructure are likely to exacerbate, rather than ameliorate, U.S. civil-military tensions.[25]

Second, civilian leaders should eschew subjective control. Politicizing the military does not engender healthy civil-military relations, nor is it ultimately likely to benefit individual civilian factions. Rather, objective controls and military professionalism remain the strongest pillars of good civil-military relations. Civilian leaders should foster a culture of military professionalism through objective controls.

Finally, despite the less challenging threat environment of the post–Cold War period, civilian leaders should resist public declarations that the country will never again face the kind of significant external threats that justify traditional, external military missions. The overly optimistic rhetoric of Russian and American civilian leaders about the diminished need for military force in the post–Cold War world may have contributed to the current problems in Russian and American civil-military relations by calling into question the countries' respective armed forces' traditional external mission. Civilian leaders need to remind the public of the inevitability of future conflicts in order to bolster healthy civil-military relations. While this does not mean that the Russian and U.S. militaries must remain wedded to fighting a major conventional or nuclear war, it does suggest that their primary mission ought to remain the traditional one of external war-fighting.

NOTES

This essay draws heavily on my forthcoming book, tentatively entitled *Soldiers, States, and Structure: Civilian Control of the Military in a Changing Security Environment.* I would like to thank Andrew Bacevich, Kurt Campbell, and Mary Jo Desch for their helpful comments.

1. Samuel P. Huntington, *Political Order in Changing Societies* (New Haven: Yale University Press, 1968), 194.

2. See Harold Lasswell, "The Garrison State," *American Journal of Sociology* 46 (January 1941): 455–68. A more recent example is Jack Snyder, "Civil-Military Relations and the Cult of the Offensive, 1914 and 1984," in Steven E. Miller, ed., *Military Strategy and the Origins of the First World War: An International Security Reader* (Princeton: Princeton University Press, 1985), 108–46.

3. The extensive literature on the external consequences of military doctrines includes Barry R. Posen, *The Sources of Military Doctrine: France, Britain, and Germany Between the World Wars* (Ithaca, N.Y.: Cornell University Press, 1984), and Jack Snyder, *The Ideology of the Offensive: Military Decision Making and the Disasters of 1914* (Ithaca, N.Y.: Cornell University Press, 1984). There is also an impressive literature in comparative politics that looks at the domestic consequences of military doctrines, notably Alfred Stepan, *The Military in Politics: Changing Patterns in Brazil* (Princeton: Princeton University Press, 1971). My objective in both this essay and my forthcoming book is to combine the insights of these two literatures.

4. Samuel P. Huntington, *The Soldier and the State: The Theory and Politics of Civil-Military Relations* (Cambridge: Harvard University Press, 1957), 83–85.

5. Stanislav Andreski, "On the Peaceful Disposition of Military Dictatorships," *Journal of Strategic Studies* 3 (December 1980): 3–4. As he observes elsewhere, "'the devil finds work for idle hands': the soldiers who have no wars to fight or prepare for will be tempted to interfere in politics. Taking a long-term view, it seems that there is an inverse connection between strenuous warfare and praetorianism." *Military Organization and Society* (Berkeley and Los Angeles: University of California Press, 1968), 202.

6. On the importance of strong civilian institutions to good civil-military relations, see Huntington, *Political Order in Changing Societies*, 1–31.

7. Huntington, *The Soldier and the State*, 80–81.

8. This section draws from my "U.S. Civil-Military Relations in a Changing

International Order," in Don Snider and Miranda Carlton-Carew, eds., *U.S. Civil-Military Relations: In Crisis or Transition?* (Washington, D.C.: Center for Strategic and International Studies, 1995), 166–84.

9. George F. Kennan best represents the nonmilitary perspective on the Cold War; see his *Memoirs: 1925–1950* (Boston: Atlantic Monthly Press, 1967), 271–97 and 354–67. The military reading of the Cold War was clearly articulated in National Security Council Paper #68 (NSC-68), entitled "United States Objectives and Programs for National Security" (issued on 14 April 1950), which redefined the American strategy of containment. For a discussion of these two perspectives, see John Gaddis, *Strategies of Containment: A Critical Appraisal of Postwar American National Security Policy* (New York: Oxford University Press, 1982), 89–126.

10. This section draws from my "Why the Soviet Military Supported Gorbachev and Why the Russian Military Might Only Support Yeltsin for a Price," *Journal of Strategic Studies* 16 (December 1993): 455–64.

11. Condoleezza Rice, "The Party, the Military and Decision Authority in the Soviet Union," *World Politics* 40 (October 1987): 80–81.

12. In addition to Stepan's work, this section draws upon Alain Rouquie's excellent *The Military and the State in Latin America*, trans. Paul Sigmund (Berkeley and Los Angeles: University of California Press, 1987).

13. A recent article that discusses the French influence on Latin American national-security doctrines is Carina Perelli, "From Counterrevolutionary Warfare to Political Awakening: The Uruguayan and Argentine Armed Forces in the 1970s," *Armed Forces and Society* 20 (Fall 1993): 25–49. For a fuller discussion of the doctrine of revolutionary war, see the section on France below.

14. The best work on the internal consequences of military doctrines has been done by scholars examining the military dictatorships of Latin America's Southern Cone; see especially Stepan, *The Military in Politics,* and Rouquie, *The Military and the State.* In addition, excellent work has been done by David Pion-Berlin; see his *Ideology of State Terror: Economic Doctrine and Political Repression in Argentina and Peru* (Boulder, Colo.: Lynne Rienner, 1989), "The National Security Doctrine, Military Threat Perception and the 'Dirty War' in Argentina," *Comparative Political Studies* 21 (October 1988): 382–407, "Latin American National Security Doctrines: Hard- and Softline Themes," *Armed Forces and Society* 15 (Spring 1989): 411–29, and, with George A. Lopez, "Of Victims and Executioners: Argentine State Terror, 1975–1979," *International Studies Quarterly* 35 (March 1991): 63–86.

15. Stepan, *The Military in Politics,* 168.

16. On this period, see especially Alistair Horne, *A Savage War of Peace: Algeria, 1954–1962,* rev. ed. (New York: Penguin, 1987); Peter Paret, *French Revolutionary Warfare from Indochina to Algeria: The Analysis of a Political and Military Doctrine* (New York: Praeger, 1964); and Paul-Marie de la Gorce, *The French Army: A Military-Political History,* trans. Kenneth Douglas (New York: Braziller, 1963).

17. Literature of the "crisis school" includes Russell Weigley, "The American Military and the Principle of Civilian Control from McClellan to Powell," *Journal of Military History* 57 (October 1993): 27–58; Richard Kohn, "Out of Control: The Crisis in Civil-Military Relations," *The National Interest* 35 (Spring 1994): 3–17; Edward Luttwak, "Washington's Biggest Scandal," *Commentary* 97 (May 1994): 29–33; and Charles Dunlap, Jr., "Welcome to the Junta: The Erosion of Civilian Control of the U.S. Military," *Wake Forest Law Review* 29 (Summer 1994): 341–92.

18. Skeptics include Generals Colin Powell and William Odom; see "An Exchange on Civil-Military Relations," *The National Interest* 36 (Summer 1994): 23, 25–26.

19. See my "Why the Soviet Military Supported Gorbachev," 467–74.

20. Optimistic views include Stephen M. Meyer, "How the Threat (and the Coup)

Collapsed: The Politicization of the Soviet Military," *International Security* 16 (Winter 1991–92): 5–38; John Lepingwell, "Soviet Civil-Military Relations and the August Coup," *World Politics* 44 (July 1992): 539–72; Bruce Porter, *Red Armies in Crisis* (Washington, D.C.: Center for Strategic and International Studies, 1991); and Brian Taylor, "Russian Civil-Military Relations After the October Uprising," *Survival* 36 (Spring 1994): 3–29.

21. Skeptical views include Mikhail Tsypkin, "Will the Military Rule Russia?" *Security Studies* 2 (Autumn 1992): 38–73; Robert Arnett, "Can Civilians Control the Military?" *Orbis* 38 (Winter 1994): 41–57; and Thomas Nichols, "'An Electoral Mutiny?' Zhirinovsky and the Russian Armed Forces," *Armed Forces and Society* 21 (Spring 1995): 327–48.

22. "The Main Provisions of the Russian Federation Military Doctrine," *Voennaya Mysl'*, November 1993, 2–16.

23. Samuel P. Huntington, "New Contingencies, Old Roles," *Joint Force Quarterly* 1 (Autumn 1993): 38–43.

24. Almost all of the major parties contesting the Duma elections in December 1995 had high-ranking military officers on their slates. See "A Real Generals' Election," *The Economist*, 23 September 1995, 44, 46.

25. See the letter of Deborah R. Lee, assistant secretary of defense for reserve affairs, "Our Civil-Military Program Is Small, But It's Paying Big Dividends," *Washington Times*, 24 May 1995, 22.

3.
MILITARY ROLES
PAST AND PRESENT

Louis W. Goodman

Louis W. Goodman is dean of the School of International Service at American University. He earned his doctorate in sociology from Northwestern University. He is the coeditor of Lessons of the Venezuelan Experience *(1995) and of* The Military and Democracy: The Future of Civil-Military Relations in Latin America *(1989).*

The primary purpose of a military force is to provide for a country's external security. Nonetheless, ever since the advent of sizeable standing armies, scholars and politicians have debated whether the armed forces should also be used for peaceful missions benefiting the larger community. This discussion has intensified since the end of the Cold War, as the collapse of the Soviet Union has fundamentally altered the security environment facing many countries around the world. The era is now past in which large combat forces need to be deployed overseas in forward locations at high states of combat readiness. The United States, Russia, and most of their allies have initiated broad-gauged programs of military downsizing and defense conversion. In light of these changes, some have argued that there is now an "opportunity to match some of the freed resources with critical domestic needs."[1]

Such arguments have been put forth before. In the aftermath of the Second World War, many policy makers suggested that highly trained armed forces could be used for nonmilitary purposes. In many developing nations, notably in sub-Saharan Africa and South Asia, technical training of the military began as a consequence of expanded operations during the Second World War.[2] After demobilization at war's end, the military in many countries continued to provide technical training. In the 1950s, for example, the Pakistani army became actively involved in road building and dam construction, successfully curtailed massive jute-smuggling operations, and trained ex-servicemen for civilian life; in Côte d'Ivoire and several other African countries, the armed forces trained civilians for both agricultural and industrial employment; in Chile,

Colombia, Peru, and other Latin American countries, military personnel became extensively involved in agrarian training, road building, medical service, basic education, and other forms of civic action.[3] In all of these cases, military personnel possessed critical skills that were in short supply in the civilian sector. Military units and personnel trained in communications, construction, education, medicine, procurement, or transportation carried out noncombat missions perceived as socially beneficial. Finding civilians to undertake these missions was viewed as either infeasible or not cost-effective, since military personnel were already trained or the capacity for training civilians under military discipline was already in place.

With the end of the Cold War, nations confront somewhat similar choices. Many skilled soldiers face the prospect of demobilization, often in countries in which civilian capacity to carry out important social and economic roles may be in short supply. Yet post–Cold War circumstances, both domestic and international, are substantially different from those prevailing after the Second World War. In the post–Cold War world, international ideological rivalry has been replaced by cooperation and competition in the economic, social, and environmental arenas. Furthermore, the technological revolutions in telecommunications and transportation have markedly altered the nature of this competition. Individuals are more aware of the lifestyles and opportunities available to their counterparts in other countries. State and nonstate actors engage in global transactions with a speed and intimacy inconceivable at the end of the Second World War. Telecommunications technology now allows people to transmit information around the world as easily as friends exchange gossip—sometimes even more so. The commercial use of the jet engine allows one-day travel between any of the world's capital cities.

These technological changes have created a "global village" in which allies meet and interact with a frequency unparalleled in human history. Linked financial managers send currency and securities around the world electronically. Diplomats represent their nations in person when and where needed and get new instructions in an electronic instant. Business officials create "virtual corporations" so that space does not limit the scope and speed of their operations.

In this environment, military officers need counterparts in other countries who can quickly understand and adjust to rapidly changing joint efforts that may be as broad-gauged as the Gulf War and UN peacekeeping operations or as simple as binational road building and civic action. Smooth cooperation among allies is essential for the pursuit of common goals. Moreover, the strongest international alliances involve cooperation in many diverse areas—diplomatic, commercial, cultural, and military. If such cooperation entails huge transaction costs, economic alliances may be noncompetitive, and security, environmental, or social alliances may become unwieldy. Transaction costs (the inefficiencies involved in attempting to work together) are likely to be high among allies with differing political systems or among institutions whose structures or trajectories diverge. This makes it difficult for democratic nations to work easily with countries governed by authoritarian regimes. It has also contributed to the worldwide decline in defense spending and in the size of armed forces since 1989.[4] If the armed forces of nations trying to forge alliances take on markedly different roles and missions, their ability to cooperate militarily is likely to be impeded, with possible spillover into other arenas.

Potential New Roles

These pressures impinge on national choices regarding the roles and missions of the armed forces. First and foremost, armed forces are enjoined from overthrowing democratically constituted regimes. The Organization of American States (OAS) clearly stated this point in its 1991 "Santiago Commitment to Democracy," and further directed the OAS secretary general to devise "incentives" for restoring democracy in those countries where democratic regimes had been overturned.[5] For its part, the U.S. government has directed that its overseas military commands place special emphasis on encouraging foreign armed forces "to consider roles appropriate to their national requirements, roles that are supportive of civilian control and respectful of human rights and the rule of law."[6]

In other areas, norms of conduct have been established for post–Cold War military activity. For example, although drug trafficking and terrorism are regarded as extremely dangerous transnational threats to national security, most armed forces have adopted the official position that they will pursue counterdrug and counterterrorism activities only in support of such civilian agencies as the police or customs authorities. Nonetheless, the massive commitment of resources by the United States Southern Command and the armed forces of many Latin American countries to combating drug trafficking in the late 1980s and early 1990s suggests new de facto military roles. While most policy makers agree that military activity in these areas should be undertaken in support of civilian agencies, there is little consensus about what priority these activities should be assigned. Consultation among allies in the Western Hemisphere and continuing evaluation of counterdrug programs suggest that the role the military plays in fighting drug trafficking and terrorism may become less important in the future than its role in fostering development and combating poverty in the Americas.[7] Previous experience with military involvement in social development and civic-action programs, however, raises significant questions: 1) how to avoid undermining the capacity of civilian development agencies when imposing military solutions to poverty alleviation, and 2) how to draw a clear line between fostering social development and countering subversion.

While the end of international ideological conflict has led to widespread acceptance of democracy and capitalism, the need for combat-ready armed forces has not disappeared. The national-security imperatives at the close of the century are often described as "more diverse" than those that faced the international community during the Cold War. President Clinton in a July 1994 report on national security listed as "serious dangers" such security threats as ethnic conflict, rogue states, and the proliferation of weapons of mass destruction, along with such broad concerns as environmental degradation and population growth.[8] The United Nations has indicated that "the use of small arms in intrastate conflicts has been more frequent [since the end of the Cold War] than at any other period since World War I."[9] Despite the changing nature of external threats in the post–Cold War era, nations still require the capacity to use force when necessary to defend the interests of their citizens. Since armed forces cannot be assembled on short notice—especially given the contemporary need for rapid deployment, integration of military systems, and full interoperational capacity among international allies—long-term investment in national defense is still required.

This does not mean that national armed forces will have identical structures, or that the current global balance between national and regional forces will be maintained. For example, while Costa Rica, Panama, and Haiti have disbanded their respective armed forces, each has maintained its security forces and international alliances in order to protect its territorial integrity and help cope with natural disasters. Moreover, in 1995 Costa Rica and Panama both contributed security forces to OAS peacekeeping efforts in Haiti. Other countries, while retaining their armed forces, have nonetheless changed their military establishments significantly since the end of the Cold War. Between 1985 and 1994, the size of the world's armed forces dropped by a total of 16 percent, and overall military expenditures were cut by 30 percent. Moreover, many national militaries have become involved in multilateral peacekeeping operations, and some are currently attempting to promote regional cooperation through defense cooperation.[10]

The situation for countries without formal armed forces does, however, differ in several important respects from that of nations with standing armies. On the one hand, the relatively small size of the security forces in such countries decreases the power asymmetry that exists between the various armed services and civilian institutions. On the other hand, policy makers in these nations have fewer choices regarding the assignment of such smaller security forces to alternative missions than do their counterparts in countries with formal standing armies. These differences have significant implications, which will be discussed below.

The United States

Historically, democratic nations have not always strictly confined their militaries to combat missions. The United States provides a case in point.[11] The United States Military Academy at West Point once trained many of the nation's engineers, both civilian and military. The United States Army contributed to national economic development by helping explore and survey the West, choosing settlement sites, and building roads, dams, and waterways. Indeed, the Army performed many tasks now carried out by the National Weather Service and the Geological Survey. In the early twentieth century, the Army Corps of Engineers constructed the Panama Canal and was responsible for many other public works and buildings; even today, it provides water to the nation's capital. During the Depression, the Army also put together and oversaw the Civilian Conservation Corps.

The United States Navy took an active part in exploration and scientific research: its ships surveyed coasts throughout the hemisphere, explored the Amazon, laid cables, and collected scientific specimens and data from around the world. During the nineteenth century, the Navy policed the slave trade while the Army administered civil government in the Reconstruction South and in the Alaskan Territory. Later in the century the Army was often called in to deal with strikes and labor violence. American soldiers have also taken on special roles in times of emergency: they have often been called in to quell urban riots or provide relief in areas affected by floods, earthquakes, blizzards, or hurricanes. Overseas, they helped combat disease, hunger, and illiteracy, organized elections, and promoted democracy in such countries as Panama, Cuba, Haiti, and Nicaragua.

Since the end of the Cold War, the armed forces have taken on many new roles that do not directly involve fighting wars or deterring potential aggression against the United States. During the administrations of George Bush and Bill Clinton, U.S. troops became involved in peacekeeping and humanitarian operations in places like Somalia, Rwanda, Bosnia, and Haiti. The Clinton administration, in a May 1994 presidential directive on U.S. policy on reforming multilateral peace operations, laid out the first comprehensive framework officially affirming the importance of using American military forces in peace-keeping and other noncombat operations. President Clinton's July 1994 national-security report reaffirmed combat as "the primary mission of our Armed Forces," but specifically mentioned such secondary roles as combating terrorism, protecting the safety of Americans abroad, supplying military training and advice to friendly governments, assisting in disaster relief, helping with the U.S. space program, and participating in multilateral peacekeeping operations.[12]

Those countries currently undergoing democratization can draw four lessons from the U.S. experience:

1) The core mission of the U.S. armed forces has always been combat—to deter aggression and, if necessary, to fight and win conflicts in which vital national interests are threatened.

2) A longstanding secondary mission has been disaster relief—providing emergency food, shelter, medical care, and security to victims of floods, storms, droughts, earthquakes, and civil disturbances.

3) A new post–Cold War mission is the use of American forces for peacekeeping operations—promoting democratization or conflict resolution through the provision of airlift, intelligence, or communications support and, if necessary, American combat units.

4) Other missions of a transitional nature may be taken on when necessary, to be relinquished as soon as civilian authorities can assume responsibility.

Latin America

Since the end of the Cold War, many nations have moved toward democracy. Nowhere has this been more apparent than in Latin America, where since 1979 civilian presidents have been elected in 19 nations once ruled by military officers. Many of these nations have held subsequent elections that resulted in the leaders of opposition parties peacefully assuming the presidency, have promulgated new constitutions, and have undertaken popularly mandated reforms of the executive, legislative, and judicial branches of government.

Nonetheless, in many nations the military, as the largest and best-organized institution, has assumed new roles that have significantly expanded its scope of responsibility. For example, the armed forces have sometimes taken on the task of maintaining public order. Sometimes this came about through the merging of the police and the military into a single service, as occurred under Manuel Noriega's rule in Panama; at other times, it resulted from an emergency decree, as happened during Colombia's attempts to control various insurgent forces and during Peru's battle with the guerrillas of the Sendero Luminoso (Shining Path). This policing role has taken on particular significance with the rise of illegal narcotics trafficking, as troops from Argentina to Mexico have become involved in fighting the "drug war."

Troops in Venezuela, Honduras, and Argentina have been assigned the mission of "protecting the environment," planting trees, and fighting pollution. Throughout the hemisphere troops are frequently involved in various public works projects—laying roads, building dams, and constructing buildings from Brazil to El Salvador. Similarly, the armed forces are often involved in *civic action:* delivering education, health, and other services to the disadvantaged from the heights of the Ecuadorian Andes to the jungles of Guatemala.

The armed forces also provide various goods and services to public- and private-sector buyers under a variety of circumstances. In Paraguay, where many of the military's expenses are not met in the national budget, the armed forces have generated revenue on their own, engaging openly in such activities as farming and timber harvesting and less openly in smuggling. During periods of hyperinflation, the armed forces of such nations as Argentina have set up holding companies to generate revenue from real estate, manufacturing, and services. The proceeds from these activities have financed military expenses that governments could not cover owing to budgetary pressures.

From Guatemala to Argentina, the military has gotten into the business of supplying itself with munitions and military equipment, arguing that indigenous private firms simply could not provide critical goods. The products manufactured by military enterprises include advanced missile systems in Argentina, tanks and armed personnel carriers in Brazil and Chile, and shoes, clothing, canvas goods, light arms, and explosives in Guatemala, El Salvador, and Ecuador. In several cases, this manufacturing capacity has grown sufficiently to allow sales of some items to the private sector and, notably in Brazil and Chile, substantial export of military equipment abroad.

In Ecuador, for example, the armed forces not only own companies that manufacture a wide range of munitions and military equipment; they also, through their holding company DINE (Dirección de Industrias del Ejército), manufacture buses and light vehicles, industrial and consumer machinery and equipment, construction products, laminated steel, metal sheets and posts, copper piping and plumbing equipment, and oil piping. The Ecuadorian armed forces have a constitutional mandate to contribute to the nation's socioeconomic development, which has resulted in their importing cars and spare parts, exporting agricultural products, mining gold, supervising port authorities (in Esmeraldas, Guayaquil, Manta, and Puerto Bolivar), and managing a bank, an airline, and a shipping company.

These missions are as varied as those taken on by armed forces in the United States and other nations with relatively long experience in democratic rule. Now that all the OAS states have adopted democratiza- tion as national policy, the proper mission to assign the armed forces has everywhere become a subject of national discussion. Dramatic changes have taken place in several national military establishments. Both Argentina and Brazil have publicly disavowed their respective nuclear projects; moreover, Argentina has abandoned its highly publicized Condor missile venture and ended conscription. While Latin American nations continue to be involved in international arms sales, the principal suppliers (Argentina, Brazil, and Chile) have at least scaled back their participation, have privatized firms to eliminate military control, and have converted some enterprises to nonmilitary production.

With the end of the Cold War, governments around the world have reassessed the nature of their external security environments. In many cases, they have concluded that the dissolution of the Soviet Union and the concomitant abandonment of the policy of containment require that the military's roles and missions be reevaluated. While not negating the importance of the core mission of external defense, decision makers have slashed military expenditures and personnel. Today, as in the past, the armed forces of most nations have taken on many noncombat assignments. Whether the military can continue to play such a role in a manner consistent with the consolidation of democracy is a concern for civilian authorities and military officials worldwide.

Criteria for Evaluating Military Missions

The first question that we need to ask is whether the acceptance of nontraditional missions by the military enhances or diminishes prospects for the consolidation of democracy. If national well-being depends on a particular task being carried out, and no institution other than the military can undertake it successfully, then the military's assumption of that responsibility is appropriate. If, on the other hand, a particular mission does not further the national interest or can be done better or more economically by another party, then the military's involvement may have a negligible or even negative impact. For example, if education and health officials cannot deliver needed services to remote rural areas, then military involvement may be critical for promoting national integration and economic development. In contrast, if police can adequately control illegal activities, if private construction companies can build quality roads and bridges, if the agriculture ministry can mount effective environmental-protection campaigns, if private firms can manufacture vehicles, construction-grade steel, copper piping, or even military equipment, then the military's involvement in any of these activities will either contribute nothing to the democratization process or actually jeopardize it.

Another relevant question is how the assumption of a noncombat role affects the extent and nature of the military's involvement in domestic politics. If neither the state bureaucracy nor the military gains added political advantage from military involvement in civic action, internal security, education, or economic activity, then the military's successful undertaking of these tasks can strengthen democracy. If, however, the military gains a privileged position within the political system because of such activities, then the democratization process is likely to suffer.

Finally, military involvement in noncombat roles can facilitate the consolidation of democracy only if it does not detract from the military's ability to carry out its core combat mission. Any weakening of combat readiness—whether due to the corruption that may ensue from involvement in activities like narcotics control, to the diversion of critical defense resources to military-controlled industries, or to the diffusion of defense capacity as a result of overcommitment to the delivery of social services—ultimately undermines the foundations upon which democracy rests.

Three criteria determine whether a given mission can appropriately be taken up by the military:

1) Does the military's involvement shut out other parties—police, entrepreneurs, private contractors, teachers, environmentalists, health officials—from that activity, thus preventing them from developing critical skills and expanding their activities?

2) Do the armed forces by their involvement gain added privilege and become a special-interest group promoting their own institutional interests at the expense of public or private entities?

3) Does the military begin to neglect its core defense mission—one that entails considerable time and effort in planning, training, and maintaining readiness (particularly in the post–Cold War era, when strategic threats and technological capabilities are undergoing dramatic change)?

Political analysts often warn that the military will defend its narrow institutional interests without regard for the larger social good.[13] At times, the various services that make up the armed forces may so relentlessly pursue their particular corporate interests that they end up directly competing with political parties for power. As the largest, best-supplied, and most organized institution in most societies, military establishments have tremendous capacity to realize their own organizational interests if they choose to do so. The armed forces can inflict significant harm on the democratization process through the pursuit of their own narrow institutional interests or their intimidation of potential rivals.[14]

In the post–Cold War era of military downsizing, it is all too tempting to regard the armed forces as a national resource with a proven capacity to solve a wide range of societal problems. In the United States, proposals to use the armed forces to combat narcotics trafficking, help rebuild cities, or teach children in inner-city schools have been debated in the halls of Congress. Many Latin American countries obviously have a pressing need to build roads, educate citizens, provide health care, protect the environment, curtail illegal activities, and promote economic development—what is not clear is under what circumstances, if any, the military should become involved. If the armed forces are engaged in building roads while competent construction firms cannot secure contracts, or if the military supervises education in an area where local education officials could operate, then such involvement hinders the development of essential civilian institutions.

The negative impact of military involvement in national politics can easily be seen in cases where political parties have been banned or the executive branch has been taken over by the armed forces. Yet less visible, longer-term harm may be inflicted on the political system when the military takes on responsibilities in arenas where civilian public or private entities could emerge and develop critical expertise if the social or political space was not already occupied by the armed forces. For example, Ecuadorian entrepreneurs claim that extensive military involvement in the economy has inhibited their ability to promote private-sector growth. DINE officials assert that its firms' activities generate significant employment and economic benefits at no cost to Ecuador's taxpayers and offer the private sector attractive investment opportunities.[15] DINE's critics contend, however, that DINE contributions cannot be measured because critical information on those firms' operations is not made public—information that might reveal hidden subsidies or inefficiencies.[16]

> *A real danger exists that involvement in alternate missions may lead the military to neglect its core mission by failing to maintain combat readiness.*

The Ecuadorian military continues to be concerned about the civilian sector's inadequate capacity, as evidenced by the pressure it exerted in November 1995 to cancel consideration of open bids on a new oil pipeline; by its insistence that the armed forces set the terms by which the electric power industry would be privatized; and by its takeover of the nation's largest corporation, Petroecuador.[17] Such extensive military influence in Ecuador's economy could be seen either as essential, in light of the weakness of the country's civilian institutions, or as incompatible with achieving the balance of public and private power needed to deepen democratic development.

A real danger exists that involvement in alternate missions may lead the military to neglect its core mission by failing to maintain combat readiness. The difficulties the Russian army has encountered in dealing with its Chechen adversaries illustrate how a regime's own legitimacy may be called into question if its armed forces cannot carry out their core mission effectively. The 1994–95 border conflict between Ecuador and Peru shows how essential careful attention to planning, training, and combat readiness is to successfully carrying out the war-fighting mission. In this case, the Ecuadorian military's attention to terrain characteristics, force structure, and equipment requirements allowed it to defeat the armed forces of a much larger neighbor. While questions have been raised about the wide-ranging involvement of the Ecuadorian armed forces in the nation's economy, in this instance at least it received overwhelming praise for its combat prowess. That success even temporarily bolstered popular support for the relatively weak government of President Sixto Duran-Ballan (although political scandals a few months later seriously undermined the government's effectiveness).

At times, a national consensus emerges that the armed forces must take on certain internal missions owing to special circumstances, as during the terrorist campaigns in Peru carried out by the Sendero Luminoso or the insurgency in Colombia led by the Colombia Revolutionary Armed Forces. In much of Central America, the inability of civilian institutions to deliver health and educational services or to ensure security in remote regions has led to a military presence in many rural areas. In Guatemala, for example, although in 1982 the armed forces had begun to retreat from nontraditional activities, in 1986 the weakness of President Venicio Cerezo's civilian government forced the military to renew its civic-action programs in rural areas in an effort to prevent insurgents from establishing a base of support there. In Peru, Bolivia, Colombia, and Mexico, the armed forces have become involved in attempts to control illegal drug trafficking despite intense national debate regarding how well the armed forces have performed this task and what impact this has had on the political system.[18]

Setting Clear Limits

How can the armed forces take on such missions without police work, road building, munitions production, and other noncombat-related activities either becoming permanent missions or remaining in military hands far longer than necessary? From the outset, the military's undertaking of any noncombat missions must be clearly understood as transitional by all concerned. Moreover, such clearly defined *transitional missions* must come with a firm timetable for their return to civilian hands, and checks must be put in place that entail civilian authorization (by the executive and the legislature) of any extensions.

The fundamental laws that govern the nation—national constitutions, organic laws regarding the armed forces, national-security and anti-terrorist legislation, penal codes, and the like—must include provisions restricting the military's missions and specifying under what circumstances exceptions can be made. Statutes in many consolidating democracies already restrict the military's missions and lay out procedures for granting "exceptions," as when the executive or legislature proclaims an "emergency." To date the results have been mixed. Several governments in Africa, Asia, and Latin America that derive their legal heritage from the French Revolution have adopted legal structures that "protect" democracy against itself. These allow the president, police officials, and military officers to exercise "extraordinary powers" temporarily, permit the suspension of civil liberties, and require that the armed forces play a specified role in defending (ergo, defining) the "permanent interests of the nation."[19] In allowing the armed forces to serve as institutionalized guardians of the nation's long-term interests, these rules effectively mean that civilian participation in politics is carried out under the constant threat of military intervention. Since the military's effective monopoly of the use of force means that such a possibility exists in any country, the culture of the armed forces—limited and influenced by the checks and balances of a nation's legal system and political practices—ultimately determines whether such an eventuality will come to pass.[20]

Consequently, civilian authorities must have clear plans for beginning and ending whatever transitional missions are required of their armed forces. Such plans are needed to ensure that the armed forces do not take on unnecessary nonmilitary missions. Equally (if not more) important, these plans should also guarantee that due attention is paid to the core mission of maintaining combat readiness.

In developing such contingency plans, civilian authorities must address one of the most glaring deficits facing political leaders in new and fragile democratic political systems—the significant gap in expertise on defense policy between civilians and military officials. Few civilians in most newly consolidating democracies possess sufficient knowledge and understanding of the military's institutional requirements to enable them to contribute to building healthy civil-military relations. Civilian defense-policy experts are needed to interpret military needs for elected officials and to serve as interlocutors between the armed forces and society. While the post–Cold War world has seen impressive progress in the election of civilians to high office, significant gaps remain in the social and institutional infrastructures of many nations. In the area of civil-military relations, if military officers are to adhere strictly to core professional military roles, they need civilian counterparts who understand the needs of the military establishment.

The need for civilian expertise is particularly important in the post–Cold War world, where the end of superpower competition and changes in military structure driven by new information technology have created unprecedented uncertainty for military planners everywhere. Since changes in military operations favor smaller, more mobile forces relying increasingly on automation, stealth technologies, passive deception measures, and the ability to quickly incorporate improvements in military capabilities through "open-ended architectures," military officers must be certain that the civilians responsible for oversight will understand the military's needs. Without such civilian expertise, the confidence needed to undergird civil-military relations supportive of democracy can easily erode.

Indeed, the lack of such expertise in many nations has contributed to the mutual isolation of civilian authorities and military officials, and ultimately to political breakdown. Without such expertise, the frayed civil-military relations that inevitably result can lead to a hardening of positions and a desire by the armed forces to take matters into their own hands by expanding the military's missions, prerogatives, and political power. Examples include the coup attempts that took place in Venezuela in 1992 and the special role that the Ecuadorian constitution accorded the armed forces. In Venezuela, the efforts by dissident members of the armed forces to overturn civilian rule in Latin America's oldest multiparty democracy, although unsuccessful, provided a clarion call that the institutional needs of contemporary armed forces cannot be neglected if the military is to serve national objectives.[21] In Ecuador, the lack of confidence in civilian leadership during the period of "revolutionary military government" from 1972 to 1976 resulted in a constitution that gives the armed forces extraordinary prerogatives, including the duty to contribute to the nation's socioeconomic development.[22] Moving beyond such situations of resentment or impasse to civil-military relations characterized by mutual respect and confidence requires concerted efforts on the part of civilian policy makers in countries attempting to consolidate democracy. Military restraint alone will not suffice to create satisfactory civil-military relations; the importance and complexity of the military's core missions and the rapid pace of worldwide change require close collaboration between military officers and civilians knowledgeable about each other's institutional needs. This will pose a special challenge in countries where the military traditionally has been left alone to manage itself. Building the civilian expertise necessary to understand the operations of the armed forces in countries where civil-military estrangement has been the rule will be critical to efforts to consolidate democracy.

NOTES

1. Sam Nunn, "The Military's Role in Rebuilding America," *Issues in Science and Technology* 9 (Winter 1992–93): 25–28.

2. See Morris Janowitz, *The Military in the Political Development of New Nations* (Chicago: University of Chicago Press, 1964), ch. 3.

3. See Hugh Hanning, *The Peaceful Uses of Military Forces* (New York: Praeger, 1967), ch. 1.

4. See U.S. Arms Control and Disarmament Agency, *World Military Expenditures and Arms Transfers, 1993–1994* (Washington, D.C.: U.S. Government Printing Office, 1995), 1–8.

5. The OAS invoked the Santiago Doctrine in 1991 when the Haitian military overthrew the government of Jean-Bertrand Aristide, in 1992 when President Alberto Fujimori of Peru dissolved Peru's Congress, and in 1993 when Guatemalan president Jorge Serrano attempted to dissolve Guatemala's Congress.

6. For a discussion of how the U.S. armed forces have encouraged appropriate military roles in Latin America, see General Barry R. McCaffrey, "Statement Before the House National Security Committee," 8 March 1995, 1, 7–11.

7. What future roles the military could play in the Americas was discussed at the "Conference of the American Armies" in Bariloche, Argentina, in November 1995; see *Latin American Weekly Report*, 7 December 1995.

8. William J. Clinton, *A National Security Strategy of Engagement and Enlargement* (Washington, D.C.: Government Printing Office, 1994).

9. Swadesh Rana, *Small Arms and Intra-State Conflicts* (New York: United Nations, 1995), 1.

10. International Institute for Strategic Studies, *The Military Balance 1995-1996* (London: Oxford University Press, 1995).

11. For an extensive discussion of the noncombat roles taken on by the U.S. military, see Edward Bernard Glick, *Peaceful Conflict: The Non-military Use of the Military* (Harrisburg, Pa.: Stackpole Books, 1967), chs. 3-4; and James R. Graham, ed., *Non-Combat Roles for the U.S. Military in the Post–Cold War Era* (Washington, D.C.: National Defense University Press, 1993).

12. Clinton, *A National Security Strategy*, 14, 8-13.

13. Morris Janowitz, in his seminal work on civil-military relations, wrote, "The political behavior of the military, like that of any large organization, is grounded in strong elements of personal and organizational self-interest." *The Professional Soldier: A Social and Political Portrait* (New York: The Free Press, 1960), 285.

14. In *Rethinking Military Politics: Brazil and the Southern Cone* (Princeton: Princeton University Press, 1988), Alfred Stepan describes this as "military institutional prerogatives" (ch. 7) and as "articulated military contestation against the policies of civilian democratic leadership" (ch. 6).

15. DINE employs over four thousand civilians in the more than 30 companies that it controls.

16. For example, DINE's public-relations office does not provide detailed information on individual companies, and DINE's accounts are not audited by entities independent of Ecuador's armed forces.

17. See *El comercio* (Quito, Ecuador), 15 November 1995, 14 December 1995, and 26 December 1995.

18. For further discussion, see Louis W. Goodman and Johanna S.R. Mendelson, "The Threat of New Missions: Latin American Militaries and the Drug War," in Louis W. Goodman, Johanna S.R. Mendelson, and Juan Rial, eds., *The Military and Democracy: The Future of Civil-Military Relations in Latin America* (Lexington, Mass.: Lexington Books, 1990), 189-95.

19. For an extended discussion of the concept and practice of "protected democracy," see Brian Loveman, "'Protected Democracies' and Military Guardianship: Political Transitions in Latin America, 1978-1993," *Journal of Interamerican Studies and World Affairs* 36 (Summer 1994): 105-89.

20. For a provocative fictional depiction of military guardianship in the United States, see Charles J. Dunlap, Jr., "The Origins of the American Military Coup of 2012," *Parameters* 22 (Winter 1992-93): 2-20.

21. Low military salaries and lack of institutional resources in a period of economic decline were exacerbated by the isolation of Venezuela's high command from mid-ranking and junior officers, and of Venezuelan politicians from the armed forces. Louis W. Goodman et al., eds., *Lessons of the Venezuelan Experience* (Baltimore: Johns Hopkins University Press, 1995).

22. See Anita Isaacs, *Military Rule and Transition in Ecuador, 1972-92* (Pittsburgh: University of Pittsburgh Press, 1993).

II.
The Developing World

4.
ARMIES AND CIVIL SOCIETY IN LATIN AMERICA

Juan Rial

Juan Rial is a researcher at Peitho, Sociedad de Análisis Político, and a consultant with Perelli, Rial & Associates in Montevideo, Uruguay. He has conducted extensive fieldwork in Latin America and Africa on armed forces and society, and is coeditor of The Military and Democracy: The Future of Civil-Military Relations in Latin America *(1989).*

As a rule, military establishments are uncomfortable with the enforced inactivity of peacetime. Mindful of the need to justify their continued existence, they are ever vigilant against new external threats. Their discomfort is particularly evident at the close of the "age of extremes," as Eric Hobsbawm aptly calls the "short twentieth century" that began in 1914 and ended in 1991.[1] The world in the post–Cold War era has yet to experience either general peace or large-scale mass conflict. Armed conflicts continue to erupt but are limited in extent and confined to "peripheral" regions.

At the global level, governments usually employ force with restraint, viewing it primarily as an instrument of diplomacy. The application of force is often far less restrained at the local level, where it is perpetrated more often by death squads, guerrilla insurgents, or other "irregular" forces than by the state's professional armed forces. Such local-level violence often approaches the "total" levels that characterized the "age of extremes."

These considerations provide a useful framework for understanding the new role of the armed forces in Latin America and the military's evolving relationship with civil society. The mission of military forces throughout the Western Hemisphere drastically changed with the end of the Cold War. From the 1960s through the 1980s, armed forces in many Latin American countries were preoccupied with fighting subversion by Marxist guerrilla movements, often inspired or supplied by the Soviet Union or Cuba. By 1995 only a few such groups remained active, primarily in Peru and Colombia, although in January 1994 a new revolutionary movement—the Zapatista National Liberation Army—did arise in southern Mexico. In Nicaragua, the Sandinista army has largely completed its transformation into a national armed force loyal to the state rather than to a political party. Cuba, faced with the collapse of the Soviet Union in 1991, had to abandon its longtime role as the expeditionary force of international communism; in fact, by 1995 its armed forces had become virtually paralyzed owing to spending cuts and lack of munitions, gasoline, and spare parts.

At the same time, military establishments throughout Latin America have lost much—but not all—of their domestic political power. They have tended to stay on the sidelines, except in times of national crisis. Recent instances of greater political visibility include the Ecuador-Peru border conflict of early 1995; the public acknowledgment by General Martín Balza, Argentine army chief of staff, of the Argentine army's human rights abuses during the "dirty war" of the late 1970s; and General Augusto Pinochet's vehement opposition to prosecutions of high-ranking Chilean army officers for similar abuses committed during his military government (1973–89). The negative consequences of Latin America's most recent experience with military rule—economic crisis, international opprobrium, and damage to the armed forces' prestige—have left most military establishments highly disinclined to return to power.

The end of the Cold War has witnessed the rise of new security threats in Latin America unlike those of earlier decades. Accordingly, the future mission of the region's armed forces will likely focus far less on counterinsurgency operations and the "moderating" of civilian political conflicts than on traditional border defense combined with efforts to defeat "new" security threats, ranging from extreme socioeconomic underdevelopment and rampant domestic crime to the international drug trade. The ability of the armed forces to discharge these functions in a way that does not undermine governability or democratic consolidation will depend, of course, upon the successful subordination of these forces to lawful civilian authority.

Different Latin Americas

Several distinct patterns of civil-military relations can be found in Latin America. Mexico constitutes a unique case. Its military is rooted in the revolution that began in 1913 and became institutionalized during the 1930s. Mexico's central military institution is the army, which for decades has been tightly bound to the country's unique state structure and party system. Although the army portrays itself as a national and nonpartisan armed force reflecting the legitimate authority of the state, in practice it has served since the 1940s as an arm of the ruling Institutional Revolutionary Party (PRI).

Mexico's armed forces reflect the influence of both the U.S. and Latin American military models. Although they receive equipment and tactical instruction from the United States, their operational guidelines and institutional structure and ethos more closely resemble the Latin American pattern. Because of Mexico's proximity to the United States, its armed forces have taken on a policing rather than a defensive mission, and Mexico has developed neither an air force nor a navy of any size or importance. The country's proximity to Guatemala, on the other hand, has led Mexico's armed forces to adopt operational guidelines very similar to those of their South American counterparts, as was shown in the heavy-handed repression that accompanied the army's counterinsurgency efforts against the Zapatistas in Chiapas in early 1995. Although the Mexican armed forces remain formally subordinate to the civilian authorities, their autonomy has steadily increased in recent decades as the PRI has declined in strength and authority. They have tried to deepen their professional separation from the PRI by adopting behavior appropriate to a military loyal exclusively to the state.

The countries of Central America and the Caribbean display a variety of civil-military relations. Armed forces in many of these countries follow the traditional Latin American practice of constant meddling in domestic politics. The Guatemalan armed forces epitomize this pattern: more than ten years after the return of elected civilian rule, they remain the country's most powerful domestic political actor. The Honduran armed forces also exemplify this "traditional" pattern, although their domestic political influence is less than that of their counterparts in Guatemala.

At the other extreme are the Cuban armed forces; although, like their Guatemalan counterparts, they wield significant political influence, they are also totally committed to supporting the civilian government. The Cuban military is totally subordinated to Fidel Castro's totalitarian regime: its *raison d'être* is to defend the regime against all challenges, foreign or domestic. It has also maintained a strong profile in recent years, despite its dwindling resources.

In the place of professional military forces, other Central American and Caribbean countries for a long time had U.S.-created, quasi-military police forces, usually called "national guards." They were responsible for maintaining order, preserving the economic and social status quo, and keeping the incumbent rulers in power. All of these national guards eventually came to unfortunate ends. Some fell to revolutionary insurgencies, as happened in Cuba in 1959, the Dominican Republic in 1965, and Nicaragua in 1979. The revolutionary governments of Cuba and Nicaragua replaced their national guards with professional, Soviet-style armies, whereas the Dominican Republic established a new professional armed force in 1965 modeled after the U.S. Army. Following the Sandinistas' electoral defeat in 1990, the Nicaraguan army underwent profound changes and by 1995 had made considerable progress toward becoming a nonpartisan military force.

In Panama during the late 1970s and the 1980s, Generals Omar Torrijos and Manuel Antonio Noriega tried to transform the National Guard into a small professional army *a la sureña* (along South American lines).[2] The United States destroyed this force in the wake of the "intervasion" of 1989. In 1994, Haiti's army suffered a fate similar to that of Panama, this time as the result of a U.S.-brokered agreement between Haiti's military rulers and deposed civilian president Jean-Bertrand Aristide.[3] Shortly after resuming office in October 1994, Aristide reduced Haiti's army of seven thousand troops to a musical band of fewer than two dozen members. He also vowed to submit a formal request to the new parliament, elected in June 1995, to abolish the institution.[4] Haiti and Panama thus join Costa Rica, which abolished its army in 1948, as Latin American countries without a full-fledged military force.

During the 1980s, El Salvador, like many of its neighbors, replaced its National Guard with a professional military force. Nonetheless, as only part of that army achieved significant operational capacity, it ultimately failed in its efforts to neutralize the ongoing guerrilla insurgency of the leftist Farabundo Marti National Liberation Front. As a result, the army was forced to accept a U.S.-brokered diplomatic settlement in 1990 between the government and the guerrillas, which initiated a new stage in El Salvador's democratic transformation. Once a dominant political force in El Salvador, the army has seen its political influence decline in the 1990s as both its budget and its mission have contracted.

Unlike the military forces of Central America, which were established largely along U.S. lines, those of South America trace their origins mainly to Europe and especially to Germany. Their institutional ethos is rooted in the early-nineteenth-century South American wars of independence, which accorded these forces a privileged status as founders of both nation and state.[5] Most did not become professionalized until the late nineteenth century—in the Venezuelan case not until the 1930s—under the guidance of foreign instructors, usually either French or German (both, in the case of Brazil).

At least until the 1960s, almost every South American military force viewed itself as a *poder moderador*—a "moderating power" responsible for defending the constitutional order against any damage that might be inflicted on it by squabbling civilian factions.[6] Military officials justified occasional seizures of power as temporary intermissions or "cooling-off periods," after which democratic normality would be restored. Chile and Uruguay largely escaped the South American propensity for military coups, as these two countries boasted the most highly developed state institutions and most stable party systems in the region. Chile and

Uruguay experienced military rule only twice—briefly during the 1930s and again for a longer time beginning in the early and middle 1970s. In the latter case, the armed forces overthrew elected governments to preempt what they perceived as efforts by powerful left-wing forces to subvert the constitutional order and establish Soviet-aligned socialist regimes. In contrast, other South American countries saw the pendulum swing frequently between civilian and military rule.[7]

Although some military governments in South America during the 1960s and 1970s implemented radically new economic and social policies, most could not be characterized as "foundational" regimes that broke decisively with the past. Indeed, their self-justification and legitimacy rested upon their stated pledge to restore democratic rule as soon as was practicable, and they did not see themselves as a permanent alternative to democratic rule. In Uruguay, civilian president Juan María Bordaberry (1971–76), who had presided over a military regime since 1973, did try in 1976 to establish such a foundational political system, but the armed forces removed him from power, as they favored a "limited democracy" along Brazilian lines. Chilean dictator Augusto Pinochet also spoke of setting up a foundational regime to supplant Chile's traditional democratic system, but the 1980 constitution that he pushed through established a legal procedural framework that thwarted such plans and laid the groundwork for the country's subsequent return to democratic rule.

The military's reluctance to establish a lasting alternative to democratic governance made an eventual return to democratic normality inevitable. By and large, the troops left their barracks during times of national crises to restore public order and "moderate" conflicts among contentious political forces. As the crises that had compelled the armed forces to intervene politically abated, so did the justification for continued military rule.[8] Thus it is hardly surprising that during the 1980s all of Latin America's military governments gave way to freely elected successors.

A Zone of Peace

Latin American states have engaged in few cross-border armed conflicts during the twentieth century. One exception was the Chaco War of 1930–32, in which Bolivia and Paraguay fought for control of an arid and sparsely populated region thought (erroneously, as it turned out) to contain large oil reserves. Bolivia's defeat shattered its liberal regime and brought to power short-lived military governments of both the Left and the Right; in the long run, however, this defeat paved the way for the 1952 National Revolution that extended democracy to the lower classes. In contrast, whereas Paraguay's military also seized power following the war, the prestige garnered by its victory helped it to hold on to power and eventually made possible the lengthy authoritarian regime of General Alfredo Stroessner (1954–89).

Another exception to Latin America's modern tradition of interstate peace is the long-running border dispute between Ecuador and Peru. Peru has long denied Ecuador's claim to be an "Amazonic" country and has resisted Ecuadorian efforts to gain access to the Amazon region at Peru's territorial expense. In 1941 the two countries fought a brief war over the question, which Ecuador lost after Peru invaded its southern El Oro province and besieged its second-largest city, Guayaquil. Anxious to maintain hemispheric stability with war looming in Europe, the United States intervened diplomatically to defuse the conflict. Both countries accepted the U.S.-brokered 1942 Protocol of Rio de Janeiro, which effectively denied Ecuador access to the Amazon.[9]

Yet the border dispute has continued to fester. In 1960 Ecuador's populist president, José María Velasco Ibarra, denounced the 1942 Rio Protocol as null and void since it had been imposed on Ecuador by the guarantor states (Argentina, Brazil, Chile, and the United States), but he took no action to abrogate it. The dispute flared up again 20 years later in 1981, when Ecuadorian troops occupied the contested region, only to be driven out within three days by the Peruvian army. Fighting broke out anew in 1995 but was brought to a halt two months later with the signing of the Itamaraty Declaration and the deployment of a four-power observer force (Momep). Since then, both nations have worked toward resolving the disputed border issue through diplomatic means.[10]

The only other twentieth-century cross-border dispute to result in armed conflict was the brief 1969 Soccer War between El Salvador and Honduras (fueled by border, trade, and migration disputes). Although Venezuela and Colombia have engaged in minor naval altercations over conflicting fluvial and maritime claims, these engagements did not give rise to armed conflict. Such occasional flare-ups aside, all twentieth-century military conflicts between Latin American states have been limited in time, space, and resources. This holds true, too, for the 1982 Falklands/Malvinas war, the only armed conflict between a Latin American state and a power outside the Americas, as fighting between Argentina and Great Britain remained restricted to the disputed islands.

Several diplomatic disputes over territorial claims continue to fester. Nicaragua claims ownership of Colombia's San Andrés and Providencia islands; Guatemala claims Belize's territory as its own, though it has recognized Belize as a state; and Venezuela claims territories currently held by Guyana and by Trinidad and Tobago. Relations between Bolivia and Chile have been strained ever since the War of the Pacific (1879–84), when Bolivia lost its coastal territories to Chile, as Bolivia still longs for sovereign access to the Pacific Ocean.[11]

Latin American states have limited their involvement in extra-hemispheric armed conflicts. During the Second World War, Brazil sent an army division to assist in the Allied campaign in Italy, and Mexico contributed several patrol and training aircraft to Allied efforts in the Pacific theater. Only Colombia participated in the Korean War, sending an infantry battalion.

In recent years, Latin American countries have confined their extraregional military activities to participation in UN-sponsored peacekeeping missions. Argentina and Uruguay have been the most active participants in such efforts. Some nine hundred Argentine troops have served in Croatia since 1991, and an additional four hundred have been stationed in Cyprus since 1994. Hundreds of Uruguayan troops participated in UN peacekeeping operations in Cambodia in 1992–93 and in Mozambique in 1993–94, and a battalion is currently stationed in Angola. Other Latin American countries have contributed troops to UN observer missions in Kashmir, Haiti, and several African countries. During the Persian Gulf War, Argentina contributed two frigates to the allied forces fighting Iraq.

In short, Latin America has had no modern experience of the type of "total war" that affects all of society. Recent interstate armed conflicts have been limited to brief and rather inconsequential border disputes. Such peripheral conflicts have been nearly invisible to citizens of the contending countries, much like the colonial wars of independence that many European powers fought after 1945.

Yet acute domestic conflict—even internal warfare—has wracked nearly every Latin American country in recent years, leaving no social class untouched. Time has not healed the wounds left by some of these conflicts, particularly the urban-based "dirty wars" in Argentina, Chile, and Uruguay during the late 1970s, and the rural-based insurgencies in El Salvador and Nicaragua during the 1980s and in Guatemala from the late 1950s to the mid-1990s.[12] Since 1980, some twenty-five thousand Peruvians have died at the hands of the Sendero Luminoso (Shining Path), a Maoist guerrilla movement whose renowned brutality is reminiscent of Cambodia's Khmer Rouge. Thousands more civilians were killed during the Peruvian army's counterinsurgency sweeps through the countryside. Colombia, for its part, has endured almost constant guerrilla violence since the 1960s. The far-ranging influence and considerable power of Colombia's guerrilla movements and drug-trafficking cartels have significantly restricted the government's operative sovereignty over the national territory, large parts of which are effectively outside government control.

From Dictatorship to Democracy

Military interventions in Latin American politics have taken various forms. Most have followed the "institutional model," in which the armed forces *as an institution* seize and wield governmental power—recent examples include Ecuador (1972–79), Brazil (1964–84), Argentina (1976–83), and Uruguay (1973–84). In each case, a junta of top-ranking officers exercised joint power, although individual junta members occasionally tried to rise above their colleagues in influence and control.

Several Latin American countries have also experienced the "personalist model" of military rule. In this case, the armed forces as an institution limit their political role mainly to supporting their leader as supreme dictator or *caudillo*, after the fashion of Spanish dictator Francisco Franco (1939–75)—Chile under General Augusto Pinochet (1973–89) is the best example. Paraguay between 1954 and 1989 under General Alfredo Stroessner had what Max Weber called a prebendary and patrimonial regime.[13] In Panama, General Omar Torrijos (1968–81) and then-General Manuel Antonio Noriega (1982–89) led similar *caudillista* regimes, although the military as an institution participated actively in both governments. The Haitian armed forces under General Raoul Cédras ruled in like fashion between 1991 and 1994.

Other Latin American regimes fell somewhere between these two models or evolved from one type to another. For example, the military junta that seized power in Peru in 1968 was initially more personalist than institutional, as the armed forces deferred to a single leader, General Juan Velasco Alvarado. Yet many other military officers held influential political posts as cabinet ministers, public-enterprise directors, or middle-level managers of state enterprises. In 1975, the personalist Velasco regime gave way to a more fully institutionalized military government. This regime, led by General Francisco Morales Bermúdez, soon embarked on a transition to democratic rule.

During the late 1970s, the U.S. government adopted new foreign-policy guidelines that contributed to subsequent democratic transitions in Latin America and elsewhere. Respect for human rights became a touchstone of President Jimmy Carter's foreign policy and a prime criterion for U.S. support and assistance to particular Latin American governments. This policy shift was accompanied by dramatic improvements in communications technologies, which magnified the new policy's impact.

The Carter administration did not apply its policy toward dictatorial regimes evenly throughout Latin America, however. In Central America, for instance, the U.S. government tended to support military regimes embroiled in internationalized civil wars with Soviet-supported communist guerrillas. Democratic governance and respect for human rights loomed larger in U.S. policy toward South American governments, which faced less dire threats of leftist subversion than did their Central American counterparts. U.S. criticism of South American military regimes for human rights violations helped to isolate these regimes internationally and to eventually persuade their leaders to hand over power to elected civilian successors.

Latin America's new democratic governments faced continuing problems bequeathed to them by their authoritarian predecessors. This authoritarian legacy posed particular problems when human rights abuses remained fresh in the collective memory, even when amnesty laws formally absolved those responsible for committing them.

Military Missions Today

The fall of dictatorial regimes in Latin America coincided with the end of the Cold War, the waning of the communist movement, and a global technological revolution in communications and financial transactions. These changes left a deep imprint on Latin America's armed forces, which lost their traditional role as a moderating power and often had to account for their rather dark past. They could not hope to compete with the armed forces of developed countries (which were equipped with advanced technology), as became clear during the Falklands/Malvinas war between Argentina and Great Britain. Moreover, they could no longer use the threat of ongoing communist subversion to justify high defense budgets, demands for advanced weaponry, and occasional forays into the political arena.

These epochal developments provoked a fundamental rethinking of the role of the military throughout Latin America and especially in South America. Latin American armed forces, which are highly unlikely to disband voluntarily, must somehow justify their continued existence. Most Latin American constitutions require the government to maintain a military force.[14] According to the constitution or the organic law regulating the military, the armed forces' two basic tasks are to ensure national security and to defend the nation's constitution and its laws. In some countries, either the constitution or organic law makes the armed forces responsible for preserving public order during national emergencies; sometimes, the military is also required to contribute to the country's social and economic development.

Legal changes have broadened the mission of some armed forces to include law-enforcement tasks traditionally assigned to the police. In some cases—such as the ongoing struggle against international drug traffickers—the armed forces have acquired these police functions not through legislative enactment but simply owing to incremental role expansion spurred by necessity. Often, military commanders have been reluctant to assume this responsibility. Odds against success in fighting the drug trade are high, as is the potential threat of drug-related corruption within the armed forces. Crop-eradication programs inevitably bring conflict with farmers and undermine popular support for the armed forces in rural areas. Moreover, it is difficult to control drug-related activities in border regions.[15]

Although conditions vary widely among Latin American countries, certain tasks are common to virtually every military force in the region. In the first place, many—perhaps most—of these forces must guard against border violations by neighboring states and be prepared to use force to repel any foreign incursions, as the February 1995 border war between Peru and Ecuador attests. Although most neighboring Latin American countries reached agreement long ago on their common borders, some continue to assert conflicting claims to the same territory (as discussed above), which can lead to conflict.[16]

Second, many Latin American armed forces face ongoing challenges from subversive guerrilla movements. In 1995, leftist guerrilla groups remained active in Colombia and Peru. A similar movement in Guatemala—the Guatemalan National Revolutionary Union—has paled in significance and now seeks a negotiated settlement with the government. In Mexico a new revolutionary group, the Zapatista National Liberation Army, emerged in early 1994; however, its ideology is based not on Marxism but rather on notions of social justice. The Zapatistas to date have relied more on the international news media than on guns to advance their cause, and the government has preferred negotiation over military action in its efforts to defuse the Zapatista challenge. Subversive groups no longer pose a threat to civil order in most other Latin American countries, and the armed forces limit themselves to monitoring organizations that profess an antiregime or antistate ideology.[17]

"Police" operations—especially against international drug traffickers—constitute a third common area of military activity. The armed forces of Mexico, the Andean countries, and some Central American countries have pursued aggressive antidrug operations of varying degrees of effectiveness. Drug trafficking remains one of the region's most profitable activities, however, despite increased police seizures of drug shipments. In some countries, such as Bolivia, drug revenues have made the difference between national economic solvency and default.

Apart from these antinarcotics operations, the armed forces occasionally help the civilian police maintain public order in times of social unrest. In fact, the roles and missions of the police and military have become increasingly difficult to distinguish—a development with negative implications for the democratization process. Thus many Latin American armed forces are becoming increasingly "policified," while police forces are becoming increasingly "militarized." The danger lies in the fact that the maintenance of internal order and the defense against external threats are entirely different tasks. Combining them runs the risk of eroding the military's professional ethos and of reducing its accountability and subordination to elected civilian authorities.

Fourth, Latin American armed forces occasionally help their governments carry out social and economic development programs. In previous years, governments tended to view such "civic-action" or "nation-building" activities as part of a larger strategy designed to blunt the popular appeal of armed guerrilla movements. Recently such activities have largely served to improve the military's public image, especially in the poorer countries. Because these missions have very limited military content, however, the armed forces have not always embraced them wholeheartedly.

Fifth, the armed forces occasionally participate in international peacekeeping missions. As described above, several Latin American governments (such as those of Argentina and Uruguay) maintain observer missions in countries (both within the region and outside it) that have recently experienced armed conflict.

Finally, many Latin American armed forces have taken up "self-support" activities, particularly the management of productive enterprises. Most of the military-run state enterprises producing defense-related goods have either gone bankrupt or been sold to private investors. Argentina, for instance, has sought private buyers for its Domecq shipyards and has signed a preliminary agreement with U.S. aircraft manufacturer Lockheed to modernize an aeronautics plant in Córdoba. Brazil's Embraer aircraft company is in deep financial trouble, and the country's main tank manufacturer has gone bankrupt. Latin American armed forces are now shifting to more commercial activities, such as banking and hotel management, to raise revenues both for the military establishment and for individual officers.

Political Control of the Armed Forces

In most Latin American countries, either the constitution or some fundamental law designates the nation's president as commander in chief of the armed forces, but civilian leaders have usually been careful to grant the military a significant degree of autonomy.[18] At the same time, military subordination to elected civilian authority is becoming the regional norm. An elected civilian president can directly exercise a measure of "subjective control" by appointing only officers who enjoy his personal trust to senior staff positions.[19] Military subordination can also be ensured indirectly by imposing limits on military spending, either through presidential control over the defense budget or through international pressure. In virtually every Latin American country, the military's share of the national budget has declined in recent years. Between 1985 and 1993, defense spending as a share of gross national product (GNP) fell in Argentina from 2.9 percent to 1.7 percent; in Chile from 6.8 percent to 2.1 percent; and in El Salvador from 4.4 percent to 1.6 percent.[20] The international community and especially the United States have been increasingly visible and influential in encouraging Latin American military officers not to transgress their proper authority. Foreign countries can decisively influence the military's behavior by either limiting arms sales or restricting the supply of credit to finance such purchases.

Institutional measures to ensure military subordination to civilian authority in Latin America are rather antiquated, except in Argentina. It matters little whether civilians or military officers control the defense ministry, for this agency usually is little more than a clearinghouse for personnel management, logistical support, and basic services (such as health care) for military personnel. Since defense ministers are responsible for serving as liaisons between the armed forces and the civilian authorities, they occasionally become involved in sensitive disputes over military culpability for earlier human rights violations. Patricio Rojas, defense minister under Chilean president Patricio Aylwin in the early 1990s, clashed with Chile's powerful army over ongoing efforts to prosecute military officers responsible for the assassination in 1976 of former Chilean diplomat Orlando Letelier. At the height of this dispute in 1993, army commander Augusto Pinochet ordered ten thousand troops, clad in full combat gear, into the streets of Santiago in an obvious attempt to intimidate the government.[21]

Achieving military subordination to civilian authority is made even more difficult by the frequent absence of a civilian elite knowledgeable about military issues and capable of exercising effective oversight. In Latin America as in other developing regions, the task of overseeing the armed forces is a thankless one that creates powerful enemies and rarely enhances political careers. Jealous of their institutional autonomy, military commanders are normally reluctant even to share their plans with the defense ministry, much less to seek its approval. Civilian defense ministers often find it very hard to monitor and discipline the armed forces. Budgetary disputes can be treacherous, and the infrequency of large purchases of military equipment limits the government's negotiating leverage over the armed forces. Typically, the defense minister must negotiate with a closed military establishment that has been very slow to adopt the modern procedural guidelines characteristic of civilian agencies.

The insularity of the Latin American armed forces further buffers them from effective civilian control. Most have strict internal regulations governing enlistments, promotions, and retirements, especially among the officer corps. All restrict access to their professional command levels to graduates of national military academies.[22] Each military service controls its own promotions, although some of these require formal presidential approval. Promotion decisions are typically based on seniority, objective merit (as measured by examinations or performance reviews), or purely subjective criteria. Promotions to general or admiral rank require legislative approval, but it is seldom denied. The age of mandatory retirement depends on the highest rank attained and the length of command experience.[23]

Latin American legislatures normally shun involvement in military matters. They rarely examine the details of defense-budget requests or inquire into the mission or activities of the armed forces. Military-budget submissions are normally referred not to the legislative defense committee, as one might expect, but instead to budget committees or other panels having jurisdiction over social or economic policy. Other than approving the military budget, legislatures often limit their involvement in defense matters to approving promotions and authorizing participation in international peacekeeping operations or in joint military maneuvers with foreign forces. Legislative debates over military promotions usually focus on the human rights records of the candidates, and discussion of military involvement in foreign peacekeeping operations—especially those involving U.S. troops—mainly provides a forum for leftist legislators to vent their criticism. Rarely does more substantial discussion of military matters take place within legislative councils.

The Armed Forces and the Economy

The free-market institutions now prevalent throughout Latin America have sharply limited the autonomy, operations, and even size of the region's armed forces. In the absence of serious external threats, governments have cut military spending. Lower defense budgets have generally not been accompanied, however, by commensurate downsizing of the armed forces. Because the military has resisted overall force reductions, budgetary cutbacks have resulted instead in pay cuts for existing military personnel, forcing them to make up the difference by neglecting their official duties to take on second jobs in the private sector or engaging in corruption.

Consequently, many of the region's armed forces have experienced a real decline in operational capacity. Frequently, military installations are fully staffed only from 7:00 a.m. to 1:00 p.m., when officers and enlisted men depart for their second jobs, leaving only a skeleton work force behind. Operational capacity is also undermined by the wide dispersion of troops and installations throughout the national territory (even though modern communications technology makes such deployments unnecessary) and by obsolete equipment and inadequate training. Argentina and Brazil, for instance, each have just two aircraft carriers, both in dry dock, and many of their other ships cannot put out to sea because they lack the necessary crews. Moreover, many pilots have lost their flight qualifications owing to insufficient flying time.

Traditionally, Latin American armed forces have derived their incomes from a variety of sources. Military spending accounts for less than 2 percent of Latin America's aggregate GNP and 14 to 30 percent of total state spending. In the past, many armed forces supplemented their state budget allocations with revenue from military-run enterprises of various sorts. The Ecuadorian, Guatemalan, Salvadoran, and Peruvian armed forces participated in banking and other financial services; those of Ecuador and Guatemala were involved in the cement industry; and many others, including those of Honduras, participated in agricultural and livestock enterprises.

In recent years, most Latin American armed forces have sharply curtailed their involvement in nondefense enterprises. Brazil's military-run nondefense enterprises, once the most extensive in Latin America, now account for only 0.3 percent of GNP.[24] Generally, such military enterprises are poor sources of revenue, as they are highly labor-intensive and their capital equipment is often either antiquated or obsolete.

Some Latin American countries allocate to their armed forces a fixed share of income from the country's principal export product. Since the late 1950s, the Chilean armed forces have received a percentage of Chile's copper-export revenues (in 1995 that share amounted to 10 percent). In Ecuador, the armed forces receive between 9 and 11 percent of the country's oil-export revenues.

The need for increased revenues has fueled the mounting corruption found in certain Latin American armed forces. When austerity policies deprive government agencies of their accustomed level of resources, they are likely to look elsewhere—even to illicit activities—to replace any lost funds. The Paraguayan armed forces, for instance, have long derived income from smuggling, although the country's modernization process is slowly eliminating such opportunities. Other armed forces have profited from the international drug trade, either by taking payoffs in exchange for looking the other way or by actively protecting drug traffickers. Involvement in illegal activities, although reportedly widespread, can rarely be proved. Nonetheless, several high-ranking and powerful officers—including former Bolivian military president Luis García Meza, former Panamanian strongman Manuel Antonio Noriega, and Cuban general and war hero Arnaldo Ochoa Sánchez—have been brought to trial on drug-related charges.

The Armed Forces and Society

Latin American armed forces often have rather tenuous links to civil society. In many of the hemisphere's poorest countries, the state has little institutional presence outside of the national capital. The armed forces often constitute the only visible evidence of state authority in distant and isolated sections of these countries. In these cases, the army has often forged close ties with the civilian population.[25] In more cosmopolitan areas, however, the military remains remote from civil society, and especially from the middle and upper classes. Military conscription is normally the closest point of contact between the armed forces and society. Some Latin American armed forces—those of Uruguay, the Dominican Republic since 1965, Nicaragua since 1990, and Argentina since 1995—are entirely volunteer. Most others are conscript forces, composed overwhelmingly of lower-class recruits, since the sons of the upper and middle classes usually can avoid induction. Despite this disparity, military service can benefit lower-class recruits by providing access to technical training and enhancing future employment possibilities.

The officer corps of most Latin American military forces is drawn from the lower-middle and lower classes.[26] Recruitment into the closed and self-protective officer corps provides both an opportunity for upward mobility and access to an extensive mutual-support network. The insularity and mutual protection that characterize such institutions, however, can allow or even encourage involvement by some officers in extremist populist movements.[27]

The Future

The future mission and activities of armed forces in Latin America are likely to be domestic rather than external. Confidence-building measures and diplomatic means of resolving border disputes and similar interstate tensions have sharply reduced prospects for full-blown armed conflict between Latin American states. As armed forces assume additional police functions, their roles are likely to center increasingly on maintaining domestic order and fostering the nation's social and economic development. Such missions are usually circumscribed in time and space and only tangential to the military's experience and expertise. Consequently, they should be taken on only if other state or private institutions cannot discharge them. The central task of the armed forces should remain the defense of the nation's territory against external attack and the preservation of the constitutional order. Even when such threats are not manifest, the armed forces must remain vigilant against their reappearance.

Although small countries have the option of disbanding their armed forces, such a course of action can cause significant problems. Having abolished its armed forces in 1948, Costa Rica, for example, found itself without any security force in a highly unstable region. In Panama, the abolition of the army in 1989 led to the "militarization" of its national police force. Both countries now have to rely on external protectors—especially the United States—to guarantee their national security.

Since political conditions can change rapidly, governments must try to maintain maximum flexibility and to keep their options open. By abolishing its armed forces, a government forecloses an important option. In the absence of explicit security threats, however, the armed forces cannot continue to cling to their old ways and resist all change. They can best ensure their continued survival and relevance not by reacting intransigently to changing circumstances, but instead by implementing thorough internal reforms designed to improve the military's technological sophistication and quick-response capabilities so that the armed forces can carry out "police" missions on land, at sea, and in the air. These forces should be well equipped, limited in number, and funded at current budget levels. Training should be accorded the highest priority.

Finally, governments should strive to maintain adequate oversight and control of the armed forces. Unfortunately, most governments in the region have not yet established institutional mechanisms to ensure genuine military subordination to civilian authority. Few have a strong civilian defense ministry capable of controlling the various branches of the armed forces. Brazil and Peru have recently established defense ministries that combine functions formally exercised by the various service ministries. In contrast, Chile's defense ministry remains relatively powerless to supervise the country's armed forces, as does Argentina's. In light of these conditions, most Latin American governments have sought to achieve "subjective control" over the armed forces while avoiding detailed involvement in internal military affairs.

How should Latin American governments go about ensuring genuine military subordination to civilian authority? The first requirement is a clearly defined defense policy—something most governments in the region currently lack. With advice from military experts, civilian authorities must decide what sort of military force is needed, what mission it should discharge, and what level and type of resources it needs to carry out that mission. Effective implementation of this defense policy requires developing a civilian elite knowledgeable about military issues. Governments must also formulate clear legal guidelines for military involvement in domestic-security matters. Finally, they should strive to diminish the military's "ghetto mentality" through mutual confidence-building measures and other civil-military interaction. Although some governments have already made progress in this area—by promoting educational exchanges between civilian universities and military training institutes, for example—much remains to be done.

The most important obstacles to further progress stem from the inherent bureaucratic inertia of the armed forces and from the lack of political will on the part of civilian authorities to make the necessary changes. Civilian officials have fought strenuously with their military counterparts over matters of symbolic and historic importance—such as punishment of military officers responsible for human rights abuses committed under previous military regimes—but too often have sidestepped fundamental reforms. In fact, most reform initiatives have originated within the military itself.

Genuine military subordination to civilian authority will depend heavily on the continued example of armed forces in the developed world, which have been remarkably successful in carrying out their missions under effective civilian oversight and control. (This "demonstration effect," however, might cause some demoralization in the short term by underlining the vast differences that remain between civil-military interaction in Latin America and in the developed world.) Effective military control can also be promoted by continued Latin American participation in multilateral peacekeeping missions, which helps military personnel expand their horizons by gaining a deeper appreciation of the world's complexity and cultural diversity. Finally, the main social requisite for effective military subordination is the gradual reduction of the military's ghetto mentality with respect to civil society. The rising prevalence of volunteer armed forces in Latin America might hasten a much-needed attitudinal adjustment. All of these changes will, of course, require great patience and understanding from all involved.

NOTES

1. Eric Hobsbawm, *The Age of Extremes: The Short Twentieth Century, 1914–1991* (New York: Pantheon Books, 1994).

2. As a consultant to the Panamanian Defense Force between 1987 and 1989, Argentine colonel Mohammed Ali Seineldin assisted in the formation of an elite corps.

3. A U.S. delegation led by former president Jimmy Carter and including Senator Sam Nunn of Georgia and General Colin Powell, former chairman of the U.S. Joint Chiefs of Staff, convinced Haitian general Raoul Cédras and his followers of the wisdom of ceding power to Aristide—and of the folly of resisting the U.S. invasion that would ensue if they refused.

4. Douglas Farah, "From Death to Life," *Washington Post*, 20 September 1995, A14.

5. Alfred Vagts maintains that every armed force is at least partially responsible for producing the order that it exists to defend; see his *History of Militarism: Romance and Realities of a Profession* (New York: Norton, 1959). The military tends to view itself as the creator of an order that is subsequently defined by law, and thus feels responsible for protecting this order. On this point, see Walter Benjamin, *Zur Kritik der Gewalt und andere Aufsätze* (Frankfurt am Main: Suhrkamp, 1971).

6. Samuel Finer uses this term in *The Man on Horseback: The Role of the Military in Politics*, 2nd rev. ed. (Boulder, Colo.: Westview, 1988). The notion of a *poder moderador* arises from nineteenth-century Spanish military regulations, which state that the armed forces should take on a moderating role to preserve public order when violent conflict among internal political factions threatens to escalate into civil war.

7. On military authoritarianism, see David Collier, ed., *The New Authoritarianism in Latin America* (Princeton: Princeton University Press, 1979); Juan J. Linz, *The Breakdown of Democratic Regimes: Crisis, Breakdown, and Reequilibrium* (Baltimore: Johns Hopkins University Press, 1978); Guillermo O'Donnell, *Bureaucratic Authoritarianism: Argentina, 1966–1973, in Comparative Perspective*, trans. James McGuire (Berkeley: University of California Press, 1988); and Alfred Stepan, *The Military in Politics: Changing Patterns in Brazil* (Princeton: Princeton University Press, 1971).

8. See Juan Rial, "Transitions in Latin America on the Threshold of the 1990s," *International Social Science Journal* 43 (May 1991): 285–300.

9. The 1942 Rio Protocol obligated both parties to resolve their differences by peaceful

means, laid out reference points for demarcating the border between the two countries, specified that Ecuador would be allowed navigational access to the Amazon similar to the concessions granted Brazil and Colombia, and named the United States, Argentina, Brazil, and Chile guarantor nations. In 1945 a joint boundary-demarcation commission, assisted by a U.S. air force aerial survey and arbitration by a Brazilian naval officer, demarcated the border along 1,600 kilometers (about 95 percent) of the boundary between the countries. This settled the issue as far as Peru was concerned, but in 1950 Ecuador declared that new topographical information showed that mistakes had been made in demarcating the border along 78 kilometers of the Cordillera del Cóndor. The fighting in 1981 and 1995 discussed below occurred in this disputed area. For a summary of this border dispute, see *Latin American Weekly Report*, 23 February 1995, 75; the text of the 1942 Rio Protocol is reproduced in *Latin American Regional Report: Andean Group*, 9 March 1995, 6.

10. In signing the Itamaraty Declaration and agreeing to the Momep observer force (made up of military officers from the four guarantor nations), Ecuador appeared to recognize the validity of the 1942 Rio Protocol, although it still maintains that this does not apply to the disputed 78 kilometers in the Cóndor range. Relations between the two countries warmed after the signing in July of a demilitarization accord and in October of a framework for future negotiations. Moreover, Momep's mandate has already been extended twice (currently through February 1996). However, a peaceful settlement has been jeopardized by arms purchases by both sides and alleged splits within the Ecuadorian military on what approach to take to settling this dispute. See *Latin American Weekly Report*, 10 August 1995 and 25 January 1996; and *FBIS Latin America*, 22 November 1995, 39.

11. This dispute potentially involves Peru as well, as a protocol in a Chilean treaty with Peru prohibits Chile from ceding the former Peruvian province of Arica (gained in the War of the Pacific) to any third party.

12. Genaro Arriagada analyzes the military's rationale for such operations in traditionally stable countries, such as Chile and Uruguay, in *El pensamiento político de los militares* (Santiago, Chile: Centro de Investigaciones Socioeconómicas, 1981). See also Carina Perelli, "From Counterrevolutionary Warfare to Political Awakening: The Uruguayan and Argentine Armed Forces in the 1970s," *Armed Forces and Society* 20 (Fall 1993): 25–49, and *El discurso militar* (Montevideo, Uruguay: Ebo-Clade, 1987).

13. According to Max Weber, prebendary or patrimonial regimes gain and hold power by distributing material benefits (or prebends) in return for the recipients' loyalty and obedience. See Max Weber, *Economy and Society: An Outline of Interpretive Sociology* (Berkeley and Los Angeles: University of California Press, 1978).

14. Only the oldest Latin American constitutions—especially those of Argentina and Uruguay—follow the traditional liberal practice of making only oblique reference to the military. In contrast, all the modern Latin American constitutions contain a specific section on the role of the armed forces. See Juan Rial, "Providing for the Common Defense: What Latin American Constitutions Have to Say About the Region's Armed Forces," in Douglas Greenberg, Stanley N. Katz, Melanie Beth Oliveiro, and Steven C. Wheatley, *Constitutionalism and Democracy: Transitions in the Contemporary World* (Oxford: Oxford University Press, 1993), 235–48.

15. For example, during the fall of 1995, Venezuela on several occasions sent military detachments into Colombian territory in the Perija mountain range in pursuit of peasants cultivating poppy. This resulted in strong protests from the Colombian government.

16. Some countries—Paraguay, Uruguay, Panama, and the Dominican Republic—have not experienced such conflicts. Brazil has had minor territorial disputes with its neighbors but none significant enough to warrant military action. Similar ongoing disagreements that exist between Chile and Argentina and among Chile, Peru, and Bolivia are also unlikely to result in armed confrontation. Latent frontier problems exist in Central America as well, but there seems to be little inclination to settle these by force. In fact, most Latin American countries have shown determination to avoid such conflicts in the future.

Argentina hopes, for instance, to settle peacefully its dispute with Britain over the Falklands/Malvinas.

17. In late November 1995, police and military units in Peru cracked down on a resuscitated Revolutionary Tupac Amaru Movement, which had engineered political kidnappings in La Paz, Bolivia, and was planning similar operations in Lima. Among those arrested and tried for treason was an American human rights activist.

18. Bolivia and Paraguay have a separate military commander in chief, who directs the entire military apparatus. In the event of armed conflict, the president becomes chief of staff and the defense minister assumes a purely administrative role. The Honduran joint chiefs remain in full de facto command of the armed forces, while in Uruguay the president and the defense minister are jointly responsible for commanding the armed forces.

19. See Samuel P. Huntington, *The Soldier and the State: The Theory and Politics of Civil-Military Relations* (Cambridge: Harvard University Press, 1957).

20. See the 1990–94 editions of International Institute for Strategic Studies, *The Military Balance* (London: Oxford University Press, 1990–94); and World Bank, *World Development Report 1994* (Washington, D.C.: World Bank, 1994).

21. In November 1993 the two officers accused of having ordered the Letelier assassination—Generals Manuel Contreras Sepúlveda (former head of the Chilean secret police) and Pedro Espinoza Bravo (Contreras's former deputy)—were convicted and sentenced to prison terms of seven and six years, respectively. The Supreme Court subsequently ruled in June 1994 that a 1978 amnesty law did not apply in this case and in May 1995 upheld the convictions. After unsuccessful efforts by the army to block their imprisonment failed, Contreras and Espinoza were finally incarcerated in June and October 1995, respectively, in a prison outside Santiago specifically constructed to house convicted military officials.

22. Although officers trained in other Latin American countries or in the United States might attain professional status on an exceptional basis, they are rarely promoted to the highest ranks. Latin American countries that lack their own military academies tend to have small and poorly institutionalized armed forces, such as Panama's now-disbanded National Guard.

23. Chile and Peru constitute two notorious exceptions. Chile's 1980 constitution allowed military junta members who participated in the 1973 coup d'état to retain their commands indefinitely. Of the four original junta members, only army commander General Augusto Pinochet still directed a branch of the armed forces in 1995. The Fujimori government in Peru issued a decree in June 1993 allowing military-service chiefs to retain their commands at the president's discretion, even if the incumbent has passed the mandatory retirement age.

24. Antonio Carlos Pereira, "El desafío de una fuerza militar de un país que quiere ser una potencia: Brasil," *Documentos de la VI Conferencia del Proyecto Relaciones Militares en América Latina del Programa de Iniciativas Democráticas de American University* (Montevideo, Uruguay: Peitho, 1992).

25. This linkage between the level of socioeconomic development and civil-military interaction is evident in rural areas of Guatemala and Peru. In both countries the army has armed peasant farmers, creating "Self-Defense Patrols" (Patrullas de Autodefensa) in Guatemala and "Peasant Patrols" (Rondas Campesinas) in Peru to fight leftist guerrillas.

26. See Juan Rial, "El reclutamiento del cuerpo de oficiales en el Uruguay" (working paper, Peitho, Montevideo, Uruguay, 1994). In Chile and Peru, however, naval officers are recruited from higher social classes.

27. The extremist political activities of Lieutenant Colonel Aldo Rico and Colonel Mohammed Alí Seineldin in Argentina or Colonel Hugo Chávez in Venezuela illustrate this point.

5.
CONTROLLING ASIA'S ARMED FORCES

Carolina G. Hernandez

Carolina G. Hernandez *is president of the Institute for Strategic and Development Studies in Quezon City, the Philippines, and professor of political science at the University of the Philippines. She serves on the steering committee of the Council for Security Cooperation in the Asia Pacific (CSCAP) and as co-chairperson of CSCAP-Philippines.*

The end of the Cold War brought about many changes, not only in international relations but also in the domestic politics of many countries around the world. The collapse of communism in Eastern Europe and the Soviet Union gave rise to new regimes that promised to democratize their societies. In Asia the movement toward democratization had a variety of sources. As happened in much of Latin America, the failure of authoritarian regimes to promote economic development, eliminate corruption, and ensure political stability gave rise to new democratic governments in such Asian countries as Pakistan, Bangladesh, and the Philippines. In contrast, the very economic success fostered by authoritarian regimes in South Korea and Taiwan gave birth in these countries to a wide range of social and political forces that eventually chafed under authoritarian rule and led the push for democratization.

Irrespective of its origins, the movement toward political liberalization and democratization must be accompanied by a restructuring of the military's role in politics if it is to endure. This political imperative coincides with a military one brought about by the changed security environment of the post–Cold War era. The need to restructure the military's mission entailed by these two imperatives—one domestic and the other international—has profound implications for the future of civil-military relations in democratizing countries around the globe. This chapter focuses on how this issue is being played out in contemporary Asia. Given the size and diversity of the region, I will approach the issue thematically, drawing illustrative examples from those Asian countries (primarily in East and Southeast Asia) where democratic regimes are being consolidated, prodemocratic movements have emerged, or the military's role is undergoing significant change.

Asian militaries have performed a variety of roles in the modern era. Although many were organized or modernized by the colonial powers, some, like the Indonesian military, turned against the colonial regime during the independence movement. Such actions conferred upon the military a great deal of popular legitimacy, which, in combination with institutional variables and other factors favorable to the military in these societies, induced the general population to accept military intervention in politics.

Lack of experience in democratic governance on the part of indigenous political elites contributed to their inability to cope with the diverse challenges posed by nation-building and economic development. In particular, these weak postcolonial governments could not ensure internal order and stability in situations marked by strong ethnic and religious rivalries. Moreover, these new countries lacked strong political institutions, such as political parties, autonomous legislatures and courts, and a free press, that might have exerted some control over the military. This created a situation that allowed the military in many Asian countries, as elsewhere in the developing world, to step in and impose order.

Consequently, the two decades following decolonization witnessed the rise of authoritarian governments either in partnership with the military or solely under military control. The ability of these authoritarian governments to promote social harmony, internal order, political stability, and economic development varied considerably. Authoritarian regimes in South Korea and Taiwan proved to be the most successful in this regard; their Indonesian and Thai counterparts also made considerable progress in promoting economic development and national unity, and, in the Indonesian case, in providing political order and stability. In contrast, authoritarian governments in Pakistan, Bangladesh, Burma, and the Philippines proved largely unsuccessful in achieving these goals.

By the early 1990s several Asian countries had moved away from the authoritarian model and toward democratization. South Korea, the Philippines, and Taiwan can now be considered *consolidating democracies*, having installed civilian governments in relatively free elections with large-scale participation. In December 1992, with the victory of Kim Young Sam in the presidential election, South Koreans elected their first civilian government since the ouster of Syngman Rhee in 1960, and in June 1995 they participated in the first direct elections for local government. The Philippines in May 1992 held presidential, parliamentary, and local elections, which brought a peaceful transfer of power from President Corazon Aquino to her successor, Fidel Ramos. Taiwan in December 1995 held its third parliamentary elections since the lifting of martial law in 1987, paving the way for its first direct presidential election in March 1996. Thus both elites and the citizenry in these countries seem to have reached a consensus that there is no effective alternative to democratic governance. Moreover, popular participation seems to be growing not only in politics but also in civil society in all three countries.

In several other Asian countries, however, the progress of democratization is still uneven. For example, in Thailand, where political parties and a bicameral legislature seem to have become institutionalized, many legislators (notably in the upper house) and local chief executives are still appointed, thus setting limits on popular participation in the selection of the country's political leaders. Constitutional amendments to redress this situation are currently being discussed; if passed, they would bolster the democratization process.

In Pakistan and Bangladesh the transition to democracy has taken place in a fashion approximating what Samuel Finer called the "transit of regimes," in which the military haltingly disengages from direct rule while attempting to control the political coloration of successor regimes.[1] In Burma and China prodemocracy movements have arisen to challenge authoritarian regimes but have been largely suppressed. In Indonesia the military regime, although faced with the imminent problem of succession after the passing of the aged President Suharto and his cohort of independence-era generals, seems for now firmly in control.

External and Domestic Factors

As noted above, the end of the Cold War fundamentally altered the global and regional strategic environment: this change is having a major impact on the role of the military in both developed and developing countries. In Asia the end of superpower competition facilitated a warming of relations between such regional rivals as Russia and China, India and China, and even Japan and Russia. It also contributed to a reconciliation between the member states of the Association of Southeast Asian Nations (ASEAN) and Vietnam and to the resolution of the Cambodian problem.

Moreover, the end of the Cold War brought about a drawdown in the number of U.S. forces stationed in the Pacific theater. Some uncertainty has been introduced in the region owing to the elimination of the deterrent effect of bipolar competition. In this altered strategic environment, a number of Asian countries, notably China and the ASEAN states, have restructured their military forces. Similarly, the decline of the communist threat at the global level and the concomitant erosion of support for indigenous communist parties has led some countries, such as the Philippines, to reevaluate the domestic-security role of the military.

According to the comprehensive and multidimensional concept of security prevalent in East Asia, the role of the military is not limited to defending the country against potential external threats. Rather, in countries such as Indonesia, the armed forces have been given major domestic responsibilities. Such a broad view of the military's role, however, may be incompatible with the redistribution of power to civilian authorities inherent in the democratization process.

An expansive view of security constitutes a potential problem in civil-military relations for consolidating democracies. If the military is not to overstep its boundaries, its sphere of responsibility must be clearly delineated, and successor civilian governments must prove that they can be both effective and competent. The military's domestic responsibilities should be limited to quick-response operations, such as disaster relief, in which military units are withdrawn to the barracks immediately after the crisis abates. Its duties must not be broadly extended to include the sort of long-term nation-building tasks allocated to the Indonesian armed forces according to that country's "dual function" (military and socioeconomic) doctrine.

In recent years the major donor countries of the Organization for Economic Cooperation and Development—notably the United States, Japan, and Great Britain—have attempted to encourage a reduction in the military's political influence in developing countries by linking foreign aid to the recipient country's pursuit of "good governance" and democratization. This constitutes a reversal of the Cold War policy of supporting any allied authoritarian regime with large infusions of military and economic assistance, which greatly increased the wealth of ruling elites in such countries as Pakistan, Bangladesh, and the Philippines. Donor countries have now made the extension of official development assistance conditional upon a diminution in the political role of the military, including its withdrawal from ruling coalitions, and the reduction of the defense budget. Such preconditions have been placed on aid going not only to democratizing countries like Pakistan and Bangladesh but also to authoritarian states such as Burma, where the State Law and Order Restoration Council (SLORC) has balked at relinquishing any of its power.[2] Given the serious economic difficulties that face most of these governments, this type of linkage has often been successful in encouraging reform in civil-military relations.

The Consequences of Economic Development

The rapid industrialization and modernization that both South Korea and Taiwan experienced in the 1970s and 1980s significantly expanded popular participation in their economies. A sizeable middle class came into being that was better educated, more traveled, and thus better informed. If economic empowerment indeed promotes self-confidence and self-assertiveness among those whom it benefits, then economic development should unleash socioeconomic forces supportive of political liberalization and democratization and demands for greater political participation.

In both South Korea and Taiwan, modernization gave birth to the dynamic forces behind the democratization process. In Thailand as well, the leaders of the prodemocracy movement have been drawn from the middle class: intellectuals, business and management elites, and other professionals. In Indonesia the grassroots human rights movements seeking to foster adherence to the rule of law are also led by middle-class professionals. The leading opponents of the SLORC in Burma as well as the leaders of the movement to restore democracy in the Philippines come from similar backgrounds. For example, mass opposition to President Ferdinand Marcos in the Philippines, which culminated in the "people power" revolt of 1986, grew by leaps and bounds only after the Filipino middle class joined in the "parliament of the streets."[3] Nonetheless, the middle class cannot always be counted on to act as a force for political liberalization and democratization, as societal and temporal variables affect its precise role in these processes.

Economic development also provided the military with opportunities to tap new sources of wealth. Authoritarian governments that acquired political control over newly created wealth transferred significant resources to the military in an effort to buy its loyalty and support. For example, the Bangladesh government led by Lieutenant General Hossain Mohammed Ershard increased the defense budget by an average of 18 percent while the total annual budget rose by only 14 percent. The rate of increase of military salaries and perquisites was such that the real incomes of military personnel were twice those of their civilian counterparts. Military elites gained access to lucrative positions in the public and private sectors: active or retired military officers headed 14 of the 22 largest corporations and held about one-third of the diplomatic posts overseas.[4] The military also benefited from foreign aid through commissions received from foreign suppliers of goods and services funded by official development assistance. In this way, military elites became part of the country's *nouveau riche.*[5]

In Pakistan, rewards to the military during the rule of General Zia ul-Haq included an institutionalized system of appointment of military elites to senior positions in the civilian bureaucracy, parastatal enterprises, and private businesses, which in turn gave them privileged access to governmental contracts. Moreover, military officials were posted to diplomatic positions in the Gulf states. Finally, the government allotted plots of land to military elites at below-market prices, which enabled them to build luxury homes that could be sold at huge profits.[6]

Similar trends can be found in Thailand and Indonesia. The Thai military is particularly known for its rent-seeking activities, notably in natural-resource extraction and cross-border trade with Burma and

Cambodia. The government has not been able to curtail these activities, especially in remote border areas, although, following the fall in May 1992 of the government headed by General Suchinda Kraprayoon, some initial attempts were made to reduce the military's presence in business corporations. The efforts to reduce the military's penetration of state enterprises slowed after the interim government of Anand Panyarachun gave way in September 1992 to the elected government of Prime Minister Chuan Leekpai. When the military fought a "vigorous rear-guard action to maintain its influence" in politics, the government chose not to force the issue.[7]

The Indonesian military's dual function gives it easy access to influential and potentially lucrative governmental positions.

The Indonesian military's dual function gives it easy access to influential and potentially lucrative governmental positions. Military elites in Indonesia have become ministers, governors, regents of provincial subdivisions, district and village heads, members of parliament, ambassadors, and managers of state enterprises.[8]

In the Philippines, the military during the period of martial law reaped its share of largess in the form of membership on corporate boards, privileged investment opportunities, and appointment to civilian positions that facilitated rent-seeking activities.[9] Military officers also began to move into the new and expensive residential enclaves that had sprouted in metropolitan areas such as Manila. These officers' legitimate sources of income were obviously inadequate to pay for such housing, not to mention the expensive private schools that their children attended or the luxury consumer goods purchased by their wives. Even those rebel military officers who lambasted corruption among public officials are known to have profited from illegal numbers games, gold-panning operations, and logging concessions.[10] Moreover, the proceeds from these activities helped fund the various abortive coup attempts against the Aquino government.

The People's Liberation Army (PLA) in China has also been rewarded for its loyalty in the wake of Tiananmen Square. The defense budget has increased at a steady pace, as has disguised military spending on research and education and the revenues brought in by "self-help" activities in the growing number of military-affiliated businesses (currently estimated at seven thousand).[11] The PLA has grown ever more politically autonomous as the post-Deng succession has unfolded, a trend that has been enhanced by the fact that the PLA has more Long March veterans among its officials than does the Chinese Communist Party.

Even consolidating democracies like Taiwan and Korea continue to provide their militaries with sizeable military budgets. In Taiwan, when the military retirement fund is added in, some 40 percent of the total government budget goes to the military.[12] As for South Korea, even after the end of authoritarian rule the military continued to press for increases in its budget (e.g., an increase of 25 percent in the 1992 budget).[13]

The military's access to economic opportunities and to the fruits of economic development not only serves to enrich its officers but also profoundly shapes civil-military relations in democratizing societies, as will be discussed below.

The Philippine and South Korean Experiences

Democratizing leaders often promulgate policies that directly affect the military's role. During the difficult transition period, radical efforts to curtail the military's power and influence may backfire or even reverse the advance toward democracy, as such measures are likely to antagonize the military command and motivate military elites to intervene in politics. Such governmental actions include drastic reductions in the military budget, restraints on the military's autonomous economic activities, civilian intrusion into the military's sphere of professional responsibility, removal of military elites from civilian positions, forced retirement of generals with long service, and prosecution of human rights abuses and criminal activities in which military personnel have been involved. In addition, the recruitment of civilian government officials unacceptable to the military or the adoption of policies that are perceived as undermining the military's ability to discharge its functions (such as counterinsurgency) also generates resentment toward the government among military ranks.

The Philippine and Korean experiences are instructive in this regard. In the Philippines, Corazon Aquino before coming to power witnessed the military's incarceration of her husband, Senator Benigno Aquino, Jr., and his subsequent assassination while in military custody. Moreover, military troops stood on the other side of the barricades during the public demonstrations against the Marcos regime—an experience that marked her view of the military as well as that of other members of her cabinet who had been anti-Marcos activists. The military viewed President Aquino and her cabinet with suspicion, especially those members seen as left-leaning, and this lack of mutual trust made it more difficult to sort out the military's role in the immediate postauthoritarian period. Even military reformists and their civilian counterparts, who had been major players in the events culminating in Marcos's ouster, felt unjustly excluded from the inner circle of power in the Aquino administration. The persistence of communist insurgency during her tenure and the government's prosecution of those within the military accused of human rights abuses fueled military discontent.

The series of unsuccessful coup attempts in the Philippines stemmed from these and other factors.[14] Coup participants cited several reasons for joining the coup effort:

- failure of the government to deliver basic services, especially in the rural areas;
- graft and corruption in the government and the military;
- excessive grandstanding by politicians and unfair criticism, even humiliation, of the military at their hands;
- bureaucratic inefficiency, which exacerbates the alienation and impoverishment of the people;
- poor and unresponsive military leadership, characterized by an "old boys'" network and factionalism, together with inadequate financial and logistical support for soldiers in the field;
- uneven treatment of human rights abuses committed by the military and the communist rebels;
- government softness in dealing with the communists and left-leaning elements;
- lack of good government; and
- failure of the civilian leadership to effectively address the country's economic problems.

According to military officers who opposed the coups, however, the plotters were motivated by other reasons, including

- obsession with the power that they thought they had won but had to hand over to Corazon Aquino in February 1986;
- desire on the part of the coup leaders to retain the privileges that they enjoyed during the Marcos years, and the prospect of possible financial gain or increased power through a coup;
- personal grievances or the perception that their career had reached a dead end;
- strong fraternal or personal ties among themselves that went back to their academy days;
- naive idealism, especially among younger officers; and
- a messianic complex.

The coups proved unpopular with the general public. Opinion polls repeatedly indicated overwhelming opposition to the coups, even though many respondents agreed with the plotters' complaints about the political and military leadership and supported their demands for more effective government.[15] The 1992 elections were also on the horizon by the time the last phase of the 1989 coup was drawing to a close in October 1990. Given the unpopularity of the coups and their repeated failure to win political power, the coup leaders' civilian supporters may have chosen to switch to the electoral route to power, thus leaving the military rebels without the necessary financial support. Moreover, President Aquino opted to respond to those military demands that she considered legitimate, such as increases in pay, appointment of relatively young officers to the highest military posts, removal of cabinet officials to whom the military strongly objected, and a more even handling of cases involving violation of human rights. These measures facilitated the normalization of civil-military relations during the remainder of her term.

Under President Ramos, the adoption of a more open and less conditional national reconciliation with rebels of all stripes through the peace process and an amnesty program, together with the forging of a broad political coalition that broke the executive-legislative stalemate, furthered the normalization of civil-military relations. Ramos's own military background (as the former military chief of staff) meant that the military trusted him more than it had his predecessor and that he had a better understanding of civil-military relations. He appointed retired officers to key positions in his inner circle of power and in the civilian bureaucracy, and he undertook a military modernization program greatly appreciated by a military that had been badly crippled by reliance on outdated weaponry. The widely circulated rumor that his administration supported the candidacy of military rebels running in the 1995 elections even enabled some of them to win, which in turn gave them a stake in the present system and an opportunity to push through legally some of the policies that they had wanted to impose through the coups.

In contrast to the conciliatory approach taken in the Philippines, in South Korea President Kim Young Sam began clipping the military's wings soon after his election in 1993. He replaced both the army chief of staff and the defense security commander, broke tradition by appointing a general of less than four-star rank as defense minister, and dismissed a number of senior generals from the armed forces. He moved to break up the powerful secret society Hanahoe (One-Mind Society)—a fraternity of elite generals who had graduated from the Korean Military Academy—stripped the Defense Security Command (the three-service military intelligence agency) of all powers not strictly military in nature, and replaced the military brigades guarding the Blue House with civilian police.[16] Scores of other secret societies within the military have also been disbanded, and "political" generals within the military have been purged.

The Kim administration's efforts to bring an end to military corruption and to place the military firmly under civilian control have so far proved to be popular with the rank and file.[17] The measures outlined above have weakened the military establishment to the point that few South Koreans believe the military capable of mounting another coup.[18] In a few instances, however, the military did succeed in pressuring civilian leaders to oust certain ministers that the military leadership particularly distrusted: one prominent casualty was the education minister, who was immediately fired by President Kim in June 1995 following her disparaging remarks before a military audience about the army's role during the Korean War.[19]

Impact on Civil-Military Relations

The factors discussed above have reshaped the role of the military in democratizing Asian societies in a variety of ways and to different degrees. As already noted, fundamental changes in the strategic environment have forced governments all over the globe to redefine the role of the military. Although the absence of an external threat has undercut the justification for a large military and a sizeable defense budget, the new strategic environment has necessitated force restructuring, including military modernization.

In China the end of the Cold War brought about a normalization of the Sino-Russian border, spurred a restructuring of the PLA, and changed the nature of China's arms modernization. Having lost the leverage it once had between the two superpowers, China now appears to be staking out an independent role for itself that is to be made credible by the buildup of a blue-water navy and the creation of a modern air force. Its ambitious military modernization plan, its new competition with four of its Southeast Asian neighbors over potential marine resources in the South China Sea, and the general inscrutability of its foreign-policy goals mean that China constitutes a potential security threat in the region. Indeed, China could be making a bid to become the dominant actor in Asia once its modernization goals are met, depending on how other regional powers react to the new strategic environment and how such issues as the North Korean nuclear-weapons program are ultimately resolved. The increasing political autonomy and economic interests of the PLA will likely diminish the ability of Chinese political leaders to control the military, particularly during the upcoming period of political succession.

In the case of Thailand, the country's military modernization program coincided with the end of the Cold War. Having abandoned its confrontational stance toward Vietnam, Thailand no longer stands as a "front-line" state in the battle against communism. Yet in the absence of strong institutions outside the military and bureaucracy, the Thai military's share of political power remains considerable despite the country's prodemocracy movement. The military is not likely to give up its share of valuable timber, gems, and other natural resources or the lucrative cross-border trade. Moreover, it is not clear whether the prodemocracy movement that originated in the Thai middle class will continue to gain support in the future. For these reasons, the military will most likely have the upper hand in its dealings with civilian authorities for the time being.

Indonesia's military remains the most organized and institutionalized political entity in the country. Its "dual function" doctrine, which is deeply entrenched in the political culture and widely accepted by the military and citizenry alike, remains largely unchallenged. At the same time, the growing influence of religion and ethnicity in Indonesian politics has generated consternation in military circles, especially as President Suharto is perceived as playing the Islamic and ethnic cards to counterbalance the military's power. Having witnessed the violence of ethnically based repression in the aftermath of Sukarno's downfall, military elites have become staunch supporters of secularism. As the guardians of the Indonesian nation, military officials are loath to see another round of civil turmoil that would jeopardize the country's secularly based national unity.

Similarly, the changing concept of security is reshaping the military's mission, even in those countries that have long embraced the more comprehensive view of security. In Indonesia and Thailand, younger officers have begun to articulate the need for a new institutional mission. In the Philippines, changes are already under way, as the police and military have been separated in both organization and mission. The waning of the communist and Muslim insurgencies has provided an opportunity to reduce the military's size at the same time that the withdrawal of the United States from its military bases in the country has prompted the crafting of a new external focus. This new focus, however, is not primarily to resist external aggression but rather to protect Philippine marine resources from illegal fishing by better-equipped boats from neighboring countries such as Japan, China, and Korea.

The missions of the militaries in South Korea and Taiwan still emphasize resistance to external aggression owing to the security threats posed by North Korea and the People's Republic of China, respectively. The possibility that a nuclear power might emerge on South Korea's northern border is likely to ensure that the South Korean military remains a strong force even as it comes under increasing civilian control. In addition, the persistence of a major external threat might enable the military to parlay its strategic importance into political influence, as was evidenced in the 1995 reorganization of the South Korean cabinet.

As discussed above, rapid economic development facilitated the process of political liberalization and democratization in a number of Asian countries and helped bring into being various Asian prodemocracy movements. At the same time, however, economic growth under authoritarian rule has benefited those who served as the regime's guardians: high-ranking military elites in Thailand, Indonesia, South Korea, Taiwan, and elsewhere have siphoned off more than their fair share of the expanding economic pie. Military elites, sitting as they do at the very core of power in these societies, are able to benefit from contracts, influence peddling, mining and timber operations, and control over cross-border trade. They can count on the patronage doled out by political leaders whose very survival depends on the military's support. Even in those countries that have not prospered economically, the military has accumulated a considerable share of the nation's wealth.

The military's access to wealth directly affects civil-military relations. Military officials will usually resist any civilian attempts to cut the defense budget or limit their outside sources of income, and may even attempt to reverse the democratization process if they feel that the military's economic interests are threatened. Hence democratic transition and consolidation are more likely to go forward if the armed forces are reassured that the military's budget will be maintained at an acceptable level and that military elites will continue to receive their share of the economic pie.

Popularly supported prodemocracy movements are likely to become a force with which the military will have to reckon. However, if these movements do not increase their numerical strength and broaden the scope of their activities, the military may be able to neutralize them effectively through isolation or targeted repression. Tiananmen Square remains a powerful lesson in this regard. Effective political suppression in the wake of Tiananmen Square has weakened China's prodemocracy movement considerably. In Thailand, whether the Thai middle class can become a coherent force helping to advance democratization remains an open question, despite the apparent reduction of the military's role in Thai politics following the prodemocracy demonstrations in May 1992 that toppled the military government.[20]

Lessons and Policy Implications

Asian militaries face a variety of challenges in the post–Cold War era. If democratization indeed entails a redistribution of power in society (among institutions, among levels of government, and between civil society and the state), then the military in consolidating democracies will see its social and political roles inevitably contract as a new pattern of civil-military relations emerges. In those countries where the military faces rising prodemocracy movements, any number of outcomes are possible. For example, in Thailand the prospects for curtailing the military's power are better than in Burma, as Thailand has functioned as a "demi-democracy" (where liberalization exists without meaningful democracy) for a number of years.[21] Burma's military is unlikely to yield power in the short to medium term as long as it regards itself as the sole guardian of the national interest and views civilian politicians with deep-seated suspicion (particularly those associated with the opposition centered around Daw Aung San Suu Kyi). In China the military, which traditionally has been an important actor in periods of political succession, has become even more powerful in the present transitional period, especially as it has acquired considerable economic power.

The presence of external threats often but not always impedes the process of normalizing civil-military relations in democratizing societies. Thus the continuing external role of the military in South Korea and Taiwan might slow the process of reducing the military's influence in politics, though in both cases civilian control of the military has increased in recent years. Similarly, Pakistan's longstanding armed confrontation with India will most likely provide its military with important leverage vis-à-vis the civilian leadership.

The changing concept of security is likely to expand the role of the military, or at least refocus it away from purely internal and external defense responsibilities. Safeguards need to be established so that military involvement in nondefense matters is strictly delimited and short-term, does not involve regular or intensive interaction with the civilian population, and is under the strict control of competent civilian authorities. Functions that utilize military expertise but that are less politicized than the long-term socioeconomic activities in which the military has been involved in years past include disaster relief and the building of infrastructure (e.g., roads and bridges). Other roles that might be considered include peacekeeping and peacemaking under the auspices of such multilateral organizations as the United Nations.

While the existence of a strong middle class can bolster the democratization process, as in the South Korean and Taiwanese cases, democratizing elites must nonetheless be attentive to eliciting the military's cooperation. It is imperative that they secure the military's professional autonomy by spelling out a well-defined military mission, guaranteeing an adequate military budget, and safeguarding the military's institutional integrity (by protecting it from undue civilian interference). Such assurances should provide the military with sufficient confidence in the system to accept a reduction in its political influence, and motivate it to acquire a stake in the new democratic order. The Philippines can be considered an example in this regard, for here the government instituted policies that redefined the military's mission, separated it from the civilian police force (a demand that emanated from the military itself), and increased its budget for military modernization.

Political leaders who prove acceptable to the military understand the sensitivity of civil-military relations in democratizing societies and tend to be flexible in crafting a diminished role for the military. The respective experiences of Philippine presidents Aquino and Ramos, who inspired different levels of confidence on the part of the military and differed in their mode of interaction with the armed forces, provide instructive examples. President Aquino undertook reforms—including pay increases and the granting of other benefits—addressing what she considered to be the military's legitimate grievances. She did not, however, implement an amnesty program that might have enticed coup plotters to return to the governmental fold and hence bolstered the political stability of her administration, at least in the short term. In contrast, President Ramos adopted a general amnesty program that allowed coup plotters to return to active military service, receive back wages, and even run for elected office. This enabled reconciliation talks between the government and military renegades to go forward and fostered political stability in the short term; in the long run, however, this development could undermine the institutionalization of civilian control over the military, especially as far as junior officers are concerned. Nonetheless, political pragmatism is probably the most effective approach to stabilizing civil-military relations during a period of transition such as that experienced in the Philippines.

Finally, independent political institutions must be established that can exercise effective civilian control and oversight over the military. This inevitably takes a long time. Yet the Philippine case shows that civilian political institutions can indeed be strengthened at the same time that the military's role is being recast during democratic consolidation. In the Philippines, on balance, a normal democratic mode of civil-military relations seems to be on its way to being institutionalized; the only caveat is the marked increase in the number of retired military officers being appointed to important civilian positions, which raises concerns about a possible "silent coup." Nevertheless, although civil-military relations continue to pose a challenge for democratization in Asia, the Philippine example at least offers some hope for the future.

NOTES

1. Samuel E. Finer, *The Man on Horseback: The Role of the Military in Politics*, 2nd rev. ed. (Boulder, Colo.: Pinter Press, 1988), 279–83.

2. Baladas Ghoshal, "Democracy Treads Tightrope," *Far Eastern Economic Review*, 21 February 1991, 15.

3. The term applies to the mass demonstrations against Marcos that began in the early 1980s and lasted until his ouster in February 1986.

4. Talukder Maniruzzaman, "The Fall of the Military Dictator: 1991 Elections and the Prospect of Civilian Rule in Bangladesh," *Pacific Affairs* 65 (Summer 1992): 204.

5. Ibid., 217–18.

6. Hasan-Askari Rizvi, "The Military and Politics in Pakistan," *Journal of Asian and African Studies* 26 (January 1991): 31–32.

7. Rodney Tasker and Gordon Fairclough, "Return to Duty," *Far Eastern Economic Review*, 20 May 1993, 18–19.

8. Margot Cohen, "Marching to a Crossroads," *Far Eastern Economic Review*, 3 September 1992, 28.

9. See the report issued by the fact-finding commission that investigated the abortive coup of December 1989: Hilario Davide et al., *The Final Report of the Fact-Finding Commission* (Makati, Philippines: Bookmark Publishing, 1990), 485.

10. Ibid.

11. Lincoln Kaye, "Leadership Crossroads," *Far Eastern Economic Review*, 1 September 1994, 46.

12. Tai Ming Cheung, "Frozen in Time," *Far Eastern Economic Review*, 18 May 1989, 21.

13. Shim Jae Hoon, "Soldiering On," *Far Eastern Economic Review*, 26 September 1993, 27.

14. For an extensive analysis of the underlying causes, see Davide et al., *Final Report*, 470–75.

15. Ibid., 474 and 483, which cites a Social Weather Stations, Inc., survey of public opinion on the 1 December 1989 coup attempt.

16. Shim Jae Hoon, "The Battle Within," *Far Eastern Economic Review*, 1 April 1993, 25.

17. Shim Jae Hoon, "Meeting the Boss," *Far Eastern Economic Review*, 28 October 1993, 36.

18. Shim Jae Hoon and Ed Paisley, "Whirlwind Honeymoon," *Far Eastern Economic Review*, 24 June 1993, 18–19.

19. Shim Jae Hoon, "Out for a Gaffe," *Far Eastern Economic Review*, 1 June 1995, 26.

20. See Rodney Tasker, "Military: The Last Bastion," *Far Eastern Economic Review*, 18 January 1996, 20–21, and "Downsized: But the Thai Top Brass Is No Pushover," *Far Eastern Economic Review*, 18 January 1996, 22.

21. Chai-Anan Samudavanija and Sukhumbhand Paribatra, "Thailand: Liberalization Without Democracy," in James W. Morely, ed., *Driven by Growth: Political Change in the Asia-Pacific Region* (Armonk, N.Y.: M.E. Sharpe, 1993), 119–42.

6.
SECURITY AND TRANSITION IN SOUTH AFRICA

Jakkie Cilliers

Jakkie Cilliers, executive director of South Africa's Institute for Defence Policy (IDP), served for 14 years as an artillery officer in the South African Defence Force, resigning for political reasons in 1989 with the rank of lieutenant colonel. In 1991, he founded the IDP, which has played a formative role in guiding the South African military through the processes of transition and integration. He has written extensively on the South African military and its role in a democratic society, peacekeeping, and demobilization.

In Africa south of the Sahara, the last four decades have seen 35 major armed conflicts, which together have taken the lives of almost 10 million people. In just a few months beginning in the spring of 1994, genocidal strife and a series of epidemics spawned amid the ensuing refugee flight and disorder killed nearly a million citizens of the small country of Rwanda. The warfare, drought, and disease that plague Africa have given the continent a refugee population currently estimated at 26 million people; in a typical year, Africa absorbs nearly half of the world's emergency food aid. In the 1990s, a new wave of violence has swept Africa even as the continent underwent relegation to the status of post–Cold War political and economic backwater. In keeping with the general pattern of the postcolonial era, the bulk of this violence came in the form of civil conflict, with set-piece clashes among states relatively rare.

The era of independence and decolonization, which began in the early 1960s, was marred by a series of messy wars as various leaders and factions struggled to fill the power vacuum left behind by the retreating colonial powers. Colonialism left Africa a patchwork of states with borders drawn in European capitals, highly centralized administrative systems, and indigenous military cadres trained in the colonial regiments of European powers. The violence of the early postindependence years created a deadly legacy whose effects are still being felt. In 1990, for instance, 13 open conflicts were recorded, including major civil wars in Ethiopia, Angola, Liberia, Somalia, Mozambique, and Chad. Armed struggles between majority and minority ethnic or communal groups occurred in Uganda, Mali, Mauritania, Senegal, the Western Sahara, Sudan, and Rwanda.

Even more deadly than open warfare is the general disorder that besets sub-Saharan Africa. The various crises facing the region have been well documented: massive external debt, rapid population growth, and the bleak prospects for achieving sustainable development are the subjects of an extensive and depressing literature. Since 1989, national conferences and elections have become common phenomena, and multiparty politics has been accepted—at least in principle, and often at the urging of Western countries.

Many causes of dissatisfaction remain, however, and disillusionment with these new political arrangements seems to be growing. The upheavals have exhausted countries like Nigeria, Zaire, and Togo. Disputes brought into the open by democracy have shattered the professional, apolitical facade of the military; ethnic cleavages have forced many countries into a downward spiral of civil war, lawlessness, anarchy, and misery. Disorder—whether in the form of multisided turbulence or rule by corrupt and inept despots—has brought about a decline whose precipitousness can hardly be overstated. A recent World Bank report estimated that at the present rates of growth, it will take 40 years before the poor African states south of the Sahara regain the per-capita income levels they enjoyed in the mid-1970s.

In the fragile economic environment created by crushing foreign debt and the loss of some traditional export markets for tropical products and raw materials, droughts and famines can magnify the effects of armed conflict and give rise to major disasters. Movements of refugees and successive layers of exiles, whether fleeing famine or war, contain the seeds of future crises—which the rest of the world will not notice until they are shown on CNN.

The human diversity of the continent has long been a source of intense conflict. In sub-Saharan Africa, 52 states whose borders were drawn with no regard to ethnographic realities govern 700 million people. The Cold War, during which Africa was an arena of contention between competing international blocs, promoted political stability by reinforcing the inviolability of the colonial-era boundaries. Now this source of stability is no more. Eritrea's secession from Ethiopia, though peaceful, may be the harbinger of a bloody new age as unviable postcolonial states subdivide into ethnic ministates and clan zones, or simply melt down amid confusion, brigandage, and outbursts of genocidal violence. Fears that Africa's multinational countries will be dismembered along ethnic lines derive from the obvious failure of the unitary and centralized nation-state model left behind by colonialism, which has proved to be neither representative nor legitimate, and from the resurgence of ethnic nationalism. This latter is one of the central political phenomena of our age, and is threatening the questionable boundaries and fragile unity of nation-states from Yugoslavia to Russia, Ethiopia, Zaire, Angola, and even South Africa.

Yet there are rays of hope, even in Africa. Authoritarian regimes have suffered a marked decline in external support following the end of the Cold War. There are no more "proxy wars" between the West and the Soviet world in Africa.

Most of the former Third World, Africa included, is no longer of much strategic interest to the developed countries, either as a location for military bases or as an ideological battleground. Africa is unlikely to be the beneficiary of increased international assistance. Given the poor track record of development aid in Africa, Western donor countries and international lending institutions understandably question the efficacy of such assistance. The most telling evidence of Africa's marginalization is the comment of the U.S. Institute for National Strategic Studies in its "Strategic Assessment, 1995": "The U.S. has essentially no serious military/geostrategic interests in Africa anymore, other than the inescapable fact that its vastness poses an obstacle to deployment to the Middle East and South Asia, whether by sea or air."[1]

Africans who hope to be saved from the folly or brutality of their leaders by international peacekeepers or the guilt and pity of the rich nations are likely to be disappointed. There will be no "second colonization," even under the guise of trusteeship. The pullout of the United States and its allies from Somalia was the handwriting on the wall. Africa's leaders should be left in no doubt that they themselves are going to be largely responsible for the fate of their countrymen. If the advanced nations wish to intervene in Africa's affairs, they will do so through the conditionality requirements of international banks and agencies, not with bayonets.

Democracy and Security

Amid this bleak picture, developments in southern Africa have become a source of encouragement, led by South Africa's successful though not yet consolidated transition to democracy. Moreover, the southern African region in general—which besides South Africa includes Mozambique, Lesotho, Swaziland, Angola, Namibia, Botswana, Zimbabwe, Zambia, and Malawi—appears to be entering a period of stability and peace virtually unprecedented in modern history, particularly if the peace settlement in Angola continues on track.

With an increased number of countries in southern Africa groping toward democracy, and with the major conflicts in the region apparently resolved, stability and development may be possible. The rest of sub-

Saharan Africa, while still riven by conflicts involving massive human suffering, has also seen a considerable number of its countries make progress toward democracy over the past five years. An indispensable step in many cases has been to get the military to "return to the barracks." In some cases, military rulers have not simply withdrawn from politics, but have attempted to "manage" a return to civilian rule on their own terms.

Political stability and security are the keys to increased economic co-operation, job creation, and development in southern Africa. Although the region's prospects currently appear promising, rapid movement toward democracy and the unknotting of controlled economies, including South Africa's, may not by itself resolve profound domestic problems. Ethnic hatred, severe poverty and income inequality, hopelessness, and expectations that outstrip resources all threaten democracy by fostering antidemocratic and authoritarian attitudes, populist and xenophobic movements, and a host of other threats.

Throughout southern Africa, high levels of unemployment and relatively recent urbanization are structural sources of political and social alienation. Shortages of resources—including land, housing, and basic sustenance—reinforce this estrangement, as does the relative wealth of the small ruling elite in all the countries of the region. In the desperately poor urban and semi-urban communities of the area—South Africa's apartheid-created "townships" are probably the best-known examples—social norms have eroded, and gangs, warlords, and even nascent "revolutionary parties" thrive.

In such places, the law means little, and family and traditional authority are in sharp decline as well. Normal restraints on violence and killing have disappeared. Gangs and similar groups become politicized as they seek allies in their desperate struggle for shrinking resources. Political factions form around cleavages between rural and urban, traditional and modern, uneducated and educated, ethnic "insiders" and ethnic "outsiders." All this creates for the region a grave internal-security problem that is the hard reality of today and tomorrow.

Africa lacks the bases upon which effective, voluntary security cooperation has been founded elsewhere on the globe. There is no clear distinction between free and unfree countries, or between market-based and centrally planned economies, on which to premise an alliance system. Nor is there much of a grass-roots base of what might be called "informed citizens" to support such a system. There is, rather, a multitude of ethnic and religious divisions, and a glaring disparity between a very small, very rich elite and the poverty-stricken masses.

It is imperative therefore to temper expectations about the security benefits that the rise of poor, weak, and none-too-stable democracies can produce in southern Africa, particularly in the near future. This caveat covers not only Zambia, Lesotho, Angola, and Mozambique, but also

South Africa itself. In all these countries, as in the rest of the continent, it is more likely that the structural factors which breed violence will endure for a long time. That violent conflict defies eradication, however, does not mean that it cannot be contained: conflict management should be the watchword for the future. Most states will have to retain fairly large and expensive security establishments for this purpose. International security assistance and cooperation should be premised on liberalization (respect for human rights, military subordination to duly constituted civilian authority, and so on), rather than on the more nebulous standard of continuing "democratization."[2]

Against this background, a number of strategic considerations should be borne in mind. The first is that the keystone of greater national and regional security is progress toward a shared democratic value system among the various constituent states. Efforts should proceed on four levels. First, Africans need to stabilize their own countries. Second, cooperation on a bilateral or limited multilateral basis will be most feasible. Third, various regions, including southern Africa, need to resolve common, nagging security problems that threaten development. Last—and least urgent—is the project of laying the groundwork for a general system of security cooperation to cover the whole of Africa.

The Centrality of the State

It has become fashionable, especially among academics, to claim that the state can no longer be the key unit of analysis in thinking about how to foster greater security and stability in Africa. Those who make this claim, however, have yet to name an alternative candidate for the role. My own opinion is that the state is *not* an obsolete concept, and that students of the security problem must look with redoubled care at precisely the nature of armed forces and civil-military relations *within* the constituent countries of Africa. Few states in southern Africa have "mature" military forces or an indigenous professional military culture that accepts the supremacy of civilian and parliamentary authority over the military. Developing a military culture that can coexist with civilian supremacy and representative government is a task that should focus the minds of both Africans and their friends from the industrialized countries, and which should lead to joint and realistic strategies.

Of course, sound civil-military relations and a salutary professional military culture will not by themselves secure national or regional stability across southern Africa, but they do represent crucial building blocks for the future. Thus the nature of armed forces and civil-military relations in southern Africa merits careful examination.

In Africa, relations between the state and the military have developed in a way different from that found in most of the developed world. Three decades ago, the outgoing colonial powers left behind copies of their own military institutions. (South Africa would later do much the same in its four nominally independent "homelands" of Transkei, Bophuthatswana, Venda, and Ciskei.) At the time of independence, the new sovereignties of Africa were provided with standing military forces as an accoutrement of statehood. Yet these forces and their officers lacked a home-grown professional self-image, and had time on their hands in which to contemplate the overthrow of civilian authority, whether to serve their own self-interest or some distorted image of the "national good."

In Western Europe and the United States, unlike in Africa, military institutions were of central importance in fashioning the type of nation-state that emerged. Starting with the American and French revolutions, military service came to be seen as an integral part of republican citizenship. In the nation-states of the West, widespread (albeit not universal) reliance on compulsory national military service played a role in shaping the predominant conception of citizenship, as did such well-known social processes as industrialization, urbanization, and modernization generally.

Modern military institutions and modern parliamentary institutions arose simultaneously in the industrialized West. Military service (or at least eligibility for such service if needed) became a hallmark of citizenship, and citizenship became a hallmark of democracy. Moreover, the citizen army backed by civilian reservists served not only as a shield against foreign enemies and an instrument of national will, but also as a means for keeping the professional military class under political control.[3] A vital part of this process, at least in Europe, was the military elite's transfer of its allegiance from monarchy to new political regimes in the nineteenth century.

The experience of other nation-states that underwent industrialization, such as Japan and Russia—to say nothing of the developing countries of today—bears little resemblance to what we have been describing. In Africa, armed forces have modernized exogenously if at all, usually by importing Western or Soviet technology and copying Western or Soviet doctrines and practices. Indeed, it is questionable whether most of the countries in Africa have *ever* developed *professional* military forces in anything like the Western or even Soviet sense. Since independence, virtually every African state has been plagued by actual or threatened military interventions in politics.

Of course, the problem of coups and coup attempts is not unique to Africa. Commenting on transitions from authoritarianism to democracy in Latin America and Southern Europe since the 1970s, Guillermo O'Donnell and Philippe Schmitter write about "defusing but not necessarily disarming the military," and claim that what is "at stake in this issue is the change of the armed forces' messianic self-image as the institution ultimately interpreting and ensuring the highest interests of the nation." O'Donnell and Schmitter cite several "necessary conditions" that must be present if the armed forces are to "find and retain a 'normal' institutional status within a functioning political democracy: they must somehow be induced to modify their messianic self-image; they must be given a credible and honorable role in accomplishing (but not setting) national goals; and they must be made more impervious to the enticements of civilian politicians who turn to them when frustrated in the advancement of their interests by democratic means."[4]

The armies that were formed from colonial-era units at independence have become instruments for gathering, guarding, and dispersing largess—they exist, in short, to help maintain political or ethnic power. At the end of the 1980s, before the "third wave" of democracy reached African shores, more than two-thirds of the governments south of the Sahara either were ruled by soldiers or faced a serious challenge from politicized armed forces.

Among the many reasons for the unruliness of African militaries, one is surely the tendency to rely on long-serving, full-time forces rather than conscripts or reservists. In southern Africa, conscription has been used in Angola, Mozambique, Zimbabwe, and (until very recently) South Africa. Only South Africa, however, had an effective mobilization capability that backed its relatively small standing army of 95,000 troops with more than a half-million trained reservists, albeit drawn exclusively from "white" South Africa. In Mozambique and Angola, conscription has often meant dragooning recruits into the forces of a government with questionable legitimacy and a guerrilla war on its hands. Botswana has a standing army that it has recently expanded to a force of over 6,000 active-duty personnel organized into two brigades. Other full-time armed forces in the region include Zimbabwe's (48,000 mostly conscripted troops); Zambia's (about 24,000, all volunteers); Namibia's (7,500); and Lesotho's (2,000).[5]

The Challenge

The central problem of emerging democracies in a turbulent region such as Africa is how to ensure sufficient stability for development. Stability requires, among others things, adequate social-control mechanisms, including effective military forces. The civil-military relations problem in emerging democracies may be more urgent, but it is similar in form to the problem in more established regimes: how to ensure that the forces serving the nation fulfill only their intended purpose and do not threaten the polity.

Because of its proximity to the center of political decision making, the military is in a powerful position to influence policy through its most senior commanders and the hierarchy of officers that they head. In most developing countries, moreover, the military has resources that make it the most potent of all bureaucratic interest groups. Military establishments typically enjoy:

1) a higher degree of organizational and logistical autonomy than most of the rest of society;

2) an appropriate pool of managerial skills; and

3) a near monopoly on the use of the state's instruments of coercion.

Military forces have been and always will be susceptible to manipulation by persons or groups intent on capturing power through *force majeure*. Equally, individual military commanders may abuse their authority and turn their forces against the government, a danger that is particularly great where the military is the only efficiently organized state institution.

In view of these threats, how can civilian supremacy best be asserted and made effective? It is important to remember that where securely institutionalized civilian control exists, it is typically the product of longstanding national tradition and a complex set of formal and informal measures that affect the government, civil society, and the military itself. These set the bounds within which the military operates. For present purposes, such measures can be divided into three categories:

1) The first category are measures contained in or derived from international law, the constitution, or legislation (typically a quasi-constitutional national-security or defense act).

2) The second category are those elements that fall outside the formal ambit of the state, and so pertain to civil society. Typical of these would be the role of the media, independent academic institutes, the political traditions of the country, and the like.

3) Finally, and very important, are those elements related to the military itself—its culture, the nature of the military disciplinary system, the doctrines governing the role and tasks of the military, and so on.

Civilian supremacy is the *collective* result of *all* of these measures. The absence or weakness of even a single limiting factor—a culture of apolitical professionalism within the officer corps, for instance, or a vibrant and adequately developed civil society—can be disastrous. Such defects, moreover, must be directly and concretely addressed: Lawyers and politicians cannot fill the gap merely by writing more laws asserting civilian control.

One implication of effective civilian control is that the military leadership may have to countenance intervention by civilian officials in what it may consider to be professional military matters. Obvious examples would include policies regarding overall national strategy and defense planning; the role and mission of the military; its budget; its recruiting and training practices; its force structure; and the number and type of its arms. Civilian oversight, then, can be wide-ranging and pervasive, but accepting it is a requirement of military professionalism in a democracy.

Vitally important is a clear demarcation of the limits of the military's role and a broad consensus between soldiers and society that this role is just and appropriate. Many knowledgeable observers think that the absence of such a consensus is a major concern in South Africa at present.

It now seems as if the World Bank and the International Monetary Fund, as well as donor countries like the United States, Britain, and France, realize that measures to reform Africa's armed forces, improve civil-military relations, and demobilize former fighters in "armed struggles" need to be part and parcel of socioeconomic restructuring. In short, aid money used to get the military back to the barracks and keep them there is likely to be money well spent. The developed world could also help by forging closer ties between its own military forces and those of African countries (to achieve a salutary transfer of organizational culture); undertaking comprehensive civic-education programs for military personnel; and assisting demobilization programs.

Moreover, at a time when the strategic environment is changing rapidly, Africa is suffering from a "knowledge gap" in the areas of strategic studies, national security, and conflict management. Institutions and researchers dedicated to such topics are thin on the ground. Only in South Africa, Nigeria, and Egypt does there appear to be anything approaching systematic scholarly analysis of defense issues. South Africa's research institutions, while relatively well developed, are still almost totally reliant on information provided by the government. Independent, vigorous, and wide-ranging discussion of policy issues involving the military is essential in any country that hopes to maintain civilian supremacy and military accountability. Thus it is vital to promote the activities of nongovernmental organizations (NGOs), institutes, and research bodies that study military and defense issues. There is already a plethora of "politically correct" monitoring agencies active on the continent. What is needed are professional strategic-studies organizations that can engage the armed forces on substantive issues in ways that human rights and advocacy groups cannot.

South Africa in Southern Africa

South Africa cannot avoid being the leading nation of southern Africa. In 1992, South Africa's exports to its neighbors were worth R17.35 billion, whereas its imports from the same countries totalled only R4.12 billion (US$1=R3.60). In that same year, South Africa's port facilities handled a tonnage of goods nearly 16 times greater than that handled by all the region's other harbors combined. South Africa generates 75 percent of sub-Equatorial Africa's total installed electrical capacity. Of southern Africa's 42,000 kilometers of railway lines, 23,000 are in South Africa. Likewise, South Africa has 58,000 of the region's

87,000 kilometers of paved roads, and over 5.1 million of its 6 million motor vehicles.

Yet in 1992, South Africa's trade with Africa outside the Customs Union (Botswana, Lesotho, and Swaziland) amounted to only 7 percent of the country's overall foreign trade. By comparison, trade with the European Union was over five times greater. Although South African trade with the rest of Africa has grown considerably of late, the increase is likely to slow given the lack of credit facilities, resources, and know-how north of the Limpopo River.

South Africa is bound to its neighbors by self-interest as well as a sense of obligation for the support that many of these countries lent during the long years of struggle against apartheid. South Africa shares more than 2,000 kilometers of border with Namibia, Botswana, Zimbabwe, Swaziland, and Mozambique. Much of this frontier is porous and unguarded—sometimes even unmarked—and increasing flows of illegal immigrants, drugs, contraband, and stolen vehicles pour across it every day. The lesson is clear: instability in the region will mean instability in South Africa. For its part, the rest of southern Africa is nursing high hopes regarding South Africa's ability to boost economic and social development throughout the region. With the necessary assistance and sound leadership, South Africa can become the power-house of development for southern Africa. As we have seen, however, without an improved security environment, the outlook will be grim indeed.

The possibility that South Africa itself could become destabilized from within cannot, unfortunately, be ruled out. While South Africa is ahead of its neighbors in the development of a civil society and sophisticated mechanisms for civilian control of the armed forces, there are some nagging and potentially serious problems.

A crisis of effectiveness is threatening the police and the military in South Africa. Morale is low, society is restive (particularly in those disadvantaged quarters where a culture of entitlement has taken hold), and the police are divided among themselves (especially along lines of race). As the *Financial Mail* noted not long ago: "Racial feuding, mutinies and indiscipline in the police threaten not only the service but law and order throughout society and ultimately the prosperity of the entire nation. If the police cannot behave as police, crime will flourish, political violence will escalate, social upliftment will stall and what hope there is of attracting foreign investment will wither."[6]

Clearly, the challenge facing the South African Police Service (SAPS) is massive. Although everyone recognizes the tremendous drawbacks of using soldiers as a constabulary, there is little prospect that the government will be able to reduce the heavy reliance of the SAPS on military support across large areas of the country. Domestic law-enforcement duties will remain an unwanted, ad hoc, but constant mission of the South African National Defence Force (SANDF) for many years to come.

In no event, however, should the long-term undesirability of this situation be forgotten. In nature and ethos, military forces and police departments differ sharply—and rightly so. Any blurring of roles between the two is likely to lead to unhealthy rivalries, politicization of the armed forces, lowering of professional standards (especially on the part of the military), and other ills. If internal law and order is a bigger concern than defense against external threats—as is certainly the case in South Africa—then it would be better to shift resources from military to police budgets rather than to use soldiers as policemen.

Similar concerns should surround the emphasis that parliament, civil society, and elements within the military are placing on the use of the SANDF to support socioeconomic development programs. Once again, the real purpose of the armed forces has been lost from view: they exist as a shield against foreign aggression and an instrument of foreign policy. The greatest danger is that if forced to stagger on under heavy policing and development duties, the SANDF could become "overloaded," with consequences that presently seem unimaginable. Strained beyond its limits, the SANDF might experience rapid unionization (with labor disputes part of the process), a massive decline in operational standards, a breakdown in discipline, and effective disintegration as a fighting force and coherent institution.[7]

If the police cannot maintain law and order without the military's help and the military breaks down, who will protect society from crime and anarchy? There is a crisis brewing that we dare not ignore. As South Africa's postapartheid transition spreads its effects to the armed forces and the police, caution and restraint must be observed. More than in any other departments of government, reformers should take a "go-slow" approach. As of this writing, too much emphasis is being placed on racial balance, tolerance, human rights, women's rights, and so forth, with little or no stress on professional effectiveness. Competence, our research has shown, can earn legitimacy. Legitimacy is often undermined without competence.[8]

A second issue is the very limited resources that are currently being allocated to public-order policing and border security, both of which are the responsibility of the newly appointed commissioner of the SAPS. Although political protest per se has declined in South Africa, violent crowd incidents and mass protests are on the rise amid a culture of entitlement and raised expectations. The need for a public-order police unit may thus be greater than ever before, yet the government is considering the disbandment of the existing unit. With the approach of the local-government elections scheduled for November 1995, South Africans are asking themselves who will enforce the law and keep order in the face of phenomena like violent street blockades by thousands of taxi drivers, widespread squatter occupation of buildings and land, illegal plundering of marine and other resources, and even the taking of hostages as bargaining chips in labor disputes. Clearly, even the most legitimate, community-oriented police service in South Africa will need a public-order unit—something like France's Compagnies Républicaines de Sécurité—that can act swiftly and decisively to meet large-scale threats to domestic peace and order.

The related issues of border security, illegal immigration, and the rising tide of xenophobia in South Africa's border regions will require extensive debate and impartial analysis. There is a proven interrelationship between illegal immigration and a whole host of problems such as the smuggling of weapons, drugs, stolen vehicles, and other contraband. The problem is less the movement of people as such than it is the absence of any control over such movement into and within South Africa. Extremely tight border control, even were that politically desirable or feasible, is out of the question. What can be hoped for, however, is some significant degree of improvement over the current situation of unpoliced frontiers and an illegal-immigrant population estimated at 5 million persons (within a country of only 40 million persons altogether).

Remodeling an Army

Despite the dangers outlined above, the SANDF is currently doing a good job of dealing with the massive changes brought by the integration of the old, apartheid-era South African Defence Force (SADF) with the former guerrilla armies of the African National Congress (ANC) and the Pan-Africanist Congress (PAC), respectively, as well as the armed forces of each of the four "homelands" (Transkei, Ciskei, Venda, and Bophuthatswana). Much of the credit for this success—which has surprised most domestic and international observers—must go to the senior officers of the various forces. In the months before the historic multiracial elections of April 1994, they negotiated a detailed agreement specifying how the SANDF would be created out of the integration process that was set to follow the elections.

The agreed-on plan was for each force to present a comprehensive register of all its personnel by 26 April 1994. Guerrillas from the ANC and PAC (their numbers totalling about 28,000 and 6,000, respectively), were to report in batches of 1,500 at one of three (later two) assembly points. (Homeland troops did not have to report to these assembly points, but remained at their respective military bases and camps.) Once assembled, the former guerrillas would muster into the new SANDF and then undergo a period of training and review designed to reduce expected differences in standards of military knowledge and proficiency and to assess where each soldier might best fit in the newly organized

South African military. At each assembly point, a British Military Assistance Training Team would be on hand to ensure that the procedures used and standards applied were fair to all involved.

Sadly, much of this valuable work could soon be undone. About 40 percent of the 34,000 former guerrillas have opted not to report to the assembly points. Moreover, a small portion of those who did report have been found unfit for further service (usually on grounds of age, lack of education, ill health, and the like). Former guerrillas in both of these categories are waiting, with growing impatience, to see what kind of demobilization package the government of President Nelson Mandela is going to offer. Meanwhile, both officers and politicians privately bemoan a lack of political leadership on this issue from the Ministry of Defence. The successes achieved so far, however, will remain tenuous until tough decisions regarding demobilization and downsizing have been made.

The question of demobilization presents a huge challenge in its own right. The postintegration SANDF's optimal size is considered to be about 90,000—a figure 50,000 less than the sum total of 95,000 SADF troops, 11,000 troops from the homeland armies, and 34,000 guerrillas. The transitional plan calls for the SANDF to establish a Service Corps to offer 18 months of vocational training to any personnel wishing to be demobilized, but here too progress is lagging. The sudden release of 50,000 mostly unskilled people into an economy where unemployment already hovers at around 50 percent is not likely to turn out well.

In this context, it is especially disturbing to note that only a tiny fraction of the weapons held by the armed wings of the ANC and the PAC have been turned in. Vast quantities of arms remain hidden across the country in caches to which demobilized former guerrillas may have ready access. In the final analysis, however, disaffected ex-guerrillas are more likely to pose a straightforward law-and-order problem rather than a revolutionary political threat to the regime.

Although whites (mostly Afrikaners) continue to predominate in the officer corps of the new-model SANDF, the military's leaders have made a political transition that few thought possible. Going to great lengths to demonstrate their allegiance to South Africa's duly constituted, ANC-led government, the armed forces skillfully defused an armed revolt by rural, right-wing Afrikaners when the regime in Bophuthatswana, a conservative ally, collapsed in early 1994.

Also in March 1994, the SADF stepped in with firmness and fairness to restore order in the East Rand and KwaZulu-Natal, areas torn by factional and ethnic violence so intense that the police were powerless to stop it. The deployment in February of the misbegotten and short-lived National Peacekeeping Force—a hastily slapped-together amalgam of all the major armed factions in the country—had proved so disastrous that it was no stretch to see the military as the savior of what was rapidly becoming a desperate situation.

The third means by which the SADF proved its bona fides was its willingness to help with the printing and distribution to rural areas of badly needed ballots amid the preelection chaos of April 1994. These three events taught Mandela and his advisors that the SADF could be trusted even as they underscored the importance of having coherent and effective military forces, especially at a time when the Police Service was losing coherence and civil strife was coming dangerously close to growing out of control.

A year and a half after the epochal elections of April 1994, South Africa's military is approaching its own belated crisis of transition. Despite dramatic changes, the transformation of the SANDF as a whole remains incomplete. Strong political leadership will be needed to restore and maintain morale, guide the formulation of clear-eyed defense policy, and bind the military firmly within the democratic framework. Neither elite nor public consensus has yet been achieved on all these questions, which adds a serious though not insurmountable obstacle, since judiciously bold leadership can often create new circumstances around which a consensus can crystallize.

The Long Road to Civilian Control

Civilian control of the armed forces is the end result of a complex of interrelated measures, laws, social institutions, and customary practices. With its paucity of established democratic institutions and traditions, its massive social dislocations, and the authoritarian tendencies now regnant in some of its countries, southern Africa does not look like an especially friendly environment for the rise and consolidation of such control. In a recent article, Earl Conteh-Morgan warned: "Events in Togo, Algeria, and Zaire, in particular, serve as a grim warning that the trend towards democracy and its accompanying emphasis on respect for human rights is not irreversible. In other words, one of the perennial problems in a new African agenda is how to protect any future democratic arrangements (and their corresponding human rights gains) from being disrupted or undermined by the military."[9]

The West, led by the United States, has seized upon arms control as the centerpiece of its military-related dealings with the developing world and the best hope for conflict prevention. Yet there does not appear to be any demonstrable link between arms control and peace. While the possible spread of weapons of mass destruction to the developing world obviously worries the West, from the perspective of a developing country the focus on nuclear proliferation and biological or chemical weapons serves to divert attention from much more pressing problems, such as the need for increased engagement of Western militaries in programs designed to raise standards of training and professionalism.

There is an increased awareness across Africa that security problems must be tackled now if political stability, democratization, and prosperity are to have a chance to develop. In accepting this challenge, Africans need to adopt a cautious approach, not only regarding what is possible, but also in terms of building "up and out" from national institutions rather than trying to build "down" from regional institutions.

The international community should combine active support and encouragement for newly emerging democratic institutions with a reluctance to demand full and immediate democracy as the price of continued engagement. Africa's new-minted and mostly still-partial democracies are insecure, hesitant, saddled with adversity, and plagued by doubts about democratic institutions and free-market economies. Western policy makers should recognize the need that these countries have to proceed at their own pace, encouraged, but not goaded.

NOTES

1. Institute for National Strategic Studies, "Strategic Assessment, 1995," *US Security Challenges in Transition* (Washington, D.C.: National Defense University), 101.

2. See Guillermo O'Donnell and Philippe Schmitter, *Transitions from Authoritarian Rule: Tentative Conclusions About Uncertain Democracies* (Baltimore: Johns Hopkins University Press, 1991), 7–8. They define liberalization as "the process of making effective certain rights that protect both individuals and social groups from arbitrary or illegal acts committed by the state or third parties. It is indicative of the beginning of the transition that it triggers a number of (often unintended) consequences. . . . Democratization . . . refers to the processes whereby the rules and procedures of citizenship are either applied to political institutions previously governed by other principles (e.g., coercive control, social tradition, expert judgment, or administrative practice), or expanded to include persons not previously enjoying such rights and obligations (e.g., non-taxpayers, illiterates, women, youth, ethnic minorities, foreign residents), or extended to cover issues and institutions not previously subject to citizen participation (e.g., state agencies, military establishments, partisan organizations, interest associations, productive enterprises, educational institutions, etc.)."

3. Morris Janowitz, *Towards a New Military* (Beverly Hills, Calif.: Sage, 1975), 71, 74–76, and 83.

4. O'Donnell and Schmitter, *Transitions*, 31–32.

5. International Institute for Strategic Studies, *The Military Balance 1992–93* (London: Brassey's, 1992), 191–92, 202, 204–5, and 213–14.

6. *Financial Mail* (Johannesburg), 10 February 1995, 24.

7. See also Jakkie Cilliers, "Rethinking South African Security Architecture," *African Defence Review* 20 (December 1994): 18–19.

8. Studies conducted in the East Rand region during and after the March–April 1994 deployment of the SANDF's National Peacekeeping Force indicated that the SANDF had earned a surprising degree of public approval through effective operations designed to keep order in the townships, whereas the supposedly more "legitimate"—but incompetent—National Peacekeeping Force gained little confidence from its operations in the same area. See Jakkie Cilliers, ed., *The National Peacekeeping Force, Violence in the East Rand, and Public Perceptions* (Pretoria: Halfway House, 1994).

9. Earl Conteh-Morgan, "The Military and Human Rights in a Post–Cold War Africa," *Armed Forces and Society* 21 (Fall 1994): 69.

III.
The Postcommunist World

7.
POLAND'S ROAD
TO CIVILIAN CONTROL

Janusz Onyszkiewicz

Janusz Onyszkiewicz represents the Union of Freedom party in the Polish Parliament, to which he was elected in the first semifree elections in 1989. He served as deputy minister (1990–92) and then minister (1992–93) of defense. A mathematician by profession, he was associated with dissident movements in Poland for 25 years, and participated in the leadership of Solidarity, for which he was repeatedly imprisoned. He was Solidarity's spokesman from 1981 to 1989.

Civilian democratic control of the armed forces is too often taken as axiomatic. Rarely are questions raised as to why civilian control is so important or to what extent it can determine the success of a democratic transition and the durability of the political system.

First of all, it must be emphasized that the armed forces constitute a completely undemocratic—indeed, authoritarian—entity within the democratic state. Taken by itself, this does not necessarily mean that the military presents any real threat to the democratic political system. After all, other organizations, such as the rigidly hierarchical Catholic Church, also function in a nondemocratic manner. What makes the military different is that it is not only an extremely autocratic institution demanding complete and unconditional loyalty and commitment, but also an organization designed to bring sheer force to bear in the most efficient way possible, whenever the state requires it.

As a consequence we are faced with a situation aptly described by Samuel Finer in his book *The Man on Horseback:* "Instead of asking why the military engage in politics, we ought surely to ask why they ever do otherwise. For at first sight the political advantages of the military vis-à-vis other and civilian groupings are overwhelming. The military possess vastly superior organization. And they possess *arms.*"[1] The military's capacity to bring overwhelming force to bear makes the possibility of military takeover very real. Moreover, although outright military rule is rare and usually of short duration, the military can and often does exercise power under the veil of "transferring power to civilians." Under such circumstances, the military pulls the strings from behind the scenes in what is, in essence, military control of civilians.

As Sir Michael Quinlan, former British permanent undersecretary of defense, stated at a June 1994 seminar in Warsaw, the situation is aggravated by the fact that the military largely stands apart from society as a whole:

> The first theoretical risk comes from the fact that the armed forces constitute a coercive power which could, if it were misdirected, override all other elements of our society. The second risk comes from the fact that the armed forces invariably became, in some degree, separate and distinctive structures within our societies, and if we are not careful they may be seen by other citizens, or even see themselves, as alien institutions with interests and goals different from those of society as a whole. The central problem for democratic systems, in brief, is how to maximize the security value of our armed forces at the same time as we minimize the risk of coercive misuse and of alienation.

A number of factors set the military apart, as U.S. Representative Charlie Rose of North Carolina, leader of a House delegation to the North Atlantic Assembly, explained:

> In any country, the military represents a highly organized and disciplined group knit together by traditions, customs and working habits; but, above all, by the need to work together and to depend on each other in time of crisis and conflict—a dependence which can mean literally the difference between life and death. Such dependence builds strong bonds and loyalties and requires a degree of cohesion and coherence that few other professions can claim. It is these qualities—discipline, dedication, and loyalty—that make the military profession different and, in some respects, distinct from the rest of society.[2]

This sense of being apart from the rest of society coexists within the military with the conviction that the armed forces are the custodians of basic national values and hence understand the interests of the nation and state better than do civilian politicians. Such thinking often leads military elites to believe that they not only are authorized to, but in fact have a duty to, intervene when necessary in the nation's political life.

This phenomenon is not restricted to the so-called Third World countries but also has been seen in the postwar period in such nations as Greece, Turkey, Spain, and even France (in the French case, as recently as 1958–61 at the height of the Algerian crisis). Military leaders as different as U.S. general Douglas MacArthur and Russian general Aleksandr Lebed (commander of the Russian Fourteenth Army until he resigned in June 1995) have declared that the military owes its allegiance not to civilian political institutions but rather to the nation itself.

The potential threat that the military thus poses to democracy can be minimized if the armed forces are held to a strict standard of apolitical behavior. This means that the military cannot play any active role in domestic politics, the armed forces and its leaders cannot become involved in policy disputes, and the army barracks must be kept out of domestic political infighting. Only civilian control of the armed forces can ensure that the military remains apolitical and continues to function solely as an instrument, albeit a very important one, of state policy as set by democratically elected authorities.

Before 1989

The idea that the military should be placed under direct civilian control is new to most of Central and Eastern Europe. The practical implementation of this principle thus depends on the quite different historical contexts and military traditions of the countries in this region. On one end of the spectrum, we find countries like Belarus and Slovakia that for purely historical reasons have virtually no indigenous military traditions upon which to build. At the other end are countries like Hungary and Poland that have grand military traditions going back more than a thousand years. In between are countries like the Czech Republic, where the army never had an opportunity to gain the degree of popular support and esteem that the Polish military has long enjoyed. In Poland, as a result of the protracted struggle for national independence, the armed forces over the course of the nineteenth century became one of the nation's most celebrated and trusted institutions. Indeed, during the various national uprisings in the nineteenth century and the struggle for independence following the First World War, Poland's democratic institutions on several occasions even officially endowed the country's military leaders with dictatorial powers.

During the interwar period, the political situation in a once again independent Poland proved to be far from stable. Moreover, the proliferation of totalitarian and autocratic regimes produced a profound crisis of the democratic ideal that had spread across the European continent. Whereas in 1919 only a few countries in Europe had not become democratic, by 1939 the situation had been completely reversed. This antidemocratic mood clearly did not help to further the cause of civilian control of the military.

Following his seizure of power in 1926, Poland's charismatic leader Marshal Józef Piłsudski attempted to isolate the army from the turbulent domestic political scene in order to preserve the military as a nonpartisan and stable guarantor of the country's independence. After Piłsudski's death in 1935, the army, under the command of the inspector general, who reported directly to the president, became virtually independent of civilian authority. Although formally supervised by the president of the republic, the armed forces were effectively outside the control of both government and parliament. The Ministry of Military Affairs, staffed solely by military personnel, provided the army with whatever it needed, within budgetary limits, but had no say on either defense policy or promotions.

Under the communist political system put in place after the Second World War, the communist Polish United Workers' Party (PZPR) exercised total control over all aspects of public life and all institutions, including the armed forces. As in the other communist countries, the military in Poland was subordinated not to the state but rather to the Communist Party. The main goal of party control was, above all, to ensure that the armed forces could never challenge party rule. At times the PZPR even called upon the armed forces to prop up the communist system, as when the army was called in to subdue strikes or street demonstrations, notably in Poznań in 1956 and in Gdańsk and Szczecin in 1970. Moreover, party control ensured that all the directives and decisions issued in Moscow by the Warsaw Pact high command would be fully implemented by the Polish military.

Ruling communist parties exercised their control over the military through *political commissars*, who in Poland were organized in a special corps of *political officers*. Although formally second in command of their units, these political officers were in fact subordinated to a special department of the party's central committee, known as the Main Political Directorate of the Armed Forces. Reports written by these political officers bypassed the usual military channels and were sent directly to the appropriate central party institutions. In addition, party cells, which embraced nearly all personnel, existed at all levels of the military and in every unit. Thus the party could also exercise its control at lower levels of the military through the oversight of the local party committees. Finally, on top of this elaborate system of party control, the omnipresent counterintelligence agencies watched over the military, looking out not so much for foreign infiltration as for any hint of dissent or potential disloyalty within the ranks.

Party structures also served as a channel through which the institutional interests of the military could be articulated and subsequently conveyed to the relevant political authorities. In many respects, party-cell meetings in military units provided a forum where, at least in principle, junior officers could meet on an equal footing with generals and voice their concerns while bypassing the normal military protocol. In this way, the party took on the role normally played by labor unions, which were banned in the armed forces.

A penchant for secrecy characterized the communist system in general and the military in particular. Nothing related to military matters could be discussed publicly.[3] In Poland, the Warsaw Pact was held up as sacrosanct, and civilians were kept in the dark about its operations. As a result, after the collapse of communism in Poland, the country found itself with an extreme shortage of nonmilitary personnel with any expertise in military affairs. This penchant for secrecy also reinforced the military's isolation from the general population. Indeed, the armed forces under communism constituted a state within a state, with their own health services, holiday centers, recreational facilities, housing, canteens, and the like.

The Postcommunist Period

Early in the winter of 1989, "roundtable talks" began in Poland between the ruling Communist elite and the Solidarity-led democratic opposition. These accords paved the way for contested parliamentary elections in June 1989. Solidarity's success in these elections, together with the desertion of the Communist Party by its erstwhile parliamentary allies, resulted in the formation in August 1989 of a predominantly noncommunist government under Prime Minister Tadeusz Mazowiecki (in which the Communists held only four cabinet positions, albeit including the interior and defense portfolios).

The compromise reached during the roundtable talks changed the country's political system. As part of a complex set of trade-offs between Solidarity and the Communists, the office of the presidency was reinstated in exchange for completely free elections to the newly restored Senat (the upper house abolished in 1946). Since the accords set aside 65 percent of the seats in the Sejm (the lower house) for the Communists and their allies, the party leadership believed that even in the worst-case scenario (which ultimately came to pass), they would have enough votes in the National Assembly (both houses sitting together) to ensure that their candidate became president.

The Communists therefore insisted on granting the president special powers in military matters and foreign policy. In particular, the president received the title of "supreme commander" of the armed forces (although he did not technically assume the role of commander in chief). The Communist leadership thought that their hold on the presidency would ensure that the political situation could not deteriorate into an all-out anticommunist revolution that might provoke Soviet intervention. Indeed, despite Solidarity's impressive electoral victory, General Wojciech Jaruzelski, Communist Party first secretary and de facto military ruler since the imposition of martial law in December 1981, was elected president by the Communist majority in the parliament.

The Mazowiecki government set several military-related goals: 1) securing the military's loyalty to the new government; 2) depoliticizing the armed forces, in particular dismantling all Communist Party organs within the ranks and eliminating the political officers; 3) severing the army's ties with Moscow and bringing the Polish armed forces completely under national control; 4) instituting personnel changes in the military high command; 5) fashioning a strategic reorientation of the armed forces and changing the nation's military posture accordingly; and 6) reforming the special services, especially counterintelligence. These reforms were to be implemented incrementally, albeit over a relatively short time frame. As a first step, two former Solidarity activists were made deputy defense ministers in March 1990.

Implementation of these government initiatives to bring about civilian control of the military proved to be difficult. The military did, however, readily embrace the principle of depoliticization. Memories of army involvement in the subjugation of worker revolts in 1956, 1970, 1976, and 1981 were still fresh and, once media censorship was lifted, condemnation of these actions became nearly universal. Moreover, the military found it expedient to take a stand in favor of depoliticization at a time when tough political decisions had to be made in conjunction with the implementation of economic shock therapy. For his part, President Jaruzelski, despite the considerable power of his office, chose not to interfere in the process of restoring civilian control.

A 1991 bill on national defense introduced important legal changes in the status of the armed forces. All those in active military service were prohibited from engaging in any political activity or joining political organizations, including parties. Thus although members of the armed forces had the right to vote, anyone who chose to run for political office would have to leave active military service. Moreover, no political material of any kind could be posted or distributed in any barracks or on military premises. Finally, no political gatherings could be held on premises that were under the jurisdiction of the defense ministry.

The first test of these new rules came in the October 1991 parliamentary elections. Only a few military officials decided to run for office, and only one, a professor at the Military Technical Academy, won. No indications of unlawful political activities during the electoral campaign on the part of the military could be found. It thus appeared that the system in place worked and that there should be no problems in the future.

Work also began on fundamental organizational changes within the Ministry of National Defense. The purely military structure that this ministry had inherited from the communist era replicated that of the Soviet defense ministry. In essence, no real defense ministry had existed as such under the communist system. Other than the minister's executive staff and a few departments (such as finance and personnel), the defense ministry was really only a federation of "central institutions," such as the General Staff, the General Inspectorate for Combat Training, the General Inspectorate of Territorial Defense, the General Inspectorate of Technical Equipment, and various institutions subordinate to the quartermaster general. The commanders of the various services and military districts reported directly to the minister of defense.

Clashes with the President

In the spring of 1991 a special interministerial committee was set up to undertake an extensive overhaul of the whole system of national defense. The main task of drafting the reorganization plan for the defense ministry fell to one of the civilian vice-ministers. The aim of the reform was to separate purely military structures—henceforth to be supervised by the chief of the General Staff, who would handle combat training, operational planning, and the like—from structures handling other matters and thus able to operate like civilian institutions. In this way, it would be possible to bring civilians into the defense ministry at lower levels as well.

The draft reform bill did not meet with unanimous approval. Representatives of President Lech Wałęsa, who had been elected in December 1990 after Jaruzelski stepped down, strongly objected to having the government rather than the president exercise ultimate control over the army. This dispute was eventually settled in favor of the government, and the general guidelines of the reform were approved by all the relevant authorities, including the parliamentary Committee of National Defense.

The parliamentary elections held in October 1991 brought to power a new governing coalition headed by Jan Olszewski, who quickly clashed with President Wałęsa. In the course of this dispute, Jan Parys, the new civilian defense minister, attempted to sever the lines of communication between the president and both the defense ministry and the armed forces. Given this climate of political confrontation between the government and the president, reform of the armed forces and the defense ministry had to be shelved.

Only after the collapse of the Olszewski government in June 1992 and its replacement by a new governing coalition under Hanna Suchocka in July was the reform introduced and were detailed regulations issued to specify the lines of authority between the defense ministry's various subdivisions, including the General Staff. These regulations specified that civilian institutions would be responsible for establishing the goals and priorities of defense policy. The military would lay out the various alternative means of accomplishing these goals, and civilian politicians would decide which option to adopt.

Unfortunately, this division of labor raised expectations among some military officials that the civilian part of the ministry would be limited to supporting the army and that the military itself would be responsible for determining the extent of civilian interference in military affairs. Some even regarded the ministry as essentially external to the armed forces themselves and felt that the only link between civilian institutions and the military emanated from the fact that the chief of the General Staff would be subordinate to the minister of defense.

Meanwhile, Lech Wałęsa, out to strengthen the institution of the presidency, pressed for a new interpretation of the constitution. He thought that the largely ceremonial role of supreme commander of the armed forces given to the president by the constitution should be changed to give the president full command of the army. According to Wałęsa's plan, the chief of the General Staff, the highest-ranking military officer and the person in effective command of all forces, would take orders directly from the president without any involvement of the government.

It must be emphasized that, given the complexity of military issues in the contemporary era, no single individual can effectively control the armed forces. Thus the president's proposal would in effect have re-created the situation that had prevailed before the First World War, when neither the government nor the president had sufficient means to exercise real control over the military. Such an arrangement would have made a mockery of the principle of civilian control of the armed forces.

These efforts on the part of President Wałęsa coincided with yet another unfavorable development. It became clear that many of those in the military mistakenly believed that having the military remain apolitical meant simply that the armed forces should not support a particular political party.[4] A problem thus emerged during the electoral campaign leading up to the September 1993 parliamentary elections when President Wałęsa created the Nonparty Bloc in Support of Reform (BBWR) to ensure that he would have a large bloc of votes in parliament. Wałęsa supporters actively sought military backing for the BBWR in the elections, arguing that technically it was a political movement and not a party, and that it operated under the aegis of the president, who after all was the leader of the armed forces. Some in the military proved quite receptive to this argument, and only the firm opposition of a few civilian politicians in the defense ministry brought this solicitation of military support to a halt. In the end, only 30 officers decided to run for parliament (including two generals approaching retirement age), and only one was elected (a junior officer who duly left active service). The electoral outcome had a sobering effect on the military, as it became clear that, while the people held military officials in high esteem, they nonetheless wanted them to remain in the barracks and not enter parliament.

Reforming the Defense Ministry

After the elections, the defense portfolio in the new government went to a former military official, Piotr Kołodziejczyk, who had served as defense minister from 1990 to 1991, retiring in early 1992. Despite this appointment, pressure was building within the military to secure full independence from civilian control, a challenge that did not go unnoticed in parliament. Fortunately, the new parliament established the Standing Committee on Defense in such a way that it included many parliamentarians with considerable clout and experience in military matters. The political diversity of the committee's membership, which reflected the political composition of the parliament as a whole, did not prove to be an obstacle to reaching a consensus about the need for full and effective civilian control of the military. The committee was thus able to come up with a new bill regulating the operations and prerogatives of the defense minister, which was subsequently approved by parliament.

This bill, entitled "On the Minister of National Defense," lays down several basic principles. First, the chief of the General Staff is fully subordinated to the defense minister, and the latter, together with the government as a whole, has responsibility for the armed forces. The General Staff constitutes an integral part of the Ministry of National Defense, and the chief of the General Staff, in the name of the minister, commands the armed forces. The civilian end of the defense ministry sets financial and procurement policy, establishes research and development programs, deals with all legislative matters, and oversees the education of soldiers (to ensure that they are committed to democratic and national values). The defense minister directly supervises the departments of personnel, control (including control of combat readiness), and special services—tasks that are not allowed to be assigned to the chief of the General Staff. Command, operational planning, combat training, and the like fall within the purview of military authorities. Although the chief of the General Staff is to be consulted on all military matters, all the important decisions are to be made by the minister, who has the power to give orders to all military officials, including the chief of the General Staff. The minister also exercises disciplinary power over all military personnel.

The bill also limits the prerogatives of the defense minister. Under the legal system inherited from the communist era, the defense minister had enormous discretionary power. Since the basic decisions concerning the structure of each nation's defense ministry or armed forces emanated from the Warsaw Pact command headquarters, each nation's defense minister had to be free to implement decisions without "bureaucratic" delay—that is, without the need for *pro forma* governmental or parliamentary approval. For example, the defense minister had the right to make decisions about the organizational setup of the ministry or the military command structures without consulting even the prime minister. In contrast, by the terms of this new bill, no such decisions can be taken solely by the defense minister but instead must be approved by the cabinet as a whole.

This new bill, overwhelmingly approved by parliament, provides a sound basis for full implementation of civilian control: the military is involved in the formulation of different policy options and in laying out the means to achieve specified goals, while civilian politicians have final decision-making power and retain ultimate responsibility.

The Road Ahead

In postcommunist Poland, implementation of civilian control of the military did not proceed in a smooth and steady fashion. Rather, periods of rapid progress were followed by stagnation and setbacks. The difficulties arose in large part from the political struggle between the president, on one side, and the parliament and government, on the other, over who should exercise ultimate control over the armed forces. It did not help matters that it was the president and not the prime minister who effectively appointed the defense minister (according to the constitution, the prime minister has responsibility for appointing the ministers of defense, interior, and foreign affairs upon consultation with the president, but does not need the president's formal approval).[5]

The military does not easily accept the concept of civilian control at least in part because it views civilian politicians as having only limited experience in military affairs. Moreover, at present few civilians have the needed qualifications to work in the various institutions of the defense ministry; as a result, about 90 percent of those working in the civilian end of the ministry are in active military service. Nonetheless, what really matters is not that those employed in the defense ministry should be civilian personnel but rather that they should work in a civilian structure operating according to civilian procedures. In just a few years, those military personnel employed in the civilian end of the defense ministry have been won over to the cause of civilian control: they in turn will inevitably influence their colleagues who work in the strictly military organs.

To facilitate the process of establishing full civilian control, it is of the utmost importance that a "defense culture" be fostered among national politicians, central and local administrators, and local-government officials. Civilians must be trained to take over more positions within the defense ministry and other defense-related institutions.

Reform of the budgetary process is also crucial. The government often puts forward a poorly itemized defense budget, which makes informed debate difficult. Moreover, the defense minister is legally bound only by the overall budget and not by the itemized list, which gives him considerable spending discretion and undercuts parliamentary control.

Another very serious problem, which has not yet been adequately addressed, is the need for legislation regarding the declaration of a state of emergency or martial law, as permitted under the constitution. The extremely sensitive and complex issues surrounding the state of emergency and martial law require precise legal guidelines.

All in all, Polish politicians appear to have grasped the crucial importance of civilian control. Moreover, a strong body of informed opinion supports the idea that this principle is so fundamental that it merits inclusion in the new constitution that is now being debated in the National Assembly.

NOTES

1. Samuel Finer, *The Man on Horseback: The Role of the Military in Politics* (Boulder, Colo.: Westview, 1988), 4.

2. Charlie Rose, "Democratic Control of the Armed Forces: A Parliamentary Role in the Partnership for Peace," *NATO Review* 42 (October 1994): 13–14.

3. A leading American negotiator in the Geneva disarmament talks revealed that on one occasion, when an American expert began to cite data on Russian military potential, the head of the Soviet delegation interrupted him to ask that the civilian members of the Soviet delegation leave the room!

4. To be clear, I have contended in this essay that the military should be a mere instrument (albeit a very important one) of democratically elected civilian authorities. The armed forces must not be the object of political intrigues, nor should they meddle in political controversies or try to influence the country's political system.

5. The continuing tensions over control of the defense ministry were most recently demonstrated during the 1994 "Drawsko affair." At a September 30 luncheon briefing held at the Drawsko military training area, President Wałęsa encouraged the high-ranking military officers present to criticize Defense Minister Kołodziejczyk for failing to undertake military reform and to demand his resignation. These actions were severely criticized by those in the media and by members of parliament, who accused the president of trying to influence the composition of the government (an act that they considered incompatible with the apolitical position of the armed forces). The Sejm National Defense Committee attempted to resolve this affair by creating a subcommission to investigate the actions of those military officers present at the meeting. President Wałęsa ignored the committee's recommendation that Kołodziejczyk remain as minister of defense, and on November 10 he dismissed him after a formal request by Prime Minister Waldemar Pawlak.

8.
RUSSIA'S FRAGMENTED
ARMED FORCES

Lilia Shevtsova

Lilia Shevtsova is senior associate at the Carnegie Endowment for International Peace in Moscow and Washington, D.C. She has served as director of the Center for Political Studies of the Russian Academy of Sciences. She is also a columnist for several Russian newspapers as well as a political observer for Russian television.

Questions increasingly are being raised in both Russia and the West about the military's role in Russia's ongoing transformation. What is the military's attitude toward the current regime? What relationships exist among the armed forces, the other "force structures," and civilian political authorities? How likely is it that a Latin-American–style coup will occur? What kind of government is the Russian military likely to support in the future? Such questions have become even more pressing in light of the war in Chechnya, which marks a major turning point in Russia's political evolution.

Although Western analytical approaches can contribute to our understanding of the role of the Russian armed forces in the post-Soviet period, we can learn the most by examining the specific character of Russia's postcommunist transformation.[1] Unlike some other postcommunist countries, Russia has had to confront a whole set of problems simultaneously: state-building, democratization, free-market reform, and the creation of a new national identity. To complicate matters, the methods adopted for dealing with these problems often proved to be mutually incompatible. Moreover, Russia's transformation process began at the top, where new social interests were virtually unrepresented. As Russia lacked a true alternative political elite, those directing the transformation process have largely been drawn from the old ruling class.

A unique, hybrid regime has emerged, which, although its leaders have often espoused a liberal-democratic ideology, weaves together democratic, authoritarian, and corporatist strands. This regime assumed its current form after President Boris Yeltsin dissolved parliament in September 1993 and won a referendum on a new constitution that eliminated the previous system of checks and balances in favor of a new superpresidential order. Yet even though the constitution endowed the president with near-dictatorial authority, Yeltsin has so far proved to be a relatively weak leader, since the government has lacked effective mechanisms of management and control.

Thus the Russian military has been confronted with a situation in which the ruling elites have no clear vision of the future and Russian society remains in a state of flux. The state-building process has not yet been completed, crime is on the rise, and social structures are disorganized. The problem of national identity within the Russian Federation has not yet been resolved. In foreign policy, it has been difficult to define what the national and state interests of Russia are and to decide how much continuity should be maintained with respect to policies instituted under the former Soviet Union. Finally, Russia has been beset by a widespread sense of defeat and frustration.

All these factors weigh heavily on the military, creating disorientation and division within its ranks and inevitably pushing it toward active involvement in politics. Under the previous communist system, the military, subject to the dual control of the Communist Party of the Soviet Union and the KGB, did not take an active role in politics or the various elite struggles for power. Instead, the armed forces seemed content with an implicit contract struck with the Communist leadership: in exchange for staying out of politics, the military received all the budgetary resources needed to pursue its ambitious international goals. When the communist regime collapsed and the Soviet Union shattered into pieces, the former system of civil-military relations, including the mechanisms of civilian control, was destroyed, creating a power vacuum that has yet to be filled.

The collapse of the communist value system and the destruction of Soviet mechanisms of control and mobilization deprived the armed forces of the ideological rationale that had served as an important source of cohesion. Under the communist system, the military's primary task had been to defend the socialist heartland in the ongoing global struggle against the forces of capitalism. Expansion of the socialist sphere of influence and upholding the principle of socialist internationalism served as guiding principles that provided the military with a sense of vitality. The military, and the officer corps in particular, basked in the country's superpower status, which meant that the collapse of the USSR and the loss of territory had a profoundly demoralizing effect; it not only deprived them of their reason to continue military service but also engendered an acute sense of inferiority.

A profound sense of defeat began to permeate the armed forces, as military officers blamed the country's political leaders, both Mikhail

Gorbachev and Boris Yeltsin, for bringing the country to ruin. A growing split emerged between the new (or, more accurately, renewed) Russian ruling elite and the military. Armed forces in Central and Eastern Europe had generally supported postcommunist governments during the first phase of transition, when the goal was to liberate their country from Soviet influence and consolidate the nation. In contrast, during the early phase of Russia's transition, most of those in the armed forces rejected the values of Western liberalism and the plans for partnership with the United States and other Western powers that the post-Soviet political elite readily embraced. Thus, despite the agreement reached between Yeltsin and the group of high-ranking military personnel who controlled the armed forces after August 1991, the armed forces never became a completely loyal servant of the new ruling elite. Such a state of affairs was bound to have a significant impact on the future of both the Yeltsin regime and the Russian state itself.

Sources of Division

The economic and social problems of the armed forces, which began under Gorbachev and increased under Yeltsin, fueled the identity crisis of the Russian military. Military personnel who found themselves suddenly outside Russia's borders faced the most difficult situation. For two years they were left to fend for themselves, as Russia's new leadership had no clear idea what would happen in the newly independent states and, in particular, what role the armed forces should play under these new conditions. Russian soldiers returning from Eastern Europe, Germany, and the Baltic republics confronted similar problems. Even after their return to Russia proper, they had to cope with a myriad of problems in settling down to a new life. Thus these once elite military units became a potential wellspring of conservative and antireform sentiment opposing the Yeltsin regime.

Another problem stemmed from the social tensions that emerged within the military, the most serious of which emanated from disparities in wealth within the officer corps itself. A split has emerged between a small cadre of military leaders who have prospered in the new climate and the majority of officers, who have suffered economically and in some cases even become impoverished—a polarization that reflects the growing inequality within Russian society as a whole. As a result, according to retired colonel Yurii Deryugin, "Today's army is an army of polarities charged with the latent energy of internal conflict."[2]

In 1992 most military officers with families lived below the poverty line, as they proved even less capable than other social groups of adjusting to the new, semifree market conditions. For most of these families, military pay provided their only source of income, and in some areas, above all Siberia and the Far East, it met only 25 to 30 percent of their subsistence needs. According to data from the Ministry of Defense, 42 percent of officers' wives did not work, and only 13.5 percent of military families received financial support from their parents; 75 percent of these families did not have even minimal savings to fall back on. Moreover, despite legislation requiring that officer and enlisted pay be raised along with each increase in the national minimum wage, the Yeltsin administration delayed authorizing significant military pay increases until April 1993, in an obvious attempt to court military support prior to the anticipated confrontation with parliament. Although military officers received a pay increase of 40 percent after July 1994, they still earned only two-thirds as much as comparable personnel in the Ministry of Internal Affairs and half as much as those working for the Federal Counterintelligence Service.

Most military personnel still face barbaric living conditions. Officers generally are not provided with housing for their families: by conservative estimates, more than 16,000 naval and army officers are homeless. According to the defense ministry, military bases are extremely overcrowded (with capacity exceeded by 200 to 300 percent), and 40 percent have neither sewage nor water-purification systems. Seventy percent of military garrisons (i.e., 470 bases) are located in extremely inhospitable areas—100 within the Chernobyl contamination zone.

A very different situation prevails among generals and other senior officers. Some, primarily those who returned from Central and Eastern Europe or who remain in the newly independent states, have made fortunes by selling weaponry and other military property. Military observers have pointed out that mafia clans have formed in the Russian army, as corrupt members of the top military brass merge with criminal elements, largely through the creation of joint stock companies selling off military property. High-ranking members of the military elite have also siphoned off Western humanitarian aid to meet their personal needs.

Criminal activity is on the rise within the ranks. Homicides, rapes, thefts of state and personal property, and drug-related crimes have reached alarming proportions. Moreover, organized crime's penetration of all levels of Russian society raises the risk that criminals outside the army will "link hands" with those inside local army units. Already, heavy weapons are finding their way into the hands of local mafia clans. In such an eventuality, local army units could become a real threat, and not simply in the political realm.[3]

Another source of division that is generating discontent within the armed forces stems from the separation of military units into regular and elite troops, with the latter employed by the administration to settle domestic political disputes. Thus President Yeltsin used elite tank units in his assault on parliament in October 1993. The difference between the elite and regular troops grew even more noticeable when the latter were dispatched to Chechnya to serve as "cannon fodder." Although the fact that the elite troops are much better provided for has fueled some of the animosity toward them within the ranks, their use as the regime's de facto police force has caused the most resentment and protest.

Of course, other divisions exist within the military as well: between officers and enlisted men, volunteers and draftees, and new recruits and veterans. According to some observers, significant conflict between these groups is not only possible but inevitable and will take on an even more virulent form than the brutal hazing (*dedovshchina*) practices that have long existed within the ranks.

Other factors have aggravated the festering crisis within the Russian armed forces. The most important of these are the decline in military professionalism, the erosion in logistics and training, and the aging of equipment. The general decline in morale and the unprecedented lack of discipline increase the likelihood that weapon stocks (including nuclear ones) will be poorly maintained and that accidents will occur, with possibly tragic consequences.[4]

Finally, Russian military officers are becoming increasingly involved in political matters. Various political orientations divide the military in general and the officer corps in particular, with chauvinistic, conservative, and statist tendencies prevailing. Many political groups have formed within the officer corps, notably the Officers' Union, headed by Stanislav Terekhov, which played an active role in defending the White House (the parliament building) during the crisis of September–October 1993. Indeed, the struggle between the president and parliament between 1991 and 1993, in which each side attempted to garner military support for its cause, resulted in the politicization of the Russian military.

The September 1993 Revolution

Before September 1993, various political factions had tried unsuccessfully to draw the military into the confrontation between the president and his parliamentary opponents. Most of the officer corps chose to avoid taking sides or becoming actively involved in political squabbles. Although the rumors of a possible military coup in 1993 turned out to be false, the political situation at the time did seem to have all the elements needed to push the army to intervene: the virtual absence of effective civilian control of the military, weak political institutions and persistent institutional conflict, efforts by the major actors to enlist army support, military hostility to the Yeltsin regime and opposition to its policies, and the regime's refusal to adopt policies dear to the military.

Given all the factors favoring military involvement, why did the military not intervene in the partisan struggle for power? Some Western observers chalked it up to the military's high degree of professionalism, including its adherence to certain codes of conduct and its general reluctance to take on any new responsibilities.[5] In addition, the military may have preferred to remain a neutral observer, given its disenchantment with all the existing political forces and governing institutions.

We know that the military high command generally disapproved of the Yeltsin administration's use of elite troops—the Kantemirov and Dzerzhinskii divisions, along with units from Tula and Pskov—in its October 1993 assault on the White House, where the rebellious parliament was meeting.[6] Indeed, by all accounts, Yeltsin had great difficulty persuading his own handpicked defense minister, Pavel Grachev, and the Ministry of Defense as a whole to back him in this crisis—a fact that Yeltsin is unlikely to forget any time soon.[7]

Internal divisions within the armed forces themselves undoubtedly inhibited direct military involvement in politics during the first stage of political transformation. For example, internal divisions made it difficult to ascertain the military's overall corporate interests. Moreover, given these divisions and the political differences among military officers, the military high command feared that conflict might erupt within the armed forces themselves. Indeed, during Yeltsin's confrontation with parliament, a distinct possibility arose that clashes would break out between troops loyal to the president and those supporting parliament.

Although the military eventually intervened in support of the president during the fall 1993 crisis, this does not mean that the armed forces were solidly in Yeltsin's camp. The military clearly did not side with the president out of any newfound loyalty to its commander in chief. General antipathy toward those in parliament certainly played a role. The military had little patience for these "windbags" and all their "parliamentary nonsense." More to the point, however, parliament had rejected the military's request for pay increases and its demand that the draft quota be raised (instead, parliament endorsed legislation that excused 70 percent of the total draft pool from active duty). According to some observers, "parliament refused these requests as part of a plan deliberately aimed at increasing tension within the armed forces."[8]

Parliament Speaker Ruslan Khasbulatov and his aides chose to challenge directly the authority of the military high command by backing a group of rebellious officers headed by Colonel-General Vladislav Achalov (former airborne forces commander and Soviet deputy defense minister who had participated in the August 1991 putsch) and General Albert Makashov (former commander of the Volga-Ural military district who had run against Yeltsin on a nationalist platform in the 1991 Russian presidential election). Their plan was to split the army from its existing leadership, a move that created considerable consternation within the military high command. The crucial turn came when parliamentary leaders appointed a shadow cabinet, including Achalov as defense minister, to serve as an alternative government. This final step pushed Grachev and the military high command to put aside whatever ambivalence they felt toward Yeltsin and to provide him with armed support in his confrontation with parliament.[9] If Khasbulatov and then Vice President Aleksandr Rutskoi had pursued a less confrontational strategy toward the military high command, the army might have chosen to remain on the sidelines, and the outcome of the September revolution might have been different.

The military's initial hesitation during this crisis indicates that the armed forces in future crises will either exact a high price for their support or take matters into their own hands. Moreover, the parliamentary elections held in December 1993 showed that the military rank and file were profoundly dissatisfied with the leadership of their nominal commander in chief Boris Yeltsin, as they voted in large numbers for the ultranationalist opposition group headed by Vladimir Zhirinovsky (which received up to 80 percent of the votes cast in some army units).

The New Military Activism

That the military has a strong revulsion toward politics in general and a distrust of the government does not mean that it has no political interests of its own or that it stands completely above the political fray. Indeed, the new generation that assumed command of the Russian army after the collapse of the Soviet Union has become accustomed to operating under conditions of complete independence, having never really experienced the rigorous party scrutiny that had been the hallmark of the communist system. The *afgantsy,* as these veterans of the Afghanistan war are called, became in effect a special military caste, occupying all the top leadership positions in the defense ministry. Except for First Deputy Defense Minister Andrei Kokoshin, the post-Soviet ministerial elite all served in Afghanistan together, graduated from the same schools (i.e., the Ryazan Airtrooper School, the Armed Forces Academy, or the Frunze Academy), and attended the General Staff Academy. These *afgantsy* might well be disposed to intervene directly in politics under certain circumstances.

Russian senior officers have taken a much more active role in matters of concern to the armed forces than did their counterparts in the Soviet system. For example, the Ministry of Defense frequently clashed with the Ministry of Foreign Affairs between 1992 and 1993 over issues like the handling of the Yugoslav crisis, the negotiations with Japan over the Kuril Islands, and the withdrawal of Russian troops from the newly independent states.

The new military doctrine adopted in November 1993 after lengthy consultation and discussion sheds some light on the military's increased influence. The elaboration of this new doctrine represented an effort by the political elite to redefine Russian interests and the role of the military in the post-Soviet era. The final document emphasizes that the military's most important missions are to prevent the rise of regional security threats and to help settle whatever conflicts might break out in the former Soviet territories.[10] As far as the new doctrine's major strategic applications are concerned, there is a high degree of continuity with Soviet military thought. Thus the potential "threat spectrum" includes the American effort to modernize U.S. nuclear forces, the possible expansion of the North Atlantic Treaty Organization, increased militarization in China, and the stepped-up ambitions of the Islamic states.[11] The final document does not repudiate the use of force to achieve foreign-policy goals but instead uses the American experience in the Gulf War to justify its continued relevance. With respect to the objectives of the Russian armed forces, Lieutenant General Igor Rodionov, head of the General Staff Academy, did not rule out potential active involvement in either the "near abroad" (i.e., the former Soviet republics) or other arenas around the world.

Indeed, the Russian military continues to be active in several newly independent states. As early as 1992–93 the Russian armed forces became involved in settling the Georgian-Abkhazian conflict and establishing itself as a peacekeeping force in that region. In Moldova the Fourteenth Army played a decisive role in protecting the breakaway Transdniester Republic. The military also exerts a powerful influence in the Crimea and thus indirectly plays a major role in Ukrainian domestic politics. In Central Asia, the Russian military still serves as the major bulwark of the current regime in Tajikistan. This relatively independent role that the military plays in the "near abroad" may in the end serve as a sort of political experiment, providing the military with ideas about what it could do to solve problems within Russia itself.

The absence of strong political institutions and of mechanisms for civilian control of the military increases the likelihood that the armed forces will at some point intervene directly in the nation's political life, perhaps through a military coup. Indeed, the military has already become a low-profile power broker, without whose support none of the country's political forces can take or hold power. Thus the military's influence has increased substantially relative to the leverage that it possessed under the Soviet system.

Owing to the incomplete process of state-building and the continuing weakness at the heart of the political system, virtually no civilian control over the armed forces has been put in place during the Yeltsin administration. As political analyst Sergei Rogov has pointed out: "Virtually no military reform is being carried out here. The country's political leadership has essentially withdrawn from 'interference' in military affairs, leaving the defense department to manage its own affairs."[12] The new constitution removed the controls over the armed forces once possessed by the government, which no longer has the power to make appointments to the military high command or appoint military leaders and high-ranking generals to the defense ministry, and shifted this responsibility to the president. Moreover, both the armed forces and the "power ministries" (discussed below) are no longer subordinate to the government, which means that civilian government officials do not have easy access to reliable information about state security. The parliament, too, lost much of the authority it once had over the military budget.[13] Instead, a January 1994 presidential decree subordinated all the "force organs" (including the Ministry of Defense, the Ministry of Internal Affairs, the Foreign Intelligence Service, the Federal Security Service, and the Government Communication and Information Agency) to the president.[14] Although these changes were clearly meant to help the president survive a political crisis, they have effectively strengthened the military's independence and fueled the political ambitions of those in the other force organs.

Given the military's right to pursue its own policy initiatives and its relative freedom from effective controls, its leaders have sought to maintain longstanding organizational structures and routines, although many of these are no longer appropriate in post-Soviet Russia. Thus they have attempted to block military reform, to minimize budget cuts, and to retain inflated staffs. Despite such efforts, the defense ministry in 1994 received just 40 trillion of the 87 trillion rubles in its original budget request. The government's 1995 draft budget allocated to the military only 45 trillion of the 111 trillion rubles requested, which, given the high inflation rate, constituted a considerable cut in actual spending and forced the oft-delayed military reform to be accelerated. Under present conditions, this reform will end up being more painful for the military than it would have been had it been implemented earlier. Whether the military will end up accepting reform as inevitable or instead try to block it remains an open question.

The Chechen War

The war in Chechnya, which began in December 1994, brought to the surface or intensified various political trends that previously had gone unnoticed. Before the outbreak of this conflict, Russian politics could have moved in any of a number of different directions, including one that preserved democratic governing procedures and put in place mechanisms for reconciling divergent interests. Instead, the range of political options has narrowed considerably since the war began. The new political situation will have a major impact on the future of the Russian armed forces and other force structures.

To understand the war's impact on the armed forces, one must first examine the political leadership's goals in initiating this war and the resulting consequences. Yeltsin seems to have had several objectives in mind in undertaking this military adventure: 1) diverting public attention away from Russia's deepening economic problems and the general failure of government programs; 2) creating a new national-patriotic base of support for the regime; 3) neutralizing opponents among his former comrades in arms and preempting any opposition from his own *nomenklatura;* and 4) intimidating any autonomous republics or regions that might oppose him.

Abandoning democratic slogans, Yeltsin proclaimed "power and order" to be the hallmarks of his regime. This shift toward authoritarian rule began at the time of the September 1993 revolution, when he chose to dissolve parliament and use force against unruly deputies. The next step came with the ratification of the new constitution, which removed all restraints on presidential power and eliminated any counterbalance to one-man rule. To ensure that this new pyramidal power structure functioned as intended, Yeltsin needed not only to find a new base of support but also to restore the health of the two most important mechanisms of control—the armed forces and the bureaucracy. Without these two institutions working for him, Yeltsin, for all the near-dictatorial authority the constitution granted him, could end up as one of the weakest leaders in modern Russian or Soviet history.

Did Yeltsin achieve the goals that he set for the Chechen war? On the contrary, the Chechen operation revealed the weakness of his regime, underscored Yeltsin's inability to take charge, and precipitated a sharp drop in his popularity. Yet it appeared that the regime might be able to endure this agonizing state of affairs, given the competition between the country's various economic and political cartels, the absence of any realistic democratic alternative, and the fragmentation of the defense and security forces.

Given the strong support for opposition groups that was manifested in the parliamentary elections of December 1995, the current ruling clique might try either to postpone the presidential election (which is currently scheduled for June 1996) or to manipulate its outcome (as happened during the December 1993 national referendum to "approve" the Yeltsin constitution).[15] The threat of a coup will increase if it becomes apparent that it is the only way to bring about a change in regime. This in turn would increase the political weight of the military and security forces.

What role have the Russian armed forces played in the Chechen conflict? The decision to initiate military action clearly came not from the military high command but from Yeltsin's inner circle, which is dominated by civilians. Key presidential advisors, even some known for their democratic views, laid much of the groundwork. The military became involved only after a failed effort by the Federal Counterintelligence Service, led by Sergei Stepashin, to overthrow Chechen president Dzokhar Dudayev and capture the capital city of Grozny. Stepashin, along with Defense Minister Grachev and then–Internal Affairs Minister Viktor Erin, clearly viewed a short, successful war as a way to raise

their own political stock and consolidate their positions both within the
regime and inside their own ministries.

Right from the beginning, discontent surfaced within the armed
forces, and dissenting voices began to criticize the actions of Defense
Minister Grachev and President Yeltsin. High-ranking military officials
summoned up the courage to speak out against the war and the way in
which it was being waged. A few generals (notably Lieutenant General
Eduard Vorobiev, the first deputy army commander) resigned rather than
be held responsible for the bloodshed. General Boris Gromov, then
deputy defense minister and one of the military's most popular leaders,
sharply criticized the actions of Defense Minister Grachev—criticism
indirectly aimed at Yeltsin as well for having authorized these actions.
In particular, Gromov lambasted the decision-making process within the
ministry:

> Over the last two years, the work of the Military Collegium has taken on
> a purely formal character. Crucial decisions affecting the country's future
> increasingly have been taken by a small circle of officials—the more
> serious the task, the smaller the circle [of decision makers]. The Military
> Collegium was, in essence, shut out of the discussion of problems
> connected to the START II agreement, the Partnership for Peace program,
> and other agreements in which the Defense Ministry has a crucial stake.
> The decision to use military force in Chechnya was also made in secret
> and not taken up for discussion by the Collegium. I want to emphasize
> that I am not against imposing order in Chechnya or in the country as a
> whole but rather against using methods incompatible with the ideals of
> "constitutional order" and "democracy." . . . The army should not carry
> out political or police tasks: this is not its "profession," which explains
> the unfortunate results.[16]

Gromov went on to criticize decision makers for not having learned
from the mistakes made in Afghanistan:

> The Afghan experience should have taught us something, or so it would
> seem. In particular, [we should have learned] that the specific characteris-
> tics of a region—historical, religious, geographic, meteorological, and the
> like—must be considered before deciding on military operations. [In the
> case of Chechnya] nothing of the kind has been done. By all appearances,
> the decision [to intervene] was made spontaneously.[17]

Gromov's criticisms were echoed by other high-ranking officials.
Lieutenant General Georgy Kondratiev, also a deputy defense minister,
stated in a 20 January 1995 interview with ITAR-TASS: "Not one
meeting of the Defense Ministry Collegium has been held, and all issues
are being decided by Pavel Grachev's inner circle. . . . It seems likely
that the president has not been informed about the true state of
affairs."[18] Interviewed that same day on the television program *Nota
Bene,* Kondratiev specifically named Generals Vladimir Lapshov and

Gennadii Ivanov along with Grachev aide Elena Agapova as those within Grachev's entourage responsible for the decisions on Chechnya. He also condemned the nepotism and favoritism that characterize appointments within the defense ministry (as elsewhere in the civilian leadership): "[Lapshov, Ivanov, and Agapova] are the ones who decide everything in the Armed Forces today! Personnel issues, too! The defense minister today can do anything he wants, even appointing his relatives and friends to specific posts."[19]

The war in Chechnya has revealed the following problems: 1) the gap between the ruling clique and the majority of the officer corps; 2) the division among top military elites; 3) the defense minister's unpopularity and isolation from most of the officer corps; 4) the army's inability to carry out its assignments; and 5) the incompatibility between Russia's new strategic objectives and the army's organizational structure, mode of operations, and overall orientation. As research analyst Aleksandr Konovalov has observed: "Obviously, under the present circumstances, our armed forces cannot be easily controlled and are generally not yet capable of carrying out any successful combat operations, which is not a cause for optimism." He goes on to emphasize the damage done to Russia's armed forces: "Esteemed Chechnya strategists, due to your efforts, the potential use of force as an element of Russian foreign policy has become a lot less convincing."[20]

This was bound to have generally far-reaching geopolitical consequences. The failed blitzkrieg against Grozny was a morally unsettling and humiliating defeat for the Russian military. After such a setback, both despair and pent-up aggression permeated the ranks. In general, the continuing degradation of the military establishment has provoked considerable resentment within the armed forces and pushed the military ever closer to active political involvement. At least parts of the armed forces now form a potential opposition force that might not only support but even initiate an anti-Yeltsin coup. This represents a new stage in the evolution of the armed forces as a whole.

The failures of the initial Chechen campaign prompted a reorganization of the Russian armed forces. Political authorities needed a scapegoat for all the casualties and military blunders in this senseless war. Reorganization was also supposed to allow Yeltsin to tighten his grip on the military and eliminate potential discord within the ranks, as he ousted those popular military figures who had criticized the regime's policies. Moreover, by reducing the number of deputy defense ministers from eight to six, Yeltsin could eliminate his most vocal military critics (Generals Boris Gromov, Valeri Mironov, and Georgy Kondratiev) and replace them with others more to his liking (Generals Vladimir Churaiev and Anatolii Solomatin).

In addition, Yeltsin sought to place the General Staff under the authority of his restructured Russian Security Council.[21] Such a change effectively would have reduced the standing of the minister of defense and bolstered that of the Security Council, which would have become the coordinating body for all Russian force structures. This reform effort, whose fate depended on the struggle for power both within Yeltsin's entourage and outside it, met with strong criticism from the military and was ultimately defeated.[22]

Nonetheless, the reform effort prompted speculation in Moscow political circles (and not just among Yeltsin's opponents) that the Chechen war had actually been undertaken for the sole purpose of eliminating the military as a potential threat to the president. Such a plan seems too Machiavellian even for the current Russian leadership, given its usual inability to plan beyond the short term. Yet Yeltsin's entourage did seize on the Chechen events as a pretext to conduct a purge of the armed forces.[23] As Gavriil Popov, former mayor of Moscow, put it:

> Behind these dozens, even hundreds, of "fortuitous events," the global idea stands out: The worse [things get], the better. The Chechen operation is meant to show that the entire military establishment should be immediately sanctioned and thoroughly purged. . . . Such a purge of the army takes on added significance in light of the potential transition to a regime based on personal power. Moreover, the success of this purge and the emergence of a compliant military establishment could serve as the major argument in favor of moving from presidential to personal authoritarian rule.[24]

Prospects for a Military Coup

As noted above, the relative weakness of Russian political institutions had enabled the military to act as a behind-the-scenes arbiter courted by all the various political factions, but it had sought to avoid overt interference in the political struggle. Once the war in Chechnya began, however, the danger increased that either the military would become embroiled in an open struggle for power or conflict would break out both within the military and between it and the other force organs. Despite the military failures on the Chechen front, the public's support for the armed forces did not wane. Public-opinion polls continued to show that the military ranked above other institutions in public esteem, and that many citizens, having lost faith in civilian politicians, supported the emergence of a strong military leader.

Thus a psychological basis has been created in Russian society for accepting a military coup. Even such democratically inclined political analysts as Dmitrii Furman began to regard a military coup as not only probable but desirable.[25] Furman reasoned, first, that the military would be reluctant to initiate a war and therefore would not precipitate an increase in defense spending, and, second, that the military would still have to rely on more or less democratic institutions.[26] His argument raises two questions: 1) How ready are the Russian armed forces to take part in a coup? 2) Could the military guarantee either that democratic institutions would survive such a coup or that power would be transferred back to civilians at some point in the future?

I believe that several conditions must be present before the Russian military either would stage a coup itself or would support a civilian-initiated coup. First, a charismatic leader, preferably drawn from the military, must be found who has no ties to the present administration or at least cannot be blamed for the regime's more unpopular decisions. Second, key civilian lobbies must not only support the coup but also be responsible for organizing it, providing an ideological rationale for such a turn of events, and working out the program that the coup supporters would carry out once in power. Third, these civilian cartels must take the military's interests into consideration when planning their moves and must strike a new deal with the military that would protect its spheres of influence. The absence of even one of these conditions would reduce significantly the prospects of a successful coup. At present, as significant popular support for a coup seemingly exists and a prospective leader could undoubtedly be found, the key stumbling block is the absence of any political organization that could organize a coup or help put in place an alternative regime. Moreover, the demoralized Russian military lacks strong ties to any major civilian group.

Generals Aleksandr Rutskoi, Boris Gromov, and Aleksandr Lebed were until recently the most likely military candidates to lead any coup attempt. Lebed seemed the most promising for several reasons: 1) he does not belong to the Moscow elite and thus cannot be blamed for unpopular government policies; 2) he enjoys a strong reputation for honesty and personal integrity; and 3) he is popular both in military circles and with the public. General Lebed's own rise to prominence since 1991 is itself testimony to the very real possibility that either the military as a whole or one of its leaders may come to power in Russia.

General Lebed became well known as the military commander who brought an end to the armed conflict in the Transdniester region of Moldova (populated by large numbers of Russians) and whose troops are still holding together the fragile peace there. Earlier in his career, he served as a paratrooper in Afghanistan and, as he put it, "took Baku" (the capital of Azerbaijan) in January 1990. His role in these and other "hot spots" has earned him a large following both within and outside of the military.

A charismatic leader with a strong will and a keen intellect, Lebed initially proved rather outspoken on various political topics, although he later became more circumspect. He has sharply criticized the current political elite, both those in government and those in opposition. Asked which of Russia's politicians could be relied upon, he replied: "I cannot see any. Zhirinovsky is a minus, Gaidar too; Yeltsin is a minus and Travkin is more a minus than a plus. . . . What has changed? It is the same people [in power]—they merely swapped their [Communist] Party cards for democratic slogans."[27] He has also lambasted the defense ministry and ridiculed its program for military reform: "When the minister of defense asked me why reforms never get anywhere with me, I told him that it is because I have no interest in them."[28]

General Lebed clearly believes in authority and a strong state, saying: "There is the law of the strong. It is not openly acknowledged by many people, but it is to be found lurking in all of us. If a state is strong, it is treated with respect and reverence."[29] It is not surprising, then, that he has expressed admiration for such military strongmen as former Chilean dictator Augusto Pinochet, whom he has praised for bringing order and prosperity to Chile:

> I am not praising Pinochet in principle. But what did he accomplish? He averted the total collapse of the state and brought the army to the fore. With its help, he forced everyone to just do their job. He brutally silenced all the loudmouths. Everyone began to slave away. Chile is now a prosperous country despite its absurd geographical position. . . . This confirms the theory that says you slam your hand down on the table once, sacrifice one hundred people to the fatherland, and the issue is closed.[30]

Nor does Lebed claim to be a democrat. As he told *Newsweek:* "I am not a democrat because Russia was, is, and for some time will be an empire."[31]

Initially, Lebed denied that he had any immediate political ambitions, although he left his future options open: "I am not ruling out that at some point in the future I might assume a higher position. But I never planned on becoming president, as this is not to my liking. I am absolutely unsuited for [the presidency], as to end up there you have to negotiate diplomatically with parliament and plead with it for your authority. Such maneuvering and pandering are not for me."[32] Of course, Yeltsin's new constitution does not require that the president negotiate with anyone for his authority. In 1995 Lebed resigned his commission and took a much more active political role, standing as a candidate in the December 1995 parliamentary elections and declaring his intention to run for the country's top office in the 1996 presidential election.[33] It may be too early to tell how his party's relatively poor showing in the December 1995 elections (in which it received just over 4 percent of the vote and only five seats) will affect his chances in 1996.[34]

A political vacuum clearly exists: the only question is how and when it will be filled. Yet the future of Russia is not predetermined. Considerable obstacles stand in the way of a military coup, not the least of which is the military's lack of any tradition of direct interference in politics. Even more important are the continuing decay and lack of internal cohesion of the armed forces, which could lead to fighting between military units in the event of a coup. Moreover, civilian politicians are not particularly eager to involve the military in their plans, as this could give the military undue influence. The complexity of the problems facing the country and the failure of previous reform efforts also make many potential leaders think twice about taking on the role of a Russian Pinochet. Finally, there is a lingering fear that Yeltsin and his supporters will stop at nothing to hold on to power, as for them—especially President Yeltsin—power means life, and there can be no life without power. In particular, the strengthening of the president's security forces and of the Ministry of Internal Affairs increases the risk of armed confrontation and even civil war in the event of a coup.

Despite these mitigating factors, many fear that the military is becoming increasingly independent of civilian power structures and that change within the military has acquired its own dynamic. Despite the increasing fragmentation within the military and the variety of political opinions held by military elites, the Chechen war prompted many within the officer corps to close ranks to defend the common interests of the armed forces. Military elites began to stress the need to strengthen the Russian state, restore Russia's role as a superpower (at least in the territories making up the former Soviet Union), and maintain order; moreover, they seemed ready to back any civilian pretenders to power who appeared capable of achieving these goals.

The armed forces seem ready to guarantee noninterference in internal political affairs in return for a commitment from the civilian authorities to satisfy the military's organizational and financial needs and allow the military to handle the problems of the "near abroad." Such an agreement could easily collapse, however, if political authorities either try to involve the military in domestic political disputes or are unwilling to meet the military's demands regarding its organizational structure.

Of course, we should not assume that military involvement in politics would necessarily be directed against democracy. As Juan Linz has pointed out: "It would be a great mistake to assume that military establishments necessarily are hostile to democratic and party politics, although their mentality makes them less sympathetic to or understanding of some of the vagaries of party politics and the lack of unity of purpose and discipline so often associated with democracy."[35] For example, the army helped facilitate democratic transitions in Brazil, Peru, Greece, and Portugal, not out of any love for democracy as such but rather owing to particular circumstances (military defeat in the Greek and Portuguese cases) or the military's own reluctance to assume the complex task of running the country. What kind of regime would the Russian military be likely to back? Given the general disillusionment in Russia with the first stage of democratic transition, the Russian armed forces are most likely to back an authoritarian regime that takes a tough stance vis-à-vis the nation's problems. Still, the Russian military would be unlikely to support turning the military itself into a political weapon.

The Security Forces

During 1994–95 the Russian military began to take a back seat to the regime's burgeoning security forces. Upon coming to power, Yeltsin quickly moved to revamp the old Soviet KGB, which he viewed as a potential threat, ordering former Soviet internal affairs minister Vadim Bakatin to "dismantle and democratize" the security forces. By 1992 the former KGB had been replaced by a new Ministry of Security, headed by a career-KGB official, Lieutenant General Nikolai Golushko.[36] This ministry, which managed to hold on to most of the KGB's personnel and organizational infrastructure and to retain control over some 250,000 border troops, formed a powerful force owing to its internal discipline, organizational coherence, and relative lack of corruption and institutional decay. Although the loyalty of former KGB officers to Yeltsin personally might have been questionable, the ministry backed the president at critical junctures, notably during his armed confrontation with parliament.

Therefore, the presidential decree of 21 December 1993 abolishing the ministry and replacing it with a Federal Counterintelligence Service came as a major blow.[37] The president had undoubtedly long been concerned about the power wielded by this ministry, whose members had a long tradition of behind-the-scenes intrigue. He had to wait, however, until after he had crushed the opposition in parliament before he could take on such a potentially dangerous foe and further consolidate his power.

To head the new Federal Counterintelligence Service, Yeltsin chose not a former KGB official but rather Sergei Stepashin, who had come up through the police and fire departments. Stepashin's lack of familiarity with the job at hand made him particularly dependent on Yeltsin. Moreover, Yeltsin retained only 46 percent of those who had worked for the Ministry of Security; those who were "purged" ended up working for private security services, commercial firms, or criminal elements. Finally, Yeltsin ensured that neither the government nor parliament exercised any control over this new agency, which instead reported directly to the president.

Soon after replacing Gorbachev in the Kremlin, Yeltsin had set about creating his own security service, the Main Protection Administration (GUO).[38] Headed by KGB veteran Lieutenant General Mikhail Barsukov, this new service employed an estimated 20,000 people, yet was accountable only to the president. As this agency's mission had never been officially laid out, it began to expand its activities, creating its own intelligence and counterintelligence services and special-operations units.

The GUO even gained control over the state-owned weapons-export firm, Rosvooruzheniye, a potentially highly profitable operation. Thus this highly militarized organization, with headquarters in the Kremlin itself, acquired powers that even the KGB had never dreamed of enjoying.[39]

Skilled at playing groups off of one another, Yeltsin could not risk entrusting his personal security even to this organization. Instead, by special decree in December 1993, he created a separate Presidential Security Service (SBP) headed by Aleksandr Korzhakov, who had been his bodyguard since Yeltsin's 1986 move from Sverdlovsk to become Moscow party boss. Thus Yeltsin acquired an inner circle of security guards responsible for his personal welfare. Both Korzhakov and Barsukov would later become key political players within Yeltsin's entourage.

Other law-enforcement agencies underwent reorganization as well, notably the Ministry of Internal Affairs. The ministry's stock rose considerably after September 1993, even though it played a relatively minor role in those events (the military having secured Yeltsin's victory).[40] President Yeltsin nonetheless awarded Internal Affairs Minister Viktor Yerin a prestigious medal, for seemingly personal reasons, and since then Yerin's position in Yeltsin's entourage has appeared secure. The ministry itself—already endowed with several divisions of elite troops (including the famous Dzerzhinskii Motorized Rifle Division), task forces, and special forces (the famous "black beret" riot police)—grew even more powerful when it took over the anticorruption duties of the disbanded Ministry of Security. Nonetheless, the Ministry of Internal Affairs, which proved to be even more demoralized and corrupt than the other law-enforcement and security agencies, failed miserably when it came to combating Russia's criminal elements.

Yeltsin set out to achieve three goals through this reorganization of the security apparatus: 1) to undercut those "power ministries" and agencies that posed potential dangers to his own grip on power, in particular the former KGB; 2) to play the various military and security forces off of one another; and 3) to subordinate those forces to his personal authority while removing them from parliamentary or public control. Did these actions, however, really augment Yeltsin's personal security or effectively undermine the ability of elements within these agencies to influence policy? The events of late 1994 and 1995 point instead to the growing influence of the power ministries' leaders (Kozhakov, Barsukov, and Grachev) on public policy. Moreover, these organs became even more independent of civilian authority than they were under communism, when they had been subject to party control. In particular, Korzhakov (head of the SBP) by the end of 1994 appeared to wield ever greater influence not only on Yeltsin but on the political process as a whole.[41] Korzhakov reportedly has intervened with the government and the prime minister on a wide variety of matters ranging from high-level appointments to economic policy (e.g., sending Prime Minister Viktor Chernomyrdin a letter ordering him not to proceed with a planned reform of the oil-export system). Thus the president's security force has become an independent political entity fully prepared to use force to achieve its ends.[42]

The growing power of the security forces, and of their leaders in particular, also stemmed from the general evolution of the Yeltsin regime. Several disturbing trends can be pointed out: 1) the shift of decision making from legitimate structures either to "shadow" structures or to institutions whose role is not clearly spelled out in the constitution (such as the Russian Security Council); 2) increasing isolation of the president from his former political base and the public at large; and 3) the use of openly authoritarian methods of rule. In fact, there was mounting evidence that the Yeltsin regime was coming to resemble that of Alfredo Stroessner of Paraguay (1954–89), Mobutu Sese Seko of Zaire (1961–), or Anastasio Somoza of Nicaragua (1963–79). Each of these regimes used a mix of repression and co-optation in their dealings with the political and economic elite, sought to divide the military, and relied on personal security services.[43] Still, these regimes differ significantly from that of Boris Yeltsin to date, given the weakness of the Russian power structure and of Yeltsin personally.

Moreover, there are growing indications that the president's security forces, concerned about their future if he were to depart, are already preparing, with Yeltsin's closest aides, for the "post-Yeltsin" period. The leaders of these special services seem to have formed an alliance with Vice Premier Oleg Soskovets. As the liberal newspaper *Izvestiya* warned:

> On the surface, the president's entourage and the power structures have been abruptly strengthened. Yet this has occurred under conditions in which the president's political position is becoming more and more tenuous and his influence over crucial decision making increasingly questionable. . . . Given this situation, . . . [Yeltsin's] aides and [personal] guard need a legitimate and sufficiently powerful political figure to whom they can turn to ensure their own [continuing] influence regardless of the incumbent president's fate.[44]

Thus a coup staged by the present presidential security forces allied with Yeltsin's closest entourage may be more likely than a traditional military coup. Gavriil Popov, an eminent political observer, has warned of just such an eventuality:

> In our [present] situation, [we are more likely to see] some variant of the [historical incident involving] Pavel I, who was strangled by his closest subordinates [after ruling Russia from 1796 to 1801]. The Afghan version, in which [Prime Minister and later President Nur Mohammad] Taraki was

pushed aside by one of his deputies, could also occur given our [current] situation. . . . Undoubtedly, a group has emerged under the [current] presidential system that is confident that it can survive if Yeltsin is removed. It cannot be ruled out that this group has already "found" a successor.[45]

One possible outcome of a palace coup would be the president's being turned into a puppet rather than being removed outright. In such a scenario, the security forces would have a strong interest in weakening the military so that the armed forces would not contend with them for power. The military failures in Chechnya and the prolongation of the war in the Caucasus play right into their hands.

Any attempt by the president's security forces to consolidate an authoritarian regime either with or without Yeltsin would have a dramatic impact on Russian society. In such a tense climate, conflict would inevitably break out between individual force structures, notably between the army and the security services. Recent efforts to alleviate such conflict and promote coordination have largely failed.[46] Thus it remains very much in doubt whether Yeltsin or any likely successor could restrain the various force structures that have now become accustomed to operating on their own.

In today's Russia, influential forces—both economic cartels and criminal clans (which increasingly overlap)—stand to prosper from the continuing fragmentation of the armed forces and the tension among the diverse force structures. This in turn contributes to the general instability fueled by the problems of state-building and economic reform.

The future of Russia and the newly independent states will depend in large part on what solution to these problems is implemented by Russia's future leaders. This in turn will determine the future of the armed forces—whether they will be a guarantor of stability or will become a destructive force leading Russia toward authoritarianism or chaos.

NOTES

1. Among the most useful Western works are those dealing with the impact of liberalization and democratization on civil-military relations in the former communist countries. See in particular Timothy Colton, *Commissars, Commanders and Civilian Authority: The Structure of Soviet Military Politics* (Cambridge: Harvard University Press, 1979); Gerard Holden, "The Road to the Coup: Civil-Military Relations in the Soviet Crisis" (Occasional Paper No. 23, Peace Research Institute, Frankfurt, Germany, 1991); and David Holloway, "War, Militarism and the Soviet State," in E.P. Thompson and Dan Smith, eds., *Protest and Survive* (Harmondsworth, England: Penguin, 1980). Also valuable are works on the democratic transition process, such as Philippe Schmitter, *Military Intervention, Political Competitiveness, and Public Policy in Latin America 1950–1967* (Cambridge: Harvard University Press, 1970); Terry Karl, "Dilemmas of Democratization in Latin America," *Comparative Politics* 23 (October 1990): 1–21; Adam Przeworski, *Democracy and the Market: Political and Economic Reforms in Eastern Europe and Latin America* (New York: Cambridge University Press, 1991); and Guillermo O'Donnell,

Philippe Schmitter, and Laurence Whitehead, eds., *Transitions from Authoritarian Rule: Comparative Perspectives* (Baltimore: Johns Hopkins University Press, 1986). These works allow us to see the distinctive logic that guides the behavior of the armed forces not just in the period of stabilization but also in the period of transition from authoritarian rule. Another useful approach is to examine the influence of historical experience and traditions, the role of professionalism, and the corporate interests of the military: see Samuel P. Huntington, *The Soldier and the State: The Theory and Politics of Civil-Military Relations* (Cambridge: Harvard University Press, 1957); and Alfred Stepan, *The Military in Politics: Changing Patterns in Brazil* (Princeton: Princeton University Press, 1971). To a lesser extent, we can also learn from works focusing on social differentiation within the military; see, for example, Thomas Cox, *Civil-Military Relations in Sierra Leone: A Case Study of African Soldiers in Politics* (Cambridge: Harvard University Press, 1976).

2. Yurii Derugin, "Tevozhnye tendentsii v rossiyskoy armii" (Alarming tendencies in the Russian army), *Nezavisimaya gazeta*, 24 August 1994, 1–2.

3. Ibid.

4. Some Western analysts believe that the dangers have been exaggerated. Mary Fitzgerald states that "the most creative surges of Russian (and Soviet) military thinking have followed political or military disasters." Despite the difficult political and economic situation, the Russian General Staff continues to plan for future war contingencies: "For the short term, they have developed sophisticated technical and operational counters to the new technologies developed in Desert Storm. For the long term, they have focused most of their limited resources on creating an infrastructure that ensures rapid surge production of new military technologies as the situation warrants. For the transitional period . . . they have resurrected the concept of limited nuclear war to cope with a variety of worst-case scenarios." Mary Fitzgerald, "The Russian Image of Future War," *Comparative Strategy* 13 (April 1994): 167, 179.

5. David Holloway, writing on military and security issues one year after the collapse of the USSR, explained the military's behavior in the absence of clear civilian controls in the following way: "In the Soviet armed forces there had grown up something like a norm of professionalism, or a norm of nonintervention in politics, which recognized or claimed a certain sphere of competence for the military. . . . The military, in spite of what happened or maybe even somewhat because of what happened in August [1991], still feel bound by that norm of professional competence." George Breslauer et al., "One Year After the Collapse of the USSR: A Panel of Specialists," *Post-Soviet Affairs* 8 (1992): 320.

6. The defense ministry later claimed that some 1,300 troops had been brought into Moscow to help in the confrontation with the White House. These troops were drawn from the Taman Motor Rifle Division, the Kantemirov Tank Division, the 119th Parachute Assault Regiment, the 27th Independent Motor Rifle Brigade, the 119th Paratroop Regiment (based in Naro-Forminsk), and the Tula and Ryazan Airborne Divisions. See Stephen Foye, "Confrontation in Moscow: The Army Backs Yeltsin, for Now," *Radio Free Europe/Radio Liberty Research Report* 2 (22 October 1993): 10–15.

7. In his memoirs, Yeltsin recalled that, in the early hours of October 4, "I saw that the army, despite all the assurances of the defense minister, for some reason was not able to come quickly to Moscow's defense and fight the rebels." Yeltsin further recounts that, during the strategy session a few hours later, Grachev insisted on a direct order sanctioning the use of tanks because he did not want to assume personal responsibility. "I'll send you a written order," Yeltsin told him; he then promptly left the meeting to return to the Kremlin. Boris Yeltsin, *The Struggle for Russia*, trans. Catherine Fitzpatrick (New York: Random House, 1994), 276, 278. At 5:00 a.m., Yeltsin issued a second decree on the state of emergency, entitled "Allotting Necessary Forces and Means for Securing the State of Emergency Regime," in which he took personal responsibility for the decision to use the army in this crisis. For the text, see "Sem' blizhayshikh dney" (The next seven days), *Nezavisimaya gazeta*, 5 October 1993, 2.

8. Stephen Foye, "Civilian and Military Leaders in Russia's New Political Arena," *Radio Free Europe/Radio Liberty Research Report* 3 (15 April 1994): 3.

9. According to some reports, the Russian General Staff did not line up behind Yeltsin until 10:00 p.m. on October 3, following a series of phone calls to regional military commanders in the wake of the attacks by the pro-parliamentary forces on the mayor's office and the Ostankino television facilities. Foye, "Confrontation in Moscow," 11.

10. John W.R. Lepingwell, "The Russian Military and Security Policy in the 'Near Abroad,'" *Survival* 36 (Autumn 1994): 70–92.

11. Fitzgerald, "Russian Image of Future War," 168.

12. Sergei Rogov, "Ustoyat li vooruzhennye sily Rossii?" (Will the armed forces of Russia stand fast?), *Nezavisimaya gazeta*, 3 November 1994.

13. Prior to September 1993, the legislature was responsible for the military budget, general oversight of the military, and all organic laws on military affairs. Thus the legislature regulated the size of the armed forces (in June 1992 it stipulated that they could not exceed 1 percent of the population), the length of military service, and military pay scales.

14. A subsequent presidential edict in July 1995 strengthened presidential control over these force organs by making them subject to coordination by the president's chief of staff. Jan S. Adams, "The Russian National Security Council," *Problems of Post-Communism* 43 (January–February 1996): 39.

15. In the December 1995 elections, only Our Home is Russia, headed by Prime Minister Viktor Chernomyrdin, campaigned in support of Yeltsin; it won just 10.3 percent of the vote, which gave it 55 seats in the Duma. Two other reformist parties—Democratic Choice of Russia (headed by Yeltsin's former acting prime minister Yegor Gaidar) and Yabloko (headed by Grigory Yavlinsky)—had serious differences with Yeltsin. Democratic Choice received 3.9 percent of the vote and 9 seats, while Yabloko garnered 7 percent of the vote and 45 seats. Michael McFaul, "The Vanishing Center," *Journal of Democracy* 7 (April 1996): 90–104.

16. Aleksandr Zhilin, "Boris Gromov: 'Operatsiya gotovilas' v glubokoy tayne'" (Boris Gromov: "The operation was prepared in profound secrecy"), *Moskovskiye novosti*, 8–15 January 1995, 1, 5.

17. Ibid., 5.

18. "General Kondratyev on Differences with Grachev," Foreign Broadcast Information Service (FBIS), *Daily Report: Central Eurasia*, 23 January 1995, 13, from Moscow ITAR-TASS World Service, 20 January 1995.

19. "Claims Grachev Practicing Nepotism," FBIS, *Daily Report: Central Eurasia*, 23 January 1995, 16, from Moscow Ostankino Television, 20 January 1995.

20. Aleksandr Konovalov, "Posledstviya chechenskoy kampanii" (Impact of the Chechen campaign), *Nezavisimaya gazeta*, 14 January 1995, 2.

21. The Security Council, which was established in June 1992, brings together government ministries and agencies involved in internal and external security matters. Its primary task is to provide the president with advice, information, and alternatives on pressing security issues. Subsequent to the reorganization of January 1995, the Security Council consisted of five permanent (voting) members—the president, the prime minister, the chair of the Federative Council, the Speaker of the State Duma, and the Security Council secretary—as well as about ten consultative (nonvoting) members drawn from defense, foreign affairs, foreign intelligence, counterintelligence, border security, internal security, civil defense, nuclear energy, and finance. See Adams, "Russian National Security Council," 35–42.

22. Igor Rodionov, "Posle Chechni" (After Chechnya), *Nezavisimaya gazeta*, 9 February 1995, 3.

23. This initiative neither improved the professionalism of the armed forces nor helped

curtail the military's political role: in actuality, the reform made it more likely that the military would become increasingly involved in politics.

24. Gavriil Popov, "Komu i zachem nuzhna diskreditatsiya armii" (Who wants to discredit the army and why), *Izvestiya*, 26 January 1995, 4.

25. As Dmitrii Furman put it: "Notwithstanding the [inherent] risk and unpleasantness of a military coup, [such a coup] could play a positive role [in the development of] Russian democracy, strange as that may sound." "Nas zhdet voyennyy perevorot, polagaut rossiyskiye demokraty" (We expect a military coup, say Russian democrats), *Nezavisimaya gazeta*, 12 January 1995, 2.

26. Ibid.

27. Svetlana Gamova, "Aleksandr Lebed': Sama jizn' zastavlyaet generalov zanimat'sya politikoy" (Aleksandr Lebed: Life itself compels generals to engage in politics), *Izvestiya*, 20 July 1994, 4.

28. Aleksandr Mukomolov, "Aleksandr Lebed': '14-ya armiya v Pridnestrov'ye—chistaya politika'" (Aleksandr Lebed: "The 14th Army in Transdniestria—pure politics"), *Nezavisimaya gazeta*, 27 October 1994, 1.

29. Gamova, "Aleksandr Lebed'," 4.

30. Ibid.

31. Andrew Nagorski, "The General Waiting in the Wings," *Newsweek*, 6 February 1995, 32.

32. Mukomolov, "Aleksandr Lebed'," 1.

33. Following the publication of Lebed's remarks, Defense Minister Grachev reportedly attempted to curtail Lebed's growing influence in August 1994 by dissolving the Fourteenth Army (reducing it to a division) and hence eliminating Lebed's command position. This move backfired, as a number of generals came to Lebed's support. In the end, both Yeltsin and Grachev were forced to reaffirm their confidence in Lebed.

34. McFaul, "Vanishing Center," 91, 99.

35. Juan Linz, "Transitions to Democracy," *Washington Quarterly* 13 (Summer 1990): 155.

36. In December 1991 Yeltsin attempted to combine the KGB and the Ministry of Internal Affairs into a new Ministry of Security and Internal Affairs but was forced to abandon these plans after encountering significant political opposition.

37. The Federal Counterintelligence Service (FSK)—renamed the Federal Security Service (FSB) in April 1995—was the heir to the Second Chief Directorate of the KGB. Other former KGB directorates were reconstituted as the Foreign Intelligence Service, the Federal Agency for Government Communications and Information (FAPSI), the Military Counterintelligence Directorate (now subordinate to the FSB), and the Federal Border Service. The FAPSI, which controls the country's telecommunications networks, played a crucial role during the September 1993 events when it cut the communications lines to the White House and prevented the pro-parliamentary forces from contacting military units. See J. Michael Waller, "The KGB Legacy in Russia," *Problems of Post-Communism* 42 (November–December 1995): 3–10.

38. In a December 1993 presidential decree on executive organs, the GUO appeared with the new name of Main Administration for the Protection of the Russian Federation (GUORF).

39. The GUO was created from what remained of the KGB Ninth Directorate. It included a five thousand–member presidential regiment that was formed out of the former KGB Kremlin Guards. Alfa (an antiterrorist task force) and Vympel (the special-operations task force formerly under the KGB's foreign intelligence service) also initially came under

the authority of the GUO; in December 1993, when Yeltsin tried to transfer Vympel to the Ministry of Internal Affairs, most of its officers resigned in protest. Victor Yasmann, "Security Services Reorganized: All Power to the Russian President?" *Radio Free Europe/Radio Liberty Research Report* 3 (11 February 1994): 10–12.

40. The Ministry of Internal Affairs did send two regiments of its Dzerzhinskii Motorized Rifle Division (about three thousand men) to support the president, although it is unclear what precise role they played in these events. In addition, several "black beret" detachments participated in the fighting around the parliament building; Ministry of Internal Affairs forces were also involved in the battle for the Ostankino television studios. However, the White House was actually taken by the Alfa antiterrorist force and the Vympel special forces, former KGB units under the command of the GUO. See Foye, "Confrontation in Moscow," 10–15; and Victor Yasmann, "The Role of the Security Agencies in the October Uprising," *Radio Free Europe/Radio Liberty Research Report* 2 (5 November 1993): 12–18.

41. According to ratings by the popular television program *Summing Up,* Korzhakov ranked seventh in influence (after Yeltsin) in October 1994, fourth in November, third in December, and second (just behind Prime Minister Viktor Chernomyrdin) in January.

42. For example, General Kozhakov's security organ launched an attack on the Most financial group in an effort to undercut Moscow mayor Yurii Luzhkov.

43. Richard Snyder, "Explaining Transitions from Neopatrimonial Dictatorships," *Comparative Politics* 24 (July 1992): 379–99.

44. Irina Savvateyeva, "Oleg Soskovets," *Izvestiya*, 19 January 1995, 5.

45. Gavriil Popov, "Boris Yel'tsin i avtoritarnoye gosudarstvo" (Boris Yeltsin and the authoritarian state), *Izvestiya*, 24 December 1994, 5.

46. Instead, under Yeltsin there has been considerable duplication of effort and even direct conflict among the various force structures. In January 1994 Yurii Baturin became national security assistant (a position modeled on its American namesake) to improve coordination between the various security and defense agencies. In July 1995, following the Buddenovsk hostage crisis in Chechnya, Yeltsin initiated a major reshuffling of the power ministries. On July 28 Yeltsin signed two presidential edicts that 1) subordinated the GUO to the SBP, 2) elevated the SBP to the status of an official "state organ," and 3) placed both under the authority of the presidential staff (although the presidential staff was not given operational or personnel responsibilities with respect to these agencies). This completed the process begun in January 1993 of subordinating the power ministries directly to the president and placing the Ministry of Defense, the Ministry of Foreign Affairs, the Ministry of Internal Affairs, and the FSB under the authority of the presidential staff. In addition, key personnel changes followed in the wake of this crisis—Barsukov replaced Stepashin as head of the FSB, Yuri Krapivin (Barsukov's former deputy) became the new head of the GUO, Anatolii Kulikov replaced Yerin as minister of internal affairs, and Yerin became deputy head of the Foreign Intelligence Service. Grachev remained minister of defense, and Korzhakov continued to head up the SBP.

9.
THE POSTCOMMUNIST WARS

Charles H. Fairbanks, Jr.

Charles H. Fairbanks, Jr., is research professor of international relations at the Johns Hopkins School of Advanced International Studies in Washington, D.C., where he has been directing the Foreign Policy Institute's Study Group on Postcommunist Ethnic Conflict. He has taught political science at the University of Toronto and Yale University, and has served as a member of the Policy Planning Staff and as deputy assistant secretary in the U.S. Department of State.

We are living through what may be the twilight of an era, several centuries long, during which the use of force became ever more closely associated with the state. There are probably no symbols more strongly tied to the state than the flag and the military uniform, both of which date back only to the late seventeenth century. Everywhere that modern nation-states have arisen, one of their key tasks has been to restrict the scope of private fighting and to make themselves the sole legitimate wielders of force within their respective borders.

In much of the postcommunist world today, however, one encounters a reality that challenges all of our standard assumptions about the relations between armed forces and civilian governments. This essay will focus on the nature and role of armed forces in the new states and largely unrecognized ministates that have formed since 1991 on the territory of what used to be the Soviet Union and Yugoslavia. I will note only in passing the case of Russia; for present purposes, it shows great continuity with the state identity of the old Soviet Union. I will have much to say, however, about the 11 breakaway ministates that have arisen (and sometimes vanished again) since the dissolution of the Yugoslav and Soviet federations: Srpska Krajina in Croatia; Republika Srpska and Croat-ruled Herzeg-Bosna in Bosnia; Kosovo (which has rival ethnic-Serb and ethnic-Albanian governments, only the former of which has an army) in Serbia; the Transdniester Republic in Moldova; Abkhazia, the Adzhar Republic, and South Ossetia in Georgia; Chechnya

in Russia; Nagorno-Karabakh in Azerbaijan; and Gorno-Badakhshan in
Tajikistan.

Widely differing processes have governed the evolution of armies in
the various states that emerged after the collapse of communism. The
old Yugoslav National Army (JNA), for example, rested on a delicate
ethnic equilibrium maintained by quotas; it disintegrated along with the
Yugoslav Federal Republic in the winter and spring of 1990–91. Thus
all the new nations emerging from Yugoslavia had to construct new
armies. The Soviet army, on the other hand, had an officer corps
recruited primarily from the three Slavic nationalities (Great Russians,
White Russians, and Ukrainians). Russia, Belarus, and Ukraine all
inherited organized units from the old army that had been stationed
inside their respective borders at the time of independence. The other
post-Soviet states had to devise new armies. Most of these non-Slavic
nations had no indigenous officer cadres, since Soviet citizens who were
not Slavs generally did not follow military careers. The professional
identity of the Soviet officer corps, moreover, was strongly infused with
Russian nationalism, and such non-Slavs as did make their way into its
ranks tended to be assimilated to that ethos.

Of the inherited Belarusian and Ukrainian armies, little need be said;
what is true of the Russian army broadly applies to them as well. Like
their Russian counterpart, they are subject to considerable civilian
control, though civilian supremacy was stronger still in Soviet days.
They suffer even more from inadequate funds than the Russian army
does, because of their countries' slower-reforming economies. As in
Russia, military life is riddled with corruption, most of it having to do
with illegal trafficking in arms, supplies, and equipment from military
stockpiles. Finally, both Ukraine and Belarus, like Russia, display a
growing tendency to develop new military formations identified with
particular officials or agencies of government.

Two differences between the Russian army and its "inherited"
counterparts are worth mentioning. First, most of Ukraine's and
Belarus's officers still identify with Russia—indeed, many are Great
Russians remaining with former Soviet units that became Ukrainian or
Belarusian by virtue of their geographical posting at the time of the
USSR's collapse. In the event of conflict with Russia, the loyalty of
these officers would be in question. The second difference somewhat
offsets the first: Belarus and Ukraine do not toil under Russia's burden
of wondering whether to play an imperial role in the "near abroad," and
have thus been spared the border adventures, politicization, and
factionalization that plague the Russian army.

The remaining recognized states of the former Soviet Union and
Yugoslavia, as well as all the unrecognized ministates, have had to
improvise military forces quickly in a dangerous environment, usually
without trained officer cadres or adequate funds. In the non-Serb states

of former Yugoslavia, the Baltic states, Moldova, and the Caucasian republics, the organization of informal armed forces preceded independence, going forward against the will of Moscow or Belgrade and often of local authorities as well.

The ministates had to create armed forces even more quickly in order to fight wars of independence. Indeed, in Herzeg-Bosna, Srpska Krajina, Republika Srpska, and Chechnya, the armed force created the state. In all these areas, trained enlisted manpower and Soviet or Yugoslav military bases, equipment, and unit structures were ceded to or seized by the new authorities, although crime, general chaos, and Yugoslav or Russian interference usually prevented new units from being built directly on the foundation of old Soviet or Yugoslav units. In Georgia, for instance, the looting of military bases was so common that one sees in the countryside windmills made from aircraft propellers and pigsties made from the pontoon sections of Soviet bridging equipment.

Armenia, Nagorno-Karabakh, Serbia-Montenegro, and Croatia are special cases. Armenia and Nagorno-Karabakh (the mountainous Armenian-majority enclave in Azerbaijan) had high national morale, felt an imminent threat from the Azeris, deployed large numbers of officers with experience in the old Soviet army, and enjoyed substantial Russian help (including generals sent as military advisors). Yet even though Armenia and Nagorno-Karabakh have been able to field forces comparable in efficiency to the Soviet army, there are "armed groups" in Nagorno-Karabakh that the government has attempted to disarm, and the victories over Azerbaijan have been followed by massive looting and burning of villages.

Serbia-Montenegro started out ahead in the army-building game because more than three-fourths of the officers in the ground forces of the JNA were ethnic Serbs, and Belgrade managed to get control of most of the JNA's modern equipment as Yugoslavia broke up. With this edge in expertise and materiel, Serbia-Montenegro has created an efficient, powerful army of the familiar modern type. Croatia's swift rout of the Krajina Serbs in August 1995 demonstrates that Croatia has rebuilt a modern army in the face of far greater difficulties. Reasonably modern and well-organized forces are also being slowly constructed in the Baltic states and Slovenia. Elsewhere, however, things are fundamentally different.

Militiamen, *Condottieri*, and Brigands

When we speak of an army or military forces, we usually mean a group or groups of armed men, raised, trained, and commanded by the state, with a fixed organization and terms of service. Such armed forces normally have disciplinary rules and a clear chain of command. At least some of the commissioned and noncommissioned officers, moreover, are highly trained career soldiers. Although there may be multiple services, as well as police, security, border-patrol, or "paramilitary" forces, it is understood that the government controls all the large-scale "means of coercion." Hunters, target shooters, and criminals operating alone or in groups may legally or illegally possess firearms, but all are sharply distinguished from official forces and are normally much weaker.

The new states that I am discussing are full of armed men, some with weapons as large and sophisticated as tanks and armored personnel carriers, but many of these men do not belong to modern armies. They are not regular soldiers, but irregulars or militiamen. Their characteristic type of organization is not the modern military formation structured by impersonal commitment to the state and the chain of command, but rather a loosely bound group—often with a charismatic personality at the center—that one joins or leaves spontaneously.

The only place where I have seen this summed up in print is the Helsinki Watch *Report on the War in Abkhazia*, which notes:

> These fighters are not real soldiers in the professional sense. Typically, they serve in loose units out of personal loyalty, or for booty, or revenge on specific individuals, or a desperate hope of protecting or regaining their territory. These are, significantly, armed formations without noncommissioned officers, the disciplinary backbone of professional armies. There are no sergeants in these ranks, no one to insist on discipline among the ordinary soldiers even of a strictly military, prudential nature—to sandbag positions, dig trenches, safeguard bivouacs. . . . Actual aiming of artillery, mortars and rockets in a standard military manner is minimal because neither side is known to have employed forward spotters or fire control systems—a major factor in the extraordinary indiscriminateness of this and similar wars in the former Soviet republics.
>
> The result is a "disordered warfare" . . . high technology coupled with improvisation, weapons of great firepower which yet lack adequate control mechanisms from both the military and humanitarian points of view.[1]

Wandering through their camps and battlefields, you see that these formations, even if they are units of nominal "regular" armies, are either ignorant of or have abandoned the technical skills and routines that modern armies ordinarily employ. High-technology weapons, for instance, are used in ways that would astonish any professional military man. Because there are usually no forward observers and no fire control, artillery is used either for direct bombardment, in the eighteenth-century manner, or for terror against civilians. Rockets and jet aircraft are used in the same way.

Many of these new states defy the standard categories of civil-military relations that one finds in Western books and journals. The simple tandem of "the soldier and the state," to borrow a phrase from

Samuel P. Huntington, is replaced by a spectrum including nongovernmental irregular formations, nongovernmental formations with official
patrons, and armed formations that move in and out of the government's
ambit like Dzhaba Ioseliani's Mkhedrioni ("Horsemen") in Georgia.
Finally, there are nominally official forces, like Surat Huseinov's 709th
Brigade in Azerbaijan or Davit Zeikidze's police force in Georgia, that
actually follow a party or warlord rather than the government.

Even forces that have inherited the standard organization of modern
militaries tend to sink toward the level of the militias. This was
apparent in the Western press accounts of the Chechen War. I witnessed
the phenomenon firsthand in Bosnia, where I observed the routines of
ethnic-Serb, ethnic-Croat, and Bosnian Government forces. They were
all rather similar. The higher Serb commanders are all professionals
from the JNA, and have the bearing of veteran, highly trained officers.
Nevertheless, even their units did not dig latrines outside their living
areas and did not mark mine fields or mineswept areas—both omissions
that would make a conscientious military man blanch. Against regular
armies, as in Chechnya and the Croatian Krajina, militias usually lose.

The nebulous, ill-disciplined character of these forces can embroil the
nations that they supposedly serve in conflicts with groups of their own
people, thereby exacerbating disloyalty and secessionism. In conflicts
with other peoples, their plundering, vandalism, sexual predation, ethnic
cleansing, and general disregard for human rights can turn low-level
conflicts into bitter wars of survival. By the same token, these forces
frequently lack the military competence to settle the trouble they start:
they are too inefficient to impose order internally or to win wars
externally.

This problem is particularly acute in the unrecognized ministates,
which have to rely for assistance on criminals or intelligence agencies,
operating clandestinely and not always with the full approval of their
governments. As a result, the ministates are becoming magnets for
outlaws and other elements marginal to normal societies. As a perceptive
Russian reporter has recently written of the Transdniester Republic:
"This 'zero' land is a distinctive state that draws into itself romantics,
adventurers, and soldiers of fortune, with their unthinkable ideas and
fantastic projects, like some enormous funnel."[2]

New Realities

Scholarship and public discussion alike are still struggling to catch up
with these new realities of armed forces after communism. In the
1994–95 edition of its authoritative annual handbook *The Military
Balance*, the International Institute for Strategic Studies in London
mentions irregulars only in the sections on Georgia, Moldova, and
Azerbaijan. Yet my own reckoning, based on somewhat uneven

knowledge of the 20 newly recognized states and 11 unrecognized ministates in the former USSR and Yugoslavia, reveals a much more complicated picture. Of these 31 new political entities, 12 contain party or movement militias, 11 contain ethnic or regional militias, 8 contain armed criminal groups sufficiently powerful to be discussed in the context of military affairs, and 6 have independent warlord units that nominally operate as parts of their armies. The scale of what we are dealing with is vast. A quick survey of readily available sources on Georgia, for instance, reveals 21 armed organizations that can be listed by name, as well as others (whose number can only be guessed at) that are called simply "illegal armed formations" or "bandit formations."

The larger "militias," which usually consist of between 500 and 4,000 men arrayed in groups of 5 to 30 (a number roughly corresponding to a military platoon), tend to have a two-tier structure. There are "platoon-level" leaders or officers, who may be elected or self-appointed. Then there is the overall leader of the militia, with a small entourage that might charitably be called a staff. In many cases, there are no noncommissioned officers and nothing corresponding to field-grade officers.

Recruits are drawn through family, clan, local, or professional connections; through pay or promises of plunder; or through displays of awe-inspiring equipment. In many cases the leaders are without professional officer training. Loti Kobalia, who commanded former president Zviad Gamsakhurdia's militia in western Georgia, was a truck driver; his deputy Tengiz Bulia was a roofer. Ioseliani and Tengiz Kitovani, the leaders of Georgia's most important militias, were artists with criminal records. (Wags in Tbilisi used to call the capital's devastated downtown "Kitovani's latest sculpture exhibit.") The Serb commander in the now-reconquered enclave of Srpska Krajina who was going by the *nom de guerre* of "Captain Dragon" ran a successful bordello in Australia before returning home to join his people's 600-year-old crusade against Islam and popery.

As the outstanding televised coverage of the Chechen war illustrated, militia troops often do not wear uniforms. In Georgia, Mkhedrioni leaders wear Armani suits bulging with guns, while rank-and-file members wear distinctive civilian jackets and neck medallions. I once asked a Mkhedrioni member why he and his fellows did not wear uniforms. "We prefer American clothes," was his reply.

In most cases—including many "regular" armies—fighters serve at their own discretion; they can go home when they want to. Accordingly, such forces tend to melt away almost completely after a defeat. Mobilizations, conversely, are often accomplished through the broadcasting of televised messages about times and places of assembly.

It might be useful to sketch one militia unit, a Serb outfit involved in the fighting over Vukovar, Croatia, whose history I learned through numerous interviews in Serb-occupied Bosnia during August 1993. The leader and founder was an unemployed actor from Belgrade whom his men called simply "Chief." His best friend served as second-in-command. During the confusion surrounding the breakup of Yugoslavia and the disintegration of the JNA, the Chief got hold of a twin-barreled, 23-millimeter antiaircraft gun that he used against people and buildings, in the manner common to these ethnic wars. The Chief's command of this fearsome-looking weapon and its firepower attracted ten other young Serb nationalists.

The Chief and his crew received general strategic directions from the senior Serb commander in Vukovar, a JNA veteran and Serbian army general sent from Belgrade. Tactical decisions, however, were made on the spot without consulting higher authority. Thus when the upper ranks signed a truce with the Croats, the Chief impressed his men by declaring: "I didn't sign it, so I'm not going to obey it!" The group was not linked to any organized logistical system. They received food from friendly Serbs or took it from Croats. When they needed ammunition, they would go to a JNA supply dump and say, to take one example, "Please give us 12,000 hand grenades." Members left the unit when they "couldn't take it anymore" and wanted a respite from the front.

The complex relationships of these voluntary organizations to the state and society, to decency and crime, have been perfectly captured by the Bosnian journalist Tihomir Loza:

> Some of the gangs were created and are partly controlled by the government. But there is no absolute control, and some of them have outgrown the government. Some gangs are loyal to one faction or another within the regime, while some are independent and interested only in money. In fact, there are very narrow lines between the regular police, the military forces and the private militias.

> The anti-official mentality which has always been present in Bosnia, especially in Sarajevo, is a partial explanation. Power, even when it is not criminal, does not circulate through usual, legal ways, but through the intricate network of private or semi-private connections. The position of minister or member of the presidency does not in itself guarantee power. Furthermore, the fact that a powerful man acts as a criminal in one field does not necessarily mean he might not be completely honest and well-intentioned in another. Many gangs and militias steal and profit on the black market, but fight bravely on the front.[3]

Dubious Loyalties

If the identification between these armed forces and the nation-state is so tenuous, to what are they loyal? The tendency to break and run that many of these forces have shown, especially in the Abkhaz, Nagorno-Karabakh, Bosnian, and Krajina wars, bespeaks poor cohesion and suggests that irregular fighters are loyal mainly to themselves.

Individual fighters and whole units, moreover, have been known to change sides in midcampaign.[4]

To the extent that these *Freikorps* display loyalty, it seems to be *abstract* allegiance to an ethnic group that is not identified with a specific state, or *personal* allegiance to particular warlords or *condottieri*. Sometimes these groups are based on subethnic ties (many hard-core Mkhedrioni members, for instance, belong to Ioseliani's ancestral ethnolinguistic group); regional bonds (the case in Croatia, Bosnia, Ukraine, Georgia, Azerbaijan, Tajikistan, Chechnya); or political parties. In Russia, Georgia, Azerbaijan, and Serb-occupied Bosnia and Croatia, many political parties or movements sponsor their own armed groups.

The relation of these informal armed forces to the state is thus complex and volatile, all the more so because of the presence of mercenaries, adventurers, volunteers, or foreign formations in at least 15 of the new states or ministates. The war that raged through the winter of 1994–95 in the breakaway North Caucasian region of Chechnya, for example, was not exclusively an affair of Russian regulars versus Chechen regulars. Instead, it also drew the participation of Chechens fighting on the Russian side; Russians fighting on the Chechen side; Ukrainians fighting on both sides; Abkhazian and other North Caucasian mercenaries; plus Azeris, Afghans, Lithuanians, Arabs, Turks, and Belarusians.

In Chechnya, however, mercenaries and foreign elements had little effect on the course of the fighting. By contrast, in the wars in the Transdniester Republic, Abkhazia, South Ossetia, Nagorno-Karabakh, and Tajikistan, mercenaries, volunteers, and foreign forces and equipment have had a major and at times even decisive effect. In the Abkhazian war of secession from Georgia, for instance, the majority of "Abkhaz" forces were probably from outside Abkhazia, most had no ethnic-Abkhaz blood, and their commander at the turning point of the war was a Chechen acting under Russian sponsorship—the same Shamyl Basayev who in June 1995 led the most successful anti-Russian terrorist operation in history at Budyonnovsk.

The tendency to mix armies and nationalities in the former Soviet Union is exacerbated by the Russian army's practice of recruiting people from other republics for service in the "near abroad." In Tajikistan, for example, the Russians are recruiting Tajiks to fight Tajiks. In Armenia, the Russian forces are recruiting Armenians. The Russian peacekeeping force on the Georgian-Abkhazian border is recruiting Georgians.

While governments may pay some of the units that we are discussing, many make money on their own by stealing, selling their arms, dealing drugs, or soliciting subsidies from wealthy businessmen and foreign countries. Russian mercenaries in Abkhazia, in several attested cases, were paid by the government of the Transdniester Republic.[5]

In some of the places most wracked by militia activity (Bosnia,

Georgia, Azerbaijan, and Moldova), there now seems to be a real movement away from militias, turning them into armies or "dissolving" them by decree or disarmament. Although Russia, Tajikistan, and Chechnya have moved in the other direction, one should not dismiss the possibility of further professionalization or reprofessionalization there as well. But the militia phenomenon is due to underlying structural conditions that may be submerged or come to the surface depending on the circumstances. The fading of most (though by no means all) militias from public view in Moldova, Georgia, and Azerbaijan is connected with the success of ethnic insurgencies, so that many militias turn into "armies." With relatively stable truces holding in all three cases and a tenuous political stability in the rump states, there is no need or excuse for militias and they subside into a state of latency. They can, however, come to the surface again in favorable conditions.

Regulars and Irregulars

In addition to militias, almost all of the new states also have ordinary armies with traditional standardized, numbered units. But closer examination shows that these conventional formations have many times actually been under private control. In the case of Surat Huseinov's 709th Azeri Brigade, mentioned in passing above, a wealthy and well-connected individual twice used a private army disguised as a regular formation to mount coup attempts against the president of his country.

Around his brigade—which consisted mostly of fellow townsmen plus Russian paratroopers, all paid with money made through corrupt activities—Huseinov grouped a number of organizations within the Azeri government that were loyal to him rather than to their official superiors.[6]

The governments of other new countries are right to fear that elements of their official hierarchies could be subverted into privatized and militarized organizations dangerous to the state. Without habits of loyalty to states that are new and governments with weak legitimacy, and in the absence of money to reward obedience or a functioning judicial system to punish disobedience, it is hard to erect safeguards against the danger.

Drawing a clear distinction between public and private military forces in the post-Soviet and post-Yugoslav context is difficult for five reasons:

1) The chain of command linking bureaucratic units had already begun rusting under Brezhnev and Tito. When *glasnost'* sapped the legitimacy of the communist state and rapid political change disorganized the already-shaky governing apparatus, its component bureaucacies began to turn into independent organizations controlled by their old bosses. The bureaucratic division of labor, which the modern state had created, now turned on its maker, becoming a source of loyalties outside or even *against* the state. Military forces and security agencies, despite their

special characteristics, are also bureaucracies. They were scarcely exempt from this dynamic.

2) In revolutionary periods, public armed forces are often used for partisan or private ends rather than public purposes. This is how the Russian intelligentsia interprets the armed suppression of the Supreme Soviet in October 1993 and the Chechen War. Even if these are misinterpretations, they cause public armed forces to be seen as private.

3) Even when the bonds among them fray, the various fragments of the old state apparatus can still wield enormous power in their own right. Even if they cannot or will not enforce the law, they can still confer favors. Thus public power can be used to create private military forces such as the Moscow bankers' security services, which Yeltsin approved because they would fight for him. Indeed, private military power usually develops with the complicity of certain bureaucracies.

4) Bureaucratic units increasingly depend not on their appropriations in the state budget, but on "nonbudget funds"—that is, resources the unit acquires in exchange for services rendered to private clients. This little-understood mechanism is transforming the fundamental structure of the postcommunist states. "Nonbudget funds" are the equivalent of medieval fiefs: sources of revenue given to units of the government in order to support their operations, in a financially stringent environment, and in recompense for favors rendered. Like fiefs, such funds render bureau-cratic units partially but not totally independent of their official bosses. Georgia's security minister until September 1995, Igor Giorgadze, commanded a force far excelling the regular army in efficiency and morale, because he paid the enlisted men several times as much. The money came from giving protection to private businesses and shipments.[7]

5) The most elusive but perhaps the most powerful factor blurring the distinction between public and private military forces comes to light through a revealing paradox about the popularity of military service. Almost every one of the militias fighting for ethnic groups contains numerous mercenaries or volunteers from other areas. But the armies fighting for their own nations under the direction of the state are unpopular, as is shown by the high rates of draft evasion and desertion found in many former communist states, whether they were at peace like Russia or at war like the republics of the Caucasus and the former Yugoslavia.

The great difficulty facing transitions to democracy in the postcom-munist East is a lack of basic social cohesion. Democratic institutions, political parties, and branches of the state itself, such as regular armies, all find it hard to function in such a highly atomized environment. Here is another consequence of communism's collapse that we failed to anticipate. Many of us foresaw great difficulties, but we tended to locate them in some sort of authoritarian "political culture"—that is, in too much cohesion rather than too little.

The postcommunist world has witnessed the emergence of a kind of "antipolitics" that is more radical than antipolitics elsewhere; it goes beyond trying to replace one form of politics with another, and even beyond trying to reduce the importance of politics.[8] At its core is a near-total flight from the public world as such.

There are many signs of this flight, including the crime and corruption that are so rampant in postcommunist countries, but the one that concerns us here is the character of armed forces in this world. Their amorphousness flows from a horror of any organization that is not spontaneous or voluntary, of any obedience that is expected or compulsory, or simply of any and all forms of "political obligation."

What is causing this flight from the public world? At its root, I believe, it is a reaction against the overwhelming experience of communist rule. After decades and decades of communism's discipline and regimentation, people dread the idea of being subjected to any kind of authority that comes from outside them.

This argument about the unpopularity of armies and the state might seem to contradict what everyone knows from the evening news: the biggest new fact about the postcommunist world is the emergence of violent nationalism, bent on carving out ethnically pure states. Yet this nationalism, for all its passionate intensity, has somehow failed to build strong states. Indeed, it seems to have actually *replaced* the state after the latter lost its legitimacy. The *ethnos* functions as a surrogate for the state, which is withering away. Nationalism gives people an identity and preserves a link with some felt community without making too many demands. Indeed, what the state and its laws deny to you, the new nationalism permits and excuses: theft, rape, and crimes of revenge are central features of the wars of ethnic cleansing.

As for the forces that fight these wars, they are more dangerous to their own countrymen than to enemy states. These new armies have left great cities like Sarajevo, Tbilisi, or Baku undefended, like so many fat cattle tethered out for the hyena and the crocodile. Azerbaijan, with its vast oil and gas reserves, is ripe for conquest by the first force that seriously wants to try.

Implications for Civil-Military Relations

For reasons that should be clear by now, saying anything cogent about civil-military relations across much of the post-Soviet and post-Yugoslav worlds is exceedingly difficult. How can one discuss civilian control of the armed forces if the civilian government does not even raise or organize the armed forces? Nevertheless, it is possible to venture a few generalizations.

First, weak as the governments of many of the new states are, they are still able to confer important privileges and benefits. In the high feudal age, kings were weak but the barons still sought many things from them. Militias and political elites in today's postcommunist world often find each other useful. But the relationship differs from "normal" civil-military relations in that it is totally unstructured. It is not "constitutional," even in a broad sense; there is no "sovereign."

My second generalization describes a great paradox of postcommunist politics that has yet to be explained. Governments do not control militias, and militia-driven secessions, coup attempts, or rebellions have occurred in Croatia, Bosnia, Moldova, Georgia, Chechnya, Azerbaijan, and Tajikistan. But unlike Africa, the Middle East, and Latin America, where military regimes are a familiar phenomenon, the post-Soviet and post-Yugoslav worlds have seen no full-blown military dictatorships. I am not sure why this is so, although it is tempting to speculate that military leaders, themselves affected by the flight from the public world, want money and power more than glory and responsibility.

The result is that civilian governments are often the prisoners of militias. In Georgia, for example, President Eduard Shevardnadze had to rely on Tengiz Kitovani and Dzhaba Ioseliani in order to take power. The president managed to outmaneuver Kitovani, but Ioseliani remains so formidable that Shevardnadze has long tolerated the Mkhedrioni and their lawlessness.

Of all the items on the postcommunist political agenda, none is more urgent than the creation of serious, publicly controlled military power. So far, however, neither the citizens of the new states nor interested Westerners have been very helpful in this regard. Most of the democrats in these states are unsympathetic to the use of force; their roots are in nonviolent dissidence, not armed struggle. They have little acquaintance with the military world or military personnel: officers in Soviet-style armies were generally either upwardly mobile peasants or the sons of officers, and formed a separate professional caste. After communism fell, many democrats paid lip service to the need to refound national armies and intelligence services on a democratic footing, yet showed little interest in or enthusiasm for the actual work of doing so. Because military life, whether in militias or armies, seems *déclassé* and in many countries has been penetrated by the world of crime, the military career's lack of respectability has deepened even further.

We in the West have not helped. We admire revolutions only as long as they are "velvet," without strife or disruption. We talk about economic reform and democracy-building but never about army-building, which is the indispensable foundation of both. We are half-aware of how important the military realm is, but are prudishly reluctant to discuss it. The same is true of our attitude toward nationalism, another potentially strong state-forming force. We approach the postcommunist world with peremptory expectations of lasting change, but can barely bring ourselves to acknowledge the forces that could produce it.

This is folly. When the respectable and high-minded shun the military world, it is left open to vengeful neocommunists, criminals, crackpots, and fascists. The current state of affairs resembles Machiavelli's account of Renaissance Italy: good men are so weakened by their goodness that they relinquish their states to the wicked. Enter Ratko Mladić, Dzhaba Ioseliani, and Surat Huseinov. What is sadder still is that even these brutal characters are trivial figures with base aspirations: they are usually driven by the desire for money or raw power or by pointless grudges rather than by the ambition that builds states.

The Last Argument of Kings

It is astonishing that the chaotic former Soviet world, so similar in its disarray and corruption to Revolutionary France in 1799, has not yet given rise to a Napoleon. Perhaps this is an unlooked-for consequence of the illegitimacy of military life and the flight from the public world, or perhaps it is an underpublicized achievement of postcommunist governments building on the useful communist tradition of generals obeying commissars.

Yet even if no men on horseback appear, the absence of stable democratic institutions, genuine party systems, and legitimate ideologies means that the political destiny of many a postcommunist state is likely to be decided by "the last argument of kings," armed force. It appears that many future governments will come to power through civil wars and coups or partial coups that will change governments or policies without actually putting the military in power.

With all apologies, I will play devil's advocate for a moment and ask if this is really so bad. Looking back at history, it is hard to regret the American Revolution (which was a harsh civil war as well as an anticolonial rebellion), Ataturk's victory over the Ottomans, or the Meiji Restoration. The military intervention that brought Charles de Gaulle to the presidency of France in 1958 seems pretty clearly to have been a good thing. And to take on a much knottier question, even Napoleon's seizure of power might be defended on the ground that he gave events a new direction after the French Revolution had foundered in a way that is reminiscent of what is now happening to some postcommunist reforms. Napoleon was the creator of that enduring synthesis of revolutionary utopianism (equality before the law, religious toleration, human rights) and tradition (monarchy, religion, the appeal to honor) that made the nineteenth century a haven of relative order and decency between two agonies of war and terror. Without the amazement created by Napoleon's personal subjugation of Europe, there would have been no energy for this new departure. Conquest and usurpation have been the motor of history up until now. Are we trying to end history by pretending that it is already over?

Since 1989, the new states we are considering have seen 13 secessionist or ethnic rebellions, 5 civil wars, and 6 armed coups or quasi-coups. Eleven or twelve of the ethnic rebellions were broadly successful (as seen from the perspective of the ethnic group making them, of course). Only one of the civil wars—the first civil war in Georgia—drove the incumbents from power, and all were disastrous in the long run to most of the forces that initiated them. Of the coups or quasi-coups, only two—both mounted by the Tajik opposition against President Rahman Nabiyev in 1992, first forcing him into a coalition and then ousting him—were successful, and then only at first. In Azerbaijan, Surat Huseinov forced out President Abulfaz Elchibey, only to see power stolen by Heydar Aliyev. Military men in the postcommunist world, and those who arm and educate them, ought to know this striking record.

These facts enable us to see the other side of the argument. We have been discussing the possible utility of military intervention in politics in a situation of disintegrating states, poorly established institutions, and weak legitimacy. If the military forces that do the intervening are themselves suffering from low morale, loyalty, and competence, their involvement will just make things worse. Consider, for example, the chaos and bloodshed that followed the overthrow of President Zviad Gamsakhurdia in Georgia—an act that weakened the already-feeble inhibitions against political action outside democratic limits. Ukraine, by contrast, remained patient under a president whose incompetence was comparable to Gamsakhurdia's, but replaced him according to law and suffered no civil strife.

Democracy's prestige in the postcommunist world is not based on any lived experience of democratic governance, but rather on a widespread sense that democracy and the market are the normal way that civilized life is conducted. Where this sweet illusion has not been shattered, it is better not to touch it.

For the present, at least, the case for military activism in postcommunist politics is still unpersuasive, but the conventional Western model of civil-military relations also is not easily applicable. In this model, the armed forces as an institution are resolutely apolitical. They understand themselves as professional managers of coercion, prepared to follow the lawful instructions of the duly constituted political authorities.

This model, unexceptionable as it is in the West, does not translate well to the very different circumstances of the postcommunist world. To begin with, as Andrew Bacevich has pointed out, the conventional Western model of civil-military relations emerged out of the experience of the West in the three and a half centuries between the end of the Thirty Years' War (1618–48) and the fall of the Soviet Union, when there were fairly clear distinctions between war and peace, war and politics, war and economic life, warrior and civilian. Such distinctions are much harder to draw amid the brutal but low-intensity ethnic wars of the postcommunist world today, a world that in some ways eerily resembles early-modern Europe during the dynastic and religious wars of the sixteenth and early seventeenth centuries: civilians are both combatants and victims; soldiering and brigandage overlap; and war looks like peace, peace like war.

Another problem with the Western ideal of civilian supremacy is that it presupposes decent, law-abiding civilian government. Such supremacy becomes questionable when, as in the postcommunist world today, governments are neither liberal nor democratic and see the armed forces as potential tools of domestic repression. In Russia, various parts of the former Yugoslavia, Tajikistan, Azerbaijan, Georgia, South Ossetia, Abkhazia, Moldova, and Chechnya, rulers have used armed force to crush political opponents or to settle ethnic questions within their own borders. Is it wise to encourage militaries to give unstinting loyalty to corruption-riddled governments that came to power irregularly and lack democratic accountability? Civilian supremacy is not very appealing if the supreme civilian turns out to be someone like Vladimir Zhirinovsky.

Given the probable character of some future governments and the disorder amid which they will be functioning, there will be many dubious orders, many temptations and excruciating dilemmas. So the officers who face them, unlike Western officers, desperately need an education in political judgment. Many of them will be faced again with dilemmas like those that have recently confronted Russian generals. In October 1993, Russian generals had to decide whether to allow extremist militias to dominate Moscow streets or to disperse the elected parliament by tank fire. The generals obeyed orders then, but the disappointing outcome may have moved General Ivan Babichev, at the start of the invasion of Chechnya on 11 December 1994, to defy the hasty orders that would have begun—against the judgment of most public opinion and of the officer corps—the killing of Russian civilians. Babichev's initiative having sunk, on New Year's Eve his fellow officers received instructions from a civilian favorite of Yeltsin's for a tactically preposterous armored assault on Chechen president Dzhokar Dudayev's skyscraper headquarters, thrown together to give the defense minister, born on the first of January, a fiery birthday celebration. Those professionals faced, again, a choice: whether to send thousands of half-trained youngsters to their deaths, or to throw the country, by an open act of mutiny, into unknown waters.

Some Provocative Suggestions

The best counsel that one can offer in such bleak circumstances is that armed forces work toward *isolation* from civilian government and from crime and corruption—that is, from economic life—except in the gravest crises. For now, armed forces are wise not to respond to every civilian order to use force, but to comply only with orders for routine, nonpolitical crime prevention and measures to guard the community (as opposed to the state narrowly understood) against urgent threats to its survival. In Bosnia, Nagorno-Karabakh, and Abkhazia the armed forces were right to respond to such threats.

Because many existing "armies" are more dangerous to their countries than to the enemy, the question of civil-military relations cannot be separated from wider defense policy. Under present conditions, there are forces *both* in society and in government that are acting to privatize military power. There are grave dangers in spontaneously raised volunteer forces, but also sometimes in "professional armies." In practice, these can mean collections of autonomous legions tightly controlled by particular officials and isolated from society, like the Kremlin guard commanded by General Aleksandr Korzhakov. This force has a factional identity so strong that it took to the streets to attack a banker's security force aligned with the mayor of Moscow.

Militias of the existing type have been disastrous, but systematically recruited reserve armies of the Swiss type based on universal service have both disadvantages and advantages. On the one hand, they continue the existing diffusion of arms and military skills; on the other, they can still act—as they have done so often in history—as a check on despotism and the exploitation of society by narrow armed groups. Media coverage of the postcommunist wars has given us glimpses of so many able-bodied citizens, of both sexes, looking on helplessly as their countries writhe in the grip of militia depredations and ethnic cleansing. Student training for reserve service, like the Reserve Officer Training Corps in the United States, is worth considering. It is particularly important to involve the new middle class, which has so many other opportunities, in military service.

If armies are to protect their peoples rather than plunder them, it may also be important to work gradually to restore the prestige of military organizations and the use of force. The post-Soviet world is in a situation that is virtually without historical precedent. In most epochs of disorder, the profession of arms and the use of force have been glamorous, often too glamorous. This was the experience of tribal societies, of the Middle Ages, and, more recently, of the postcolonial Third World with its guerrilla chic. Now the profession of arms has little prestige beyond the strange glamor which, in the postcommunist world, seems to attach to criminality, plus the glamor of group defense. Both types of glamor are fading.

These suggestions, which have been formulated to be provocative, will not persuade everyone. Any policy toward military affairs must be adapted to the circumstances of individual countries, which vary enormously. Whatever the choices citizens and leaders make, they must choose in the knowledge that decisions about armed forces, more than anything else, will mold their future.

NOTES

1. Human Rights Watch Arms Project and Human Rights Watch/Helsinki Reports, *Report on the War in Abkhazia*, vol. 7, no. 7 (1994), 11.

2. Aleksey Chelnokov, "Azartnye igri v strane 'zero'" (Games of chance in country "zero"), *Izvestia*, 12 November 1994.

3. Tihomir Loza, "A People with Tolerance, a City Without Laws," *Balkan War Report*, August–September 1993, 11.

4. In August 1993, on the eve of the most decisive phase of the Abkhazian war, the commanders of the Sukhumi brigade and the Gali battalion—both units of Georgian president Eduard Shevardnadze's militia—announced that because of the "disgraceful" truce agreement with the Russians and Abkhazians, they were joining Loti Kobalia's militia then rebelling in the name of former president Gamsakhurdia. See *Georgian Chronicle*, August 1993, 6.

5. Human Rights Watch, *War in Abkhazia*, 43.

6. On Huseinov and his activities, see Thomas Goltz, "Letter from Eurasia: The Hidden Russian Hand," *Foreign Policy* 92 (Fall 1993): 111–12; and Baku Radio and Television broadcast of 11 October 1994, *FBIS-SOV*, 12 October 1994, 61.

7. Author's interview with a U.S. government official, 19 June 1995.

8. I draw here on the more complete exposition in two forthcoming book chapters: "Post-Communist Antipolitics," in Andreas Schedler, ed., *The End of Politics? Explorations in Modern Antipolitics* (London and New York: Macmillan and St. Martin's); and "Party and Ideology in the Former U.S.S.R.," in Richard Zinman and Jerry Weinberger, eds., *Left, Right and Center: Party and Ideology After the Cold War* (Ithaca, N.Y.: Cornell University Press). I have drawn upon the insights of G.M. Tamás, especially "Irony, Ambiguity, Duplicity: The Legacy of Dissent," *Uncaptive Minds* 7 (Summer 1994): 19–34.

EPILOGUE:
THE LIBERAL TRADITION

Joseph S. Nye, Jr.

Joseph S. Nye, Jr., *is dean of the John F. Kennedy School of Government at Harvard University. This text is a lightly edited version of a speech that he presented on 14 March 1995 while he was serving as U.S. assistant secretary of defense for international security affairs. A former Rhodes Scholar, he is the author of more than 100 articles and many books, most recently* Understanding International Conflicts *(1993).*

The world has changed, and views on civil-military relations have changed with it. Militaries in democratic states have lost their Cold War missions, and militaries in autocratic states have lost their preeminent roles in society. In places as diverse as Latin America, Eastern Europe, South Asia, the Pacific Rim, and the former Soviet Union, military and political leaders are being forced to confront a number of problematic trends emanating from the end of the Cold War.

Clearly, civil-military relations necessarily differ from country to country. The role of the military in China is not like that in Brazil. The Israeli military is not the same as the Czech military. Pakistan is not like Ethiopia. The end of the Cold War dramatically transformed some nations, changed the external environments of others, and barely affected others. Yet while civil-military relations are as different as the nations on Earth, they are similar in that nations in virtually all regions of the globe are currently undergoing a delicate period of transition.

Those nations now confronting the sudden absence of a long-standing external threat—countries in Western Europe and East Asia as well as the United States, for example—have sometimes found civil-military relations becoming more contentious as they grapple with how their militaries can best meet the challenges of a new era. Often the debate is fundamental, with disputes centering on what now constitutes a threat to national security.

As they struggle to define new threats, many nations have found that the role of the military in promoting security has become less important.

Today, threats to national security are often domestic. Russia's existence is threatened by internal secessionist movements. Latin America's democracies face the threat of powerful drug cartels. In the Middle East, militant Islamic radicals pose threats across borders. And in the United States, President Bill Clinton has placed a new emphasis on economic security. As a result, nonmilitary institutions (such as those involved in law enforcement, justice, and commerce) have been tapped to play a role in national security, and many militaries have seen their budgets decrease. As Michael Desch has noted at this conference, the nature of the threat environment affects a military's mission and doctrine. For many countries, the new internal focus presents a real threat to stable civil-military relations.

Many countries that are undergoing transitions to democracy are, for the first time, creating mechanisms for civilian oversight of their militaries. In Eastern Europe, Latin America, and the former Soviet Union, constitutions are being rewritten, parliaments are enacting oversight laws, and civilian defense ministries are exercising their new authority.

Many nations are finding that regional security cooperation is becoming increasingly important, yet regional military relations are still underdeveloped. This has led to a wrenching period of reevaluation of regional relations across the globe—in South Asia, the Pacific Rim, Latin America, and the former Soviet Union.

Problems on the Horizon

These trends have produced a great deal of uncertainty about what constitutes the proper role of the military in a democratic society. This uncertainty can lead to either of two extreme tendencies:

1) Military overreach, in which the people look to the military—which they view as a "man on a white horse"—for salvation, and the military becomes politicized. In Russia, pressure is being brought to bear on the military to become involved in issues of public safety, secessionism, and political intrigue. In Latin American countries, there is political pressure for the military to become involved in the drug war and in counterinsurgency. And in the United States, politicians often look to the military to help fight crime and provide disaster relief.

2) Exclusion of the military from civil society, in which civilians view the military as a threat to the stability of the nation and therefore seek to minimize its power and influence, even in areas where military expertise is germane. Militaries in both Latin America and Eastern Europe have experienced varying degrees of isolation in this way.

In the current climate of uncertainty, it is useful to reflect on what we in the United States believe the proper role of the military to be. That role is based on what is commonly referred to as the liberal tradition. The liberal tradition, which is a key product of our democratic heritage, establishes specific responsibilities for both the military and civilian leaders. The military must recognize that 1) armed forces are accountable to the rule of law and obliged to respect civilian authority, and that 2) armed forces are nonpartisan and remain above politics. Civilians are required to 1) recognize that armed forces are legitimate tools of democratic states; 2) fund and respect properly developed military roles and missions; and 3) educate themselves about defense issues and military culture.

Promoting the Liberal Tradition

A primary objective of the Clinton administration's foreign policy is the enlargement of the worldwide community of democratic nations. One means of achieving this is promoting the liberal military tradition.

An important tool in this effort is IMET, the International Military Education and Training program. Through IMET, we target key military and civilian leaders in foreign nations and bring them to the United States to teach them about the importance of the liberal tradition in our military's success.

Secretary of Defense William Perry likes to tell the story of how he recently visited Albania and saw the success of IMET firsthand. There he met an Albanian battalion commander who, thanks to IMET, had gone through Ranger training at Fort Benning, Georgia. When the commander got back to Albania, he immediately set up his own American-style training program. Secretary Perry was extremely impressed by the level of discipline his troops exhibited, and their respect for civilian authority. He also noticed that—in a first for Albania—the battalion had noncommissioned officers (NCOs), which the battalion commander had learned about in the United States.

In addition to instructing foreign military personnel about U.S. techniques through IMET, which concentrates on improving discipline, training, and combat skills, we have another related program called Expanded IMET. Expanded IMET focuses specifically on civil-military relations and emphasizes the development of professional resource-management skills, military justice, codes of conduct, and the protection of human rights.

Expanded IMET has changed the nature of civil-military relations in many countries. In Senegal, a civilian judge in the military courts worked successfully to reform the military-justice system in his country on the basis of a fundamental principle he learned in his Expanded IMET course—that the accused has rights and should be fully informed of those rights. The Naval Justice School in Newport, Rhode Island, is now offering the same course on military justice to Central European parliamentarians, government leaders, and members of the press.

Expanded IMET is the only U.S. program that teaches foreign professionals about our military-justice system: while the U.S. Agency for
International Development and the American Bar Association offer
courses on many aspects of judicial reform, military justice is not among
the topics explored.

IMET has also helped foreign militaries understand the benefits of the
transition to democracy. In Mali, officers who had participated in IMET
supported the democratic movement in their country. A U.S. Foreign
Service officer who served in Mali described the situation as follows:
"Those officers who had benefited from IMET tended to have a
heightened sense of professionalism as it related to human rights in
support of democracy. All spoke of how professional militaries act in
democracy, which they had learned not in their courses, but from
contact with the U.S. military." These same officers also sought to
improve the conditions of their NCOs. They understood that discontent
within the ranks posed a real threat to democracy in Mali and moved
quickly to improve training and living conditions for enlisted persons.

These IMET programs are among the most cost-effective steps the
United States can take; at the Pentagon they are referred to as great
"force-multipliers." It cost about $35,000 to put that Albanian through
Ranger school, give him English-language training, and teach him how
to teach others what he had learned. That small investment paid off
handsomely: the Albanian army trained hundreds of men to Western
standards, learned much about the proper role of the military in a
democratic society, and struck up better relations with the U.S. military,
once its sworn enemy.

Central Europe and Latin America

Two regions that are worth a closer look are Central Europe and
Latin America. In Central Europe, the United States is promoting the
liberal tradition with another tool—the encouragement of direct and
continued interaction between the U.S. military and other nations'
militaries. The Partnership for Peace (PFP)—in addition to everything
else it is accomplishing—is our flagship program for improving military
cooperation and for developing strong personal ties between members of
different militaries.

The PFP is working right now to help bring Central Europe closer
to the West. Many people look at the PFP and ask only one question:
When will it bring Central European countries into NATO? This
question—as important as it is—should be balanced by an appreciation
of what the PFP is currently doing to bring nations together and to
spread the liberal tradition.

The joint military exercises of the PFP bring soldiers into close
contact with the men and women they used to stare at across a divided

continent. To my mind, each joint exercise is like a hundred small IMET programs: military officers from Central and Eastern Europe see firsthand how their counterparts in the West operate. And the great untold story is how many of these exercises are under way. In 1995 alone, NATO intends to conduct up to 20 joint military exercises and 143 exercise-related activities with its new partners. These are the beginnings of the ties that bind.

These ties will undoubtedly help spread the ideas that make up our liberal tradition. So will our important military-to-military contacts with Russia and other nations that seek to move with us into the twenty-first century. We have also found fruitful our experience with our regional study centers, such as the George C. Marshall Center in Garmisch-Partenkirchen, Germany, as well as our Personal Exchange Program and the Schools of Other Nations Program, whereby American soldiers go to foreign nations' military schools and units to learn and, of course, to teach.

Latin American militaries have been affected greatly by the post–Cold War trends discussed above. Resources for Latin American militaries are shrinking as governments adopt tighter monetary policies. And countries of the region that had previously focused on the external communist threat are now reassessing the doctrines and missions of their militaries. Argentina, a bold reformer of civil-military relations, has focused on external missions like peacekeeping. Other countries, such as Brazil, have on occasion involved the military in "internal" operations to free their cities of drugs and crime. The impact of these new military missions on the armed forces requires further investigation. Such an assessment, however, should not occur only in Latin America. The United States faces similar uncertainties about what constitutes the proper role of the military. We have much to gain from a dialogue with our neighbors on these issues.

Yet the real change in civil-military relations in Latin America is more fundamental. Clearly, military missions are evolving. More important, however, the basic philosophical principles that have guided Latin American militaries are being reevaluated. In the United States, the liberal tradition has provided the basis for civil-military relations: The military is subordinate to civilian authority in all matters, and is entitled to all rights of citizenship. Latin American countries, on the other hand, have used corporatist traditions to define civil-military relations. Corporatist systems emphasize military autonomy in spheres of military competence (effectively eliminating civilian authority in military affairs), but also deny political rights to military personnel. In such a system, it is the responsibility of the military to decide, in a nonpartisan manner, the destiny of the nation. In the past, Latin American militaries were often required to evaluate the effectiveness of governments, especially in the economic sphere. When the economies of many of these countries appeared to be headed toward chaos, the military was often invited to intercede. As democratic governments become stronger, the corporatist philosophy is being rethought in many Latin American countries.

Encouraging Dialogue

One of the key goals in U.S. diplomatic relations with nations undergoing the transitions mentioned above is to help them understand the liberal tradition. This is not to suggest that the American way is the only way, but rather that we could all benefit from an exchange of views on the changing role of the military in the post–Cold War era and on civil-military relations in democratic societies. Diplomacy is a tool that can be used to encourage this dialogue.

One diplomatic initiative deserves special mention. At the end of July, Secretary Perry will host the first-ever meeting of defense ministers in the hemisphere. A truly historic event, the meeting will focus, in part, on many of the issues discussed at this conference. In terms of civil-military relations, we hope to 1) encourage dialogue among civilian and military leaders on security issues (delegations will be determined by each country, but we hope for both civilian and military participation); 2) address issues of civil-military relations, including how to develop effective civilian ministers of defense and how to promote better education for civilian leaders on defense issues; 3) encourage better relations among the region's military institutions, especially in the areas of peacekeeping, mine-clearing, and so on; and 4) help the militaries of the hemisphere focus on new missions, such as peacekeeping, humanitarian aid, and disaster relief, that promote military professionalism and stable civil-military relations.

While it remains to be seen how successful the Defense Ministerial of the Americas will be, we do know that it is not an isolated event, but part of a greater U.S. effort to promote better civil-military relations and thus improve collective security.[1] As Secretary Perry has said: "Cooperative security offers the best prospect of addressing the new problems of the post–Cold War world." Expanded IMET, the Partnership for Peace, and the Defense Ministerial of the Americas are initiatives that can avert conflict by encouraging greater dialogue and transparency among defense establishments. This dialogue must occur not only among nations but within them.

NOTE

1. Representatives from 34 governments in the Western Hemisphere attended this first defense ministerial, which was held in Williamsburg, Virginia, in July 1995. At the final session, held in the historic House of Burgesses, they adopted the Williamsburg Resolution, which confirmed the centrality of democratic government to security in the hemisphere. Argentina offered to host a second defense ministerial in October 1996. The first ministerial set an important precedent and exceeded the organizers' expectations.

INDEX

Abkhazia, 134, 137, 141, 148–150
Accountability, 56, 89, 148
Achalov, Vladislav, 115
Adzhar Republic, 134
Afghanistan, 116, 120, 123
Africa, x, xi; aid to, xx, 81, 83, 89; border conflicts in, 82; civic-education programs in, 89; civil-military relations in, xx–xxii, 85, 89; during the Cold War, xx, 82–83; colonialism in, 81–82; conflict management in, xxi; constitutions in, 40; democracy in, 95; development in, 83–85, 87, 89; ethnic conflict in, 81–82; human rights in, 94; marginalization of, 83; military in, xxii, xxix, 30, 84, 86–87, 145; political stability in, 84–85; poverty in, 82; research institutions in, 89
African National Congress (ANC) (South Africa), xxii, 7, 92, 93
Aid: to Africa, xx, 81, 83, 89; conditionality of, 69; development, xix; economic, 69; humanitarian, 113, 156; military, 69; and military elites, 70, 113; to the Philippines, 69
Albania, 153
Algeria: and the French military, 20–21, 25; human rights in, 94
Aliyev, Heydar, 147

Allende, Salvador, 18
American Revolution, 146
Amnesty, 55, 74
Angola, 10, 53, 82–84, 87
Aquino, Benigno, Jr., 72
Aquino, Corazon, xix, 67, 71–74, 78
Argentina, x, 55; armed forces in, xvii, 36–37, 59, 61, 62, 65 n. 27; civil-military relations in, xiv, 10, 18, 35, 36, 57; constitution of, 64 n. 14; coups in, 8, 9; defense spending in, 57; dictatorship in, 54; and peacekeeping missions, 53, 57, 155; territorial disputes in, 52, 64, 65 n. 16
Aristide, Jean-Bertrand, 42 n. 5, 50, 63 n. 3
Armenia, xxvi, 136, 141
Association of Southeast Asian Nations (ASEAN), 68
Aung San Suu Kyi, 77
Australia, 139
Authoritarianism, 3–6, 63, 86, 129
Aylwin, Patricio, 58
Azerbaijan, 123, 135, 136, 138, 141, 142, 144, 145, 147, 148

Bakatin, Vadim, 126
Balza, Martín, 48
Bangladesh, xviii, xix, 66–70, 79
Barsukov, Mikhail, 126, 127, 133
Basayev, Shamyl, 141

Bebler, Anton, 5, 11

Belarus, xxvi, 101, 135

Belgium, 10

Belize, 52

Bolivia, 40, 51, 52, 56, 64

Bophuthatswana, xxii, 86, 92, 93

Bordaberry, Juan María, 51

Bosnia, 22, 34, 134, 138–41, 145,
    149. *See also* Herzeg-Bosna

Botswana, 83, 87, 90

Brazil, 52, 60, 64; civil-military
    relations in, 9, 18, 35, 151, 155;
    defense ministry in, 62; demo-
    cratic transition in, 125; internal
    missions in, 18; military in,
    35–37, 50, 54, 57, 59

Bulia, Tengiz, 139

Burma, 67–70, 77

Bush, George, 22, 34

Cambodia, 10, 53, 71

Capitalism, 33, 111

Caribbean, xi, 49

Carter, Jimmy, 54, 63

Castro, Fidel, 49

Cédras, Raoul, 54, 63 n. 3

Central America, xi, xvi, 40, 49,
    50, 54, 64. *See also* Latin
    America

Central Europe, 11, 154

Cerezo, Venicio, 40

Chad, 82

Chechnya, xxiv, xxv, 24, 110, 113,
    129, 133 n. 46, 134, 136, 138,
    141, 142, 145, 148; war in, 118–
    19, 120, 121, 122

Chernomyrdin, Viktor, 128, 131, 133

Chiapas, 49

Chile, 8; civil-military relations in,
    xiv, 9, 10, 30, 36, 37, 58, 62;
    constitution of, 65 n. 23; coups
    in, 18, 65 n. 23; defense spending
    in, 57; democracy in, xxxiv, 10,
    51; domestic conflict in, 53; mili-
    tary in, xii, 18, 50, 60; under

Pinochet, 54; territorial disputes
    in, 52, 64 nn. 9, 11, 16

China, 10, 68, 71, 75–77, 117, 151

Churaiev, Vladimir, 121

Ciskei, 86, 92

Civil society, xx, 88; and democrati-
    zation, 77; development of, xxviii;
    in Latin America, xviii; and the
    military, 47, 60, 62–63, 152;
    popular participation in, 68; in
    South Africa, 90–91

Clinton, Bill, 26, 33, 34, 43, 152,
    153; administration of, 22, 26, 34,
    153

Cold War, 16, 20; and Africa, xx,
    82–83; and China, 75; civilian
    control during, 16; civil-military
    relations during, ix, xiv, 17, 25;
    end of, ix, x, xii, xiv–xvi, 12, 26,
    30, 31, 33–35, 37, 47–48, 55, 66,
    68, 75, 151; foreign aid during,
    69; French attitude toward, 20;
    and military missions, 12, 13, 15,
    22–23; and Thailand, 75

Colombia, xvi, xvii, xxxiv, 31, 35,
    40, 47, 52, 53, 56, 63

Colombia Revolutionary Armed
    Forces, 40

Communism: collapse of, ix, xxii,
    xxiv, 66, 103, 135, 143, 145;
    international, 18–20, 48; life un-
    der, 5, 127; public reaction to,
    144; in Thailand, 75

Communist party: in China, 71; in
    France, 20; in Poland, xxiii,
    102–3; in the Soviet Union (for-
    mer), xxii, 17, 111

Conflict, 51; in Africa, xx, xxi,
    81–82; in Algeria, 20; armed, 47,
    52; border, 48; East-West, x;
    ethnic, xx, 33; between Georgia
    and Abkhazia, 117; in Latin
    America, 53; militia-led, 138;
    political, xvi, xxxi, xxxiii; in the
    post–Cold War world, xiv, 27; in

the Soviet Union (former), xxiv,
xxvi; and U.S. military missions,
35; in Yugoslavia (former), xxvi
Constitutions, 88; in Africa, 40; in
Argentina, 64 n. 14; in Chile, 65
n. 23; in Ecuador, 42; in Latin
America, 57; in Poland, 106,
108–9; in Russia, 111, 117, 119,
124, 128
Contreras, Manuel, 9, 65
Corruption, xxxii, 148; in Asia, xviii,
xix; at end of Cold War, 66; in
Latin America's armed forces, 55,
60; and military cutbacks, 59; and
military missions, 38; in the Philippines, 71, 73; in the postcommunist world, 144; in Russia's
military, xxiv, 24, 126; in South
Korea's military, 74; in the Soviet
Union (former), 135, 146
Costa Rica, 33, 50, 61
Côte d'Ivoire, 30
Coups, xxxiii, 86, 146, 147; in
Argentina, 8, 9; attempted, xxvii,
8–9, 42, 71–73, 142, 145; in
Azerbaijan, 142; in Chile, 18, 65
n. 23; and civil-military relations,
xiv, 12, 23; and democratization,
xii; in Latin America, 7, 50; and
new democracies, 9; in Niger,
xxix; in the Philippines, 71–74,
79–80; in Russia, xxvi, xxv, 25,
110, 114, 117, 119, 121–25, 128,
129 n. 1, 132 n. 25; in South
Korea, 74; in the Soviet Union
(former), 12; successful, 9, 123;
unsuccessful, 4, 80 n. 9; in Venezuela, 9
Crime, xxvii, xxx; domestic, 48; and
military, 10, 145, 148, 149, 152,
155; in new democracies, 4; and
police, 90–91; in the postcommunist world, 136, 144; in Russia,
xxiv, 111, 113, 127; in Yugoslavia (former), 140

Crimea, 117
Croatia, xxvi, 10, 53, 134, 136, 139,
141, 145
Cuba, xvi, 34, 47–49
Cuban Revolution, 19
Cyprus, 53
Czech Republic, xxxiii, 101

Defense, 88, 152, 156; budget for,
xix, 17, 55, 57, 59, 69–71, 75,
77; and civilian control, xi, xxi,
xxviii, xxxi, xxxii, 89; external,
xiv, xvii, 37; in France, 21; and
Latin American legislatures, 59;
and the military, 30, 33, 48, 78;
ministry of, xxiii, xxv, xxxi,
xxxii, 5, 6, 24, 25, 58, 62, 113,
151; mission of, xv, xxx, 38; national, 6, 33, 61; in Poland, 102–
9; and police, 56, 91; policy on,
ix, xviii, xxii, xxviii, 5, 41, 43,
94, 149; prestige of, 149; in
Russia, 130–33; scholarship on,
89; spending on, 22, 23, 32, 58
Dien Bien Phu, 20
DINE (Dirección de Industrias del
Ejército) (Ecuador), 36, 39, 43
Dominican Republic, 49, 60, 64
Drug trafficking, 32, 53, 152
Dudayev, Dzokhar, 119, 148

East Asia, 5, 69, 151
Eastern Europe, 113, 129, 151, 152,
155; armed forces in, 112; civil-
military relations in, xxii, xxvii,
5, 101; collapse of communism
in, 66
Ecuador, 36, 39, 42, 43, 48, 51–53,
55, 59, 60, 63, 64
Egypt, 89
Eisenhower, Dwight, 16
Elchibey, Abulfaz, 147
Elections, 41, 82; after authoritarian-
ism, 3; in Latin America, 35; in
Nigeria, xxix; in the Philippines,

Elections *(cont'd)*
67, 73–74; in Poland, 103–6; in
Russia, 24, 29 n. 24, 116, 119,
124, 131 n. 15; in South Africa,
82, 91, 92, 94; in South Korea,
67, 74; in Taiwan, 67; and the
U.S. military, 34
Elites, 11; authoritarian, 4; in
Bangladesh, 69; business and
management, 70; civilian, xxxii;
communist, 17; and democratization, 78; in Indonesia, 70, 76;
military, xix, xxxii, 17, 70, 76,
77, 100, 113, 121, 125; in Pakistan, 69; in the Philippines, 69;
political, xxix, 67
El Salvador, 35, 36, 50, 52, 53, 57
England, 129
Erin, Viktor, 119
Eritrea, 82
Ershard, Hossein Mohammed, 70
Espinosa, Pedro, 9
Ethiopia, 82, 83, 151
European Community, xi, xxiii,
xxxiii, 5, 10, 21, 24, 53, 81, 90,
101, 153–55

Falklands/Malvinas war, 52, 55, 64
Farabundo Marti National Liberation
Front (El Salvador), 50
Finer, Samuel, 63, 68, 79, 99, 109
First World War, 27, 33, 101, 106
France, xiv, 13, 19–21, 27, 28, 89,
92, 100, 146
Franco, Francisco, 54
French Revolution, xiii, 10, 40, 146
Fujimori, Alberto, 11, 42, 65
Furman, Dmitrii, 122, 132

Gaidar, Yegor, 124, 131
Gamsakhurdia, Zviad, 139, 147, 150
Gaulle, Charles de, xiv, 19–21, 146
George C. Marshall Center, xxxiii, 7
Georgia, 134, 136, 138, 139, 141–43,
145, 147, 148

Germany, 10, 17, 20, 27, 50, 112,
129, 155
Giorgadze, Igor, 143
Glasnost', 17, 142
Golushko, Nikolai, 126
Gorbachev, Mikhail, 17, 28, 112, 126
Gorno-Badakhshan, 135
Goulart, João, 18
Grachev, Pavel, 115, 131
Great Britain, 69, 52, 55, 69
Greece, xxxiii, xxxiv, 8, 100, 125
Gromov, Boris, 120, 121, 123, 131
Guatemala, 36, 40, 42, 49, 52, 53,
56, 59, 65
Guatemalan National Revolutionary
Union, 56
Guyana, 52

Haiti, 8, 9, 33, 34, 50, 53
Hanahoe (One-Mind Society) (South
Korea), 74
Haq, Zia-ul, 70
Herzeg-Bosna, 134, 136. *See also*
Bosnia
Honduras, 35, 52, 59
Human rights, 59, 85, 89, 91, 95,
138; in Africa, 94; and democ-
racy, 154; in Indonesia, 70; mili-
tary abuses of, 7, 48, 62, 72, 73;
and Napoleon, 146; protection of,
153; respect for, 32, 54, 55, 94;
and the United States, xvii; viola-
tion of, 4, 55, 58, 74
Hungary, x, xxxiii, 101
Huseinov, Surat, 138, 142, 146, 147,
150

India, 68, 78
Indochina, 20, 28
Indonesia, 68–71, 76
Institutional Revolutionary Party
(PRI) (Mexico), 48, 49
Intelligence agencies, 138
International Military Education and
Training (IMET), 153–56

International Monetary Fund, 89
Ioseliani, Dzhaba, 138, 139, 141, 145, 146
Iran, 10
Iraq, 53
Islam, 139
Italy, 52, 146
Itamaraty Declaration, 52, 64 n. 10
Ivanov, Gennadii, 121

Japan, 24, 68, 69, 76, 86, 116
Jaruzelski, Wojciech, 103–5
Jefferson, Thomas, 11

Kashmir, 53
Khasbulatov, Ruslan, 115, 116
Khmer Rouge, 53
Kim Young Sam, 67, 74, 75
Kitovani, Tengiz, 139, 145
Kobalia, Loti, 139, 150
Kokoshin, Andrei, 116
Kołodziejczyk, Piotr, 106, 109 n. 5
Kondratiev, Georgy, 120, 121
Korean War, 16, 52, 75
Korzhakov, Aleksandr, 127, 133, 149
Kosovo, 134
Kraprayoon, Suchinda, 71
Kuril Islands, 24, 116

Lambeth, Benjamin, 8, 11
Lasswell, Harold, 12, 27
Latin America, ix, x, 145, 151; authoritarianism in, 3, 13, 18, 19, 23, 66; civil-military relations in, xi, xvi–xviii, xxvii, 5–7, 18, 31, 42, 47–48, 51, 53–55, 57–64, 152, 155; civil society in, xviii; conflict in, 53; corruption in, 60; coups in, 7; drug trafficking in, 32, 152; elections in, 35; military in, xxix, 42 n. 6, 155–56; political parties in, xvi, 35; transition to democracy in, 35, 40, 86; and the United States, 7, 49, 50, 52, 54, 57, 59, 61, 63–65, 154. *See also* Central America
Lebed, Aleksandr, 8, 24, 100, 123, 124, 132 n. 33
Lee Kuan Yew, 4
Leekpai, Chuan, 71
Lesotho, 83, 84, 87, 90
Letelier, Orlando, 58, 65 n. 21
Liberia, 82
Loza, Tihomir, 140, 150

MacArthur, Douglas, 16, 100
Makashov, Albert, 115
Malawi, 83
Mali, 82, 154
Mandela, Nelson, 7, 8, 93, 94
Marcos, Ferdinand, 70, 72, 73, 79
Marshall Center. *See* George C. Marshall Center
Marxism, 56
Mauritania, 82
Mazowiecki, Tadeusz, 103
Mexico, xi, xvi, xvii, 35, 40, 48, 49, 52, 56
Middle East, 83, 145, 152
Military missions, 10, 12–14, 26, 27, 55; in authoritarian regimes, 4; and civil-military relations, xiii, xix, 13, 18, 19, 23, 42, 66; and the Cold War, 22, 25; and democracy, 37; in France, 19, 22; in Latin America, 155; in Peru, 39, 40; in the Soviet Union (former), 17
Mironov, Valeri, 121
Mobutu Sese Seko, 128
Moldova, 117, 123, 134, 136, 138, 142, 145, 148
Morales Bermúdez, Francisco, 54
Morocco, 10
Mozambique, 53, 82–84, 87, 90

Nabiyev, Rahman, 147
Nagorno-Karabakh, 135, 136, 140, 141, 149

Namibia, 83, 87, 90
Nationalism, 21, 83, 135, 144, 145
National Liberation Front (FLN)
    (Algeria), 21
Nicaragua, xii, xxvi, 9, 34, 48, 49,
    52, 53, 61, 128
Nigeria, x, xii, xxix, 8, 9, 82, 89
Nonparty Bloc in Support of Reform
    (BBWR) (Poland), xxiii, 106
Noriega, Manuel Antonio, 35, 50, 54,
    60
North Atlantic Treaty Organization
    (NATO), xxxiii, xxxiv, 109, 117,
    154, 155
North Korea, 76
Nunn, Sam, 22, 63 n. 3

Ochoa Sánchez, Arnaldo, 60
O'Donnell, Guillermo, 63, 86, 87,
    95, 129
Officers' Union (Russia), 114
Ogarkov, Nikolai, 17
Olszewski, Jan, 105
Organization for Economic Coopera-
    tion and Development, 69
Organization of American States
    (OAS), 32, 33, 36, 42 n. 5
Ortega, Humberto, 9
Our Home is Russia (Russia), 131

Pakistan, xviii, xix, 30, 66–70, 78,
    79, 151
Pan-Africanist Congress (PAC)
    (South Africa), xxii, 92, 93
Panama, xvii, 33–35, 49, 50, 54, 61,
    64, 65
Panyarachun, Anand, 71
Paraguay, 36, 51, 54, 64, 128
Partnership for Peace (PFP), 154
Parys, Jan, 105
People's Liberation Army (PLA)
    (China), 71, 75, 76, 139
Perestroika, 17
Perón, Juan, 18
Perry, William, 153, 156

Persian Gulf War, 22, 31, 53, 117
Peru, 54; and border disputes, 48,
    52, 56, 64 nn. 9, 16; civil-
    military relations in, 11, 31, 35,
    65 n. 25; defense ministry in, 62;
    dissolution of Congress in, 42;
    guerrilla movements in, xvi, xvii,
    47, 56; military missions in, 39,
    40; transition to democracy in,
    125
Pétain, Philippe, 20
Philippines, x, xi, 70, 74; aid to, 69;
    authoritarian rule in, 67; civil-
    military relations in, xviii, 74,
    78–80; corruption in, 71, 73; coup
    attempts in, 8, 9, 72–73; democ-
    ratization in, xix, 66; elites in,
    69; military in, xix, 3, 68, 71, 72,
    76
Piłsudski, Józef, xxiii, 101
Pinochet, Augusto, 8, 9, 24, 48, 51,
    54, 58, 65, 124, 125
Poland, x, xi, xxiii, xxiv, xxxiii, 99,
    101–3, 108
Polish United Workers' Party (PZPR)
    (Poland), 102
Political culture, xxxiii, 76, 143
Political parties: in Latin America,
    xvi, 35; and the military, xxix,
    38, 39, 141; in new democracies,
    xxxiv, 143; in Poland, 102, 104;
    in Russia, xxiv, 29 n. 24, 131 n.
    15; in Southeast Asia, 67–68; in
    southern Africa, 84; in Thailand,
    68; in Western Europe, 20
Popov, Gavriil, 122, 128
Popular Front (France), 19
Portugal, xxxiii, xxxiv n. 7, 6,
    125
Powell, Colin, 22, 63
Press, 4, 11, 27, 28, 42, 43, 63–65,
    67, 72, 79, 95, 129, 130, 138,
    150, 153

Quinlan, Michael, 100

Ramos, Fidel, xix, 67, 74, 78, 79
Ratko, Mladić, 146
Religion, 76, 146
Republika Srpska, 134, 136. *See also* Yugoslavia
Rodionov, Igor, 117, 131
Rogov, Sergei, 117, 131
Rojas, Patricio, 58
Romania, 3
Rose, Charlie, 70, 100, 109, 127
Russia, x; and the Chechen war, 118–22; civil-military relations in, xi, xiv, xxiv, xxix, 6, 10, 12, 13, 23, 25, 26, 110–12, 117; constitution of, 111, 117, 119, 124, 128; crime in, xxiv, 111, 113, 127; defense in, 130–33; elections in, 24, 29 n. 24, 116, 119, 124, 131 n. 15; ethnic nationalism in, 83, 135; industrialization in, 86; internal threats to, 22; military in, xxiv, xxvi, 8, 10, 24–25, 30, 110–12, 117, 125–26, 130 n. 4, 135, 141, 143; political parties in, xxiv, 29 n. 24, 131 n. 15; political repression in, 148; prospects for military coup in, 122–24, 129; secessionist movements in, 152; and United States, 112, 117, 155
Rutskoi, Aleksandr, 123
Rwanda, 34, 81, 82

Schmitter, Philippe, 86, 87, 95, 129, 130
Second World War, 20, 30, 31, 52, 102
Secret Armed Organization (OAS) (France), 21
Sendero Luminoso (Shining Path) (Peru), 35, 40, 53
Senegal, 82, 153
Serbia, 134, 136. *See also* Yugoslavia
Serbia-Montenegro, 136
Shevardnadze, Eduard, 145, 150

Shining Path. *See* Sendero Luminoso
Sierra Leone, 130
Sinai, 10
Singapore, 4
Slovakia, 101
Slovenia, 5, 136
Solidarity (Poland), 99, 103, 104
Solomatin, Anatoliy, 121
Somalia, 34, 82, 83
Somoza, Anastasio, xxvi, 128
Soskovets, Oleg, 128, 133
South Africa, x, 3; and border security, 92; civil-military relations in, 86, 89–91; civil society in, 90–91; conflict management in, 85; and conscription, 10, 87; elections in, 82, 91, 92, 94; military in, xi, 7, 8, 93, 94; police service in, 90–92; research institutions in, 89; transition to democracy in, xxi, 83, 84; and the United States, 83, 86, 89, 94
South African Defence Force (SADF), xxii, 92–94
South African National Defence Force (SANDF), xxi, xxii, 91–95
South African Police Service (SAPS), 90, 91
South Asia, xviii, 30, 83, 151, 152
Southeast Asia, 16, 66
South Korea, xii, xviii, 9, 66, 67, 69, 70, 72, 74, 76, 78
South Ossetia, 134, 141, 148
Soviet Union, xxvi, 30, 66, 134, 151; civil-military relations in, xi, xiv, xxii, xxvii, 8, 12, 16, 17, 22, 23, 47, 111, 144–45, 152; after the Cold War, 37; collapse of, xvi, xxiv, 116, 147; Communist Party in, xxii, 17, 111; corruption in, 146; coups in, 12; legacy of, 111; role of military in, xxvii, 13, 17, 125, 141; and Third World guerrilla movements, xvi

Spain, xxxiii, xxxiv n. 7, 3, 8, 10,
    100
Sri Lanka, xxxiv
Srpska Krajina, 134, 136, 139. *See
    also* Yugoslavia
Stalin, Joseph, 17
State Law and Order Restoration
    Council (SLORC) (Burma), 69,
    70
Stepan, Alfred, xxxii, xxxiv, 6, 7,
    11, 27, 28, 43, 63, 130
Stepashin, Sergei, 119, 126
Stroessner, Alfredo, xxvi, 52, 54, 128
Suchocka, Hanna, 105
Sudan, 8, 9, 82
Suharto, 68, 76
Swaziland, 83, 90

Taiwan, xviii, 3, 66, 67, 69–71, 76,
    78
Tajikistan, 117, 135, 141, 142, 145,
    148
Terekhov, Stanislav, 114
Thailand, xviii, xix, 68, 70, 75–77,
    80
Third World, ix, xxxiv, 12, 23, 83,
    100, 149
Thirty Years' War, 147
Tiananmen Square, 71, 77
Tito, Josip Broz, 142
Togo, 82, 94
Transdniester Republic, 117, 134,
    138, 141
Transkei, 86, 92
Trinidad and Tobago, 52
Truman, Harry, 16
Turkey, xii, 6, 9, 100

Uganda, 82
Ukraine, xxvi, 24, 135, 141, 147
Umkhonto we Sizwe (MK) (South
    Africa), 7
United Nations, 33, 43, 78
United States, x; and Asia, xix, 68,
    69, 76; and Central Europe, 154;
civil-military relations in, xii, xiv,
    xv, xxvii, 3, 10, 12, 13, 15, 16,
    22, 23, 25, 26–28, 151, 152; and
    human rights, xvii; and IMET,
    153–54; and Latin America, 7,
    49, 50, 52, 54, 57, 59, 61, 63–65,
    154; military in, 30, 32, 34, 35,
    36, 38, 42, 152; and Poland, 100;
    and Russia, 112, 117, 155; and
    South Africa, 83, 86, 89, 94
Uruguay, x, xvii, 47, 50, 51, 53, 57,
    60, 64, 65

Velasco Alvarado, Juan, 54
Velasco Ibarra, José María, 52
Venda, 86, 92
Venezuela, xxxiv, 9, 10, 35, 42, 43,
    52, 64, 65
Vichy government, 19
Vietnam, xiv, 16, 68, 75
Vietnam War, 16
Vorobiev, Eduard, 120

Wałęsa, Lech, xxiii, 105, 106, 109
    n. 5
Warsaw Pact, 17, 20, 102, 107
Western Europe, 20, 86, 151
Western Sahara, 82
World Bank, 65, 82, 89

Yeltsin, Boris, xxiv, xxv, xxvi, xxix,
    11, 112, 116, 119, 130
Yugoslavia, xxvi, xxvii, 83, 134–36,
    139, 140, 143, 148
Yugoslav National Army (JNA),
    135–36

Zaire, 82, 83, 94, 128
Zambia, 83, 84, 87
Zapatista National Liberation Army
    (Mexico), 48, 56
Zhirinovsky, Vladimir, 29, 116, 124,
    148
Zimbabwe, 83, 87, 89